Condemned to death after a month-long trial in July 1942, a handcuffed Nazi saboteur leaves a U.S. military court in the custody of an Army guard. He was one of eight Germans caught while on a secret mission in the United States.

THE SECRET WAR

This volume is one of a series that chronicles
in full the events of the Second World War.
Previous books in the series include:

WORLD WAR II · TIME-LIFE BOOKS · ALEXANDRIA, VIRGINIA

BY FRANCIS RUSSELL
AND THE EDITORS OF TIME-LIFE BOOKS

THE SECRET WAR

Time-Life Books Inc.
is a wholly owned subsidiary of
TIME INCORPORATED

Founder: Henry R. Luce 1898-1967

Editor-in-Chief: Henry Anatole Grunwald
President: J. Richard Munro
Chairman of the Board: Ralph P. Davidson
Executive Vice President: Clifford J. Grum
Chairman, Executive Committee: James R. Shepley
Editorial Director: Ralph Graves
Group Vice President, Books: Joan D. Manley
Vice Chairman: Arthur Temple

TIME-LIFE BOOKS INC.

Managing Editor: Jerry Korn
Executive Editor: David Maness
Assistant Managing Editors: Dale M. Brown
(planning), George Constable, Martin Mann,
John Paul Porter, Gerry Schremp (acting)
Art Director: Tom Suzuki
Chief of Research: David L. Harrison
Director of Photography: Robert G. Mason
Assistant Art Director: Arnold C. Holeywell
Assistant Chief of Research: Carolyn L. Sackett
Assistant Director of Photography: Dolores A. Littles

Chairman: John D. McSweeney
President: Carl G. Jaeger
Executive Vice Presidents: John Steven Maxwell,
David J. Walsh
Vice Presidents: George Artandi (comptroller);
Stephen L. Bair (legal counsel); Peter G. Barnes;
Nicholas Benton (public relations); John L. Canova;
Beatrice T. Dobie (personnel); Carol Flaumenhaft
(consumer affairs); James L. Mercer (Europe/South
Pacific); Herbert Sorkin (production); Paul R. Stewart
(marketing)

WORLD WAR II

Editorial Staff for The Secret War
Editor: Anne Horan
Designer: Herbert H. Quarmby
Chief Researcher: Philip Brandt George
Picture Editor: Peggy Sawyer
Text Editors: Robert Menaker, Richard W. Murphy,
Henry Woodhead
Staff Writers: Donald Davison Cantlay,
Roger E. Herst, Brooke Stoddard
Researchers: Harris J. Andrews III, LaVerle Berry,
Kathleen Burke, Charles S. Clark, Jane Hanna,
Gregory A. McGruder, Alfreda Robertson,
Cronin Buck Sleeper, Jayne T. Wise, Paula York
Art Assistant: Mikio Togashi
Editorial Assistant: Constance Strawbridge

Special Contributor
Alexandra Gleysteen (translations)

Editorial Production
Production Editor: Feliciano Madrid
Operations Manager: Gennaro C. Esposito,
Gordon E. Buck (assistant)
Quality Control: Robert L. Young (director),
James J. Cox (assistant), Daniel J. McSweeney,
Michael G. Wight (associates)
Art Coordinator: Anne B. Landry
Copy Staff: Susan B. Galloway (chief),
Ann Bartunek, Allan Fallow, Barbara F. Quarmby,
Celia Beattie
Picture Department: Betty Hughes Weatherley
Traffic: Kimberly K. Lewis

Correspondents: Elisabeth Kraemer (Bonn); Margot
Hapgood, Dorothy Bacon, Lesley Coleman (London);
Susan Jonas, Lucy T. Voulgaris (New York); Maria
Vincenza Aloisi, Josephine du Brusle (Paris); Ann
Natanson (Rome). Valuable assistance was also
provided by: Wibo van de Linde, Janny Hovinga
(Amsterdam); Mehmet Ali Kaslali (Ankara); Pavle
Svabic (Belgrade); Helga Kohl, Martha Mader (Bonn);
Brigid Grauman (Brussels); Katrina Van Duyn
(Copenhagen); Selwyn Parker (Dublin); Robert Kroon
(Geneva); Robert W. Bone (Honolulu); Peter
Hawthorne (Johannesburg); Judy Aspinall, Jeremy
Lawrence, Pippa Pridham, Jill Rose, Pat Stimpson
(London); Trini Debelius (Madrid); Felix Rosenthal
(Moscow); Carolyn T. Chubet, Miriam Hsia, Christina
Lieberman (New York); Bent Onsager (Oslo); M. T.
Hirschkoff (Paris); Mimi Murphy (Rome); Janet Zich
(San Francisco); S. Chang Kazuo Ohyauchi (Tokyo);
Bogden Turek (Warsaw).

The Author: FRANCIS RUSSELL served in the Military
Intelligence Research Section of the British War Of-
fice in World War II and was a political intelligence
officer in the British XXX Corps in Germany after the
War. A historian and literary critic, he is the author of
The World of Dürer in the Time-Life Library of Art.
Among his other books are Three Studies in 20th Cen-
tury Obscurity, a trio of critical essays on James Joyce,
Franz Kafka and Gertrude Stein; Tragedy in Dedham:
The Story of the Sacco-Vanzetti Case; and The Great
Interlude: Neglected Events and Persons from the First
World War to the Depression.

The Consultants: COLONEL JOHN R. ELTING, USA (Ret.),
was an intelligence officer with the 8th Armored Division in World War II. A former Associate Professor at
West Point, he is the author of Battles for Scandinavia
in the Time-Life Books World War II series and of The
Battle of Bunker's Hill, The Battles of Saratoga and
Military History and Atlas of the Napoleonic Wars.

M. R. D. FOOT, an Army officer from 1939 to 1945,
received the Croix de guerre for his work with Resistance forces in Brittany. A former Professor of History at Oxford and Manchester, he is the author of the
official history of the British Special Operations Executive in France.

R. V. JONES, a pioneering force in British scientific intelligence, anticipated and countered new weapons
developed by the Germans. He was in charge of intelligence operations against the V-1 bomb, the V-2
rocket and the German nuclear developments in the
1940s. He has been Professor of Natural Philosophy
at the University of Aberdeen since 1946 and is the
author of Most Secret War.

DAVID KAHN has long been an aficionado of cryptanalysis. He is the author of The Codebreakers: The
Story of Secret Writing and of Hitler's Spies: German
Military Intelligence in World War II. He is the coedi-
tor of Cryptologia, a scholarly quarterly on the study
of codes, and is an assistant editor on the Long Island
newspaper Newsday.

EDWIN JOSEPH PUTZELL JR. served as Executive Officer
and Assistant to the Director of the Office of Strategic
Services (OSS) from 1942 until 1945. He is associated
with the law firm Coburn, Croft & Putzell.

Library of Congress Cataloguing in Publication Data

Russell, Francis, 1910-
  The secret war.

  (World War II; v. 29)
  Bibliography: p. 202
  Includes index.
  1. World War, 1939-1945—Secret service.
2. World War, 1939-1945—Cryptography.   I. Time-
Life Books.   II. Title.
D810.S7R84   940.54'85   81-9382
ISBN 0-8094-2548-3
ISBN 0-8094-2547-5 (lib. bdg.)
ISBN 0-8094-2546-7 (retail ed.)

For information about any Time-Life book, please write:

Reader Information
Time-Life Books
541 North Fairbanks Court
Chicago, Illinois 60611

CHAPTERS

PICTURE ESSAYS

CONTENTS

THE URGENT NEED FOR SECRECY

A ship sinks because of "a few careless words" in this detail from a 1943 British poster, designed to put the home front on guard against enemy eavesdroppers.

POSTERS TO KEEP CIVILIANS WARY

From this 1941 German poster, a black hulk of a spy, faceless and crude, whispers an international "pst," hoping to loosen Germany's tongue.

Two years to the day before Pearl Harbor was struck by Japanese bombs, a German spy was given a guided tour of the U.S. Army's Edgewood Arsenal in Maryland. The spy, who sent his superiors a detailed report on American weapons development, had achieved the tour by a bold expedient: He had asked for it.

By 1942 no such tour would have been possible. Secrecy shrouded every aspect of the military effort in the United States as well as in every other warring country. But if an enemy agent could no longer hope to visit arsenals, airplane factories or shipyards, he—or she—could still chat with and eavesdrop on those who worked inside them, surreptitiously picking up classified information.

To deal with that danger, all of the combatants waged propaganda campaigns that were aimed at making their citizens ever more spy-conscious. Spearheading those campaigns were carefully designed security posters. Pasted or tacked onto walls and bulletin boards wherever people gathered—restaurants and bars, bus stations, movie theater lobbies, defense plants, schools, even rest rooms— the posters hammered home a simple, unvarying message: Loose talk kills.

Each country expressed that universal message in its own distinctive graphic language. Americans tended to stress the consequences of carelessness, in one case showing a teary-eyed spaniel mourning over his dead master's uniform, which was draped forlornly over a chair "... because somebody talked!" The British dwelt on consequences too, but they usually did so with a lighter, more sophisticated touch that preferred clever verbal and visual puns to sentiment. German and Italian posters, by contrast, often took a cloak-and-dagger approach, featuring faceless spies lurking about in the shadows, eavesdropping.

All these posters taught the vital lesson that the War was being fought on the home front too, and that "the man behind the man behind the gun" had to be as discreet as the soldier in the field. "Tittle tattle," as one British poster put it, could indeed "cost the battle."

A cat-eyed German soldier glares from a 1942 American factory poster that was criticized by workers who took the figure to be an American.

IL NEMICO VI ASCOLTA

Shielding himself with a newspaper, an Allied spy strains to overhear what a soldier is telling a civilian in this Italian poster intended to remind civilians and military personnel alike that "the enemy is listening."

Schäm Dich, Schwätzer!
Feind hört mit – Schweigen ist Pflicht!

"Shame on you, bigmouth!" reads this German poster depicting a worker quacking away industrial secrets. "The enemy is listening— silence is your duty!" Nazi leaders placed great confidence in the persuasive power of posters. "Nothing is easier than leading the people on a leash," said Minister of Propaganda Joseph Goebbels cynically. "I just hold up a dazzling campaign poster and they jump right through it."

None other than Adolf Hitler—actually many shifty-eyed Hitlers—eavesdrops from the wallpaper of an English parlor.

11

A British soldier's careless words—beginning as mere waves of sound—end in a Nazi sword that skewers his comrades.

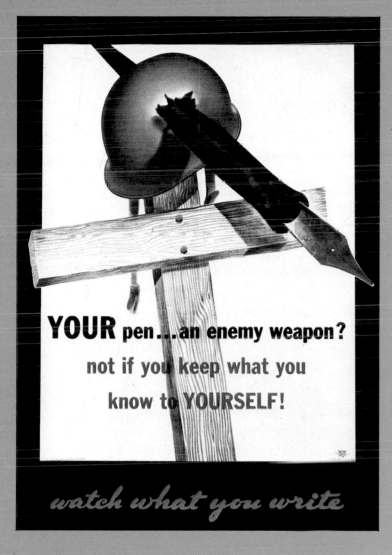

Colored blood red from its killing work, a reckless pen runs through an American soldier's helmet like a missile. American "Artists for Victory" produced 2,224 posters on a variety of wartime themes—including security—in an intensive 1942 campaign that was capped by a special exhibition held at the Museum of Modern Art in New York City.

In this French poster, deadly "repercussions" emanate in the form of neat rows of soldiers' graves from the mouthpiece of a telephone—and the "indiscretions" that have been carelessly spoken through it.

13

"Shut up!" commands an Italian patriot amid the ever-present ears of enemy spies. "He who does not shut up is a traitor."

Schweig!

A German antiaircraft gunner commands "silence!" lest casual gossip betray him to enemy planes flying overhead.

1

"In wartime," British Prime Minister Winston Churchill told American President Franklin D. Roosevelt and Soviet Premier Josef Stalin in November 1943, "truth is so precious that she should always be attended by a bodyguard of lies." Churchill happened to be speaking of a scheme to conceal Allied plans for the invasion of Europe, scheduled for the following June. But his aphorism could have been inspired by any number of operations undertaken in World War II—by Germany, Italy and Japan no less than by Churchill's government and its allies. The fate of many a battle hung on prior intelligence, and—with the urgent goal of trying to tip the balance in their own favor—the belligerent powers engaged in a multitude of operations that were themselves secret, that were intended to keep other things secret, or that represented efforts to uncover the secrets of the other side. They spied relentlessly on enemy plans, zealously guarded their own plans, sustained an unremitting drive to invent ever more effective weaponry and perpetrated giant hoaxes calculated to so confuse the enemy that he would find himself in the wrong place at the wrong time.

As the shooting war accelerated, so did the secret war—and the secret war took on an aura of unreality. "In the high ranges of secret-service work," Winston Churchill said of his nation's intelligence operations, "the actual facts in many cases were in every respect equal to the most fantastic inventions of romance and melodrama. Tangle within tangle, plot and counterplot, ruse and treachery, cross and double cross, true agent, false agent, double agent, gold and steel, the bomb, the dagger and the firing party were interwoven in many a texture so intricate as to be incredible and yet true."

Never in history had so much human brain power and advanced technology been marshaled in the service of secrecy as in World War II. Uncounted thousands of men and women took part, some as daredevils seeking adventure, others with the more modest goal of doing their patriotic duty. They came from every walk of life; among them were scientists, artists, journalists, mathematicians, linguists, doctors, lawyers, bureaucrats, inventors and dabblers in the arcane. Many of their discoveries and their deceptions played pivotal roles in the great military campaigns of the War. But much of their work was so scrupulously withheld from the public—so heavily shielded by the "bodyguard of lies" to

A BODYGUARD FOR TRUTH

which Churchill alluded—that not only did it go unknown during the War, but much of it has resisted disclosure in the ensuing decades.

For the governments waging the secret war on a grand scale, an age-old means of gathering diplomatic and military secrets was espionage, and an age-old tool for prying loose such coveted information was the spy.

The spy's duty was extremely hazardous. Alone and unloved in an alien society, he had no protection except his own wits. He existed on the edge of a precipice and knew that one mistake might send him plunging into abysmal disaster. Some spies fumbled, slipped and were caught; others were betrayed. If he was captured, the spy's own government pretended he did not exist, and he was at the mercy of his captors. The usual fate of a captured spy was execution or long-term imprisonment. Only one alternative existed—becoming a turncoat and working for his captors. The choice was a grim one, for nobody loves a turncoat—not even his new employer.

Espionage was well under way when the German Wehrmacht opened the War by crushing Poland in 1939. The previous year, when British Prime Minister Neville Chamberlain returned to London from a Munich meeting with German Chancellor Adolf Hitler and triumphantly declared "peace for our time," the chiefs of secret intelligence agencies all over Europe knew better.

Germany had two agencies already spying: the Abwehr, a branch of the OKW, or Armed Forces High Command, engaged in keeping watch on such information as the military preparedness of foreign nations; and the SD, or Sicherheitsdienst, the secret intelligence and security service of the Nazi party, responsible for both internal surveillance and espionage abroad. England also had two agencies for military intelligence, MI-5 and MI-6. In theory, MI-5 dealt with domestic security and MI-6 with foreign espionage, but in practice the concerns of the two frequently overlapped—as did the respective concerns of Germany's Abwehr and the SD. British and German agents working for all of these organizations were to match their wits against each other with increasing fervor and complexity as the War went on.

Both branches of the British intelligence service had been created early in the century, in response to the poor showing of the British armed forces in the Boer War. Because of inadequate military intelligence, the British had misjudged the strength and tenacity of the Boers and found themselves locked into a prolonged three-year conflict. Using an intelligence agency to keep the homeland secure was a legitimate and traditional enough custom, and the existence of MI-5—if not its modus operandi—was widely known. But MI-6, which snooped into the affairs of other nations, was somehow less respectable, and MI-6 shrouded its own existence, hiding a variety of bogus undertakings behind such legitimate institutions as passport control offices in foreign countries. The building that housed its central headquarters in London was fitted with secret doors and a secret stairway—and the location of even the building was a carefully guarded secret.

Not surprisingly, the quirks of such an organization were reflected in the men who ran it; indeed, it might be generally said of espionage everywhere that the characters it attracted were eccentric. The atmosphere of obscuration and mystery that cloaked MI-6 was established by its first chief, Mansfield Smith-Cumming, a one-legged Naval officer who sported a gold-rimmed monocle and wrote in green ink. Smith-Cumming, to keep his own identity as secret as the workings of his organization, gave himself a code designation—the initial of his second surname—and thus established a precedent: All subsequent chiefs of MI-6 were known only as C. Smith-Cumming was succeeded by an equal in eccentricity, Admiral Sir Hugh Sinclair, who wore a derby hat a size too small for him and indicated his indignation, if he took umbrage at something said to him in an interview, by swiveling his chair around to the wall and showing the visitor his back.

When Sinclair was dying of cancer in 1939, he recommended that the Cabinet appoint his acting C, Stewart Graham Menzies, as his replacement. Menzies was very rich and proper. He was an Eton graduate who had never attended university. Instead he had gone into the elite Grenadiers and a year later into the Life Guards. He rode to hounds for recreation and relaxed at White's, an exclusive London club for gentlemen. Menzies was clearly a perfect replacement for Sinclair. However, his career as C got off to the kind of bad start that underscored the precarious nature of espionage everywhere.

When Menzies took over in November 1939, MI-6 had given the main responsibility for British espionage to agents in The Hague, the capital of the Netherlands. There, behind the façade of His Majesty's Passport Control Office on a quiet residential street, Major R. Henry Stevens directed an extensive spy ring inside Germany. His associate was Captain S. Payne Best, who had lived for years in the Netherlands and ran an import-export business as a front for his MI-6 activities.

As Englishmen living in the Netherlands, Stevens and Best had come to the notice of German Abwehr and SD agents who spied there. Soon after the War began, the Germans decided to find a way to test them. Early in September 1939, Best and Stevens were approached by a German émigré, who offered to put them in touch with a representative of the anti-Nazi underground in Germany. After getting Menzies' approval, Best and Stevens agreed to meet the anti-Nazi and were soon introduced to a "Captain Schaemmel" of the German Army transportation corps. The first meeting was cordial, and the three men promised to stay in touch and exchange information. One meeting led to another, and soon Schaemmel had revealed that some German Army officers were concocting a plot to overthrow Hitler and restore peace with the Allies. The German was a persuasive, obviously cultured man, and his story was convincing. Intrigued, the two Britons agreed to pursue the idea further with Schaemmel at a café in a little Dutch town on the German border, five miles east of Venlo.

In midafternoon on November 9, Best and Stevens headed their blue Buick down a narrow street toward the café. Just as the Buick rounded a corner, a large, open car roared across the border from Germany and crashed through the frontier barrier pole. As its passengers sprayed machine-gun and pistol fire to pin down the Dutch border guards, the open car raced down the street and blocked the Buick. Five Germans leaped out, snatched Best and Stevens from the Buick, clapped them in handcuffs and pushed them into the open car. A Dutch intelligence officer riding with the Britons was mortally wounded. The German car screeched back across the border to sanctuary.

By coincidence, an attempt on Hitler's life had been made in the Bürgerbräukeller, Munich's most famous drinking spot, the night before. Though the would-be assassin was acting alone, the SD found it convenient to implicate the two British agents in the incident. Best and Stevens were accordingly clapped into a German jail and kept there for the duration of the War.

In London, the abduction of the two key British agents in Western Europe was a shattering blow to Menzies and MI-6. Stevens' espionage ring had been a vital conduit for Nazi secrets; now leaderless, the ring collapsed and died. Eight months later the fall of France virtually eliminated British intelligence activity on the Continent. MI-6 would have to start over, with most of the Continent under Nazi control.

The Abwehr and the SD, however, had handicaps of their own that evened the score with Britain just then. One was a misguided optimism on Hitler's part. Another was an internecine rivalry that put the Abwehr and the SD at odds with each other at home. A third—and in the long run crucial—handicap was an uncertainty in their own leadership.

During the prewar years, Hitler had nursed the quixotic dream of a union between Germany, with its great land forces, and Britain, the world's greatest sea power. Such an alliance, the Führer imagined, would be unchallengeable.

Two German policemen survey Munich's ruined Bürgerbräukeller, where Hitler escaped an assassin's bomb in November 1939. Although the crime was committed by a lone German malcontent, the Nazi police took advantage of public sentiment to fasten most of the blame for it on two British agents.

In 1935, to prevent possible damage to this plan, he forbade all spying in England. Not until two years later, when British diplomats protested that German rearmament flouted the terms of the treaty that had ended World War I, did Hitler rescind that prohibition. By 1939 Abwehr agents had begun to scatter throughout England in search of information on the location of airfields, harbors, docks and warehouses.

The kidnapping of Stevens and Best in that year was a shining triumph for the Germans, and brought kudos to the SD in particular. Adolf Hitler gratefully presented the Iron Cross to the men responsible—chief among them Captain Schaemmel, who in reality was Major Walter Schellenberg of the SD. The adroit operation near Venlo also enhanced the prestige of Schellenberg's superior, Reinhard Heydrich, who as chief of the SD was already one of Nazi Germany's most powerful men.

Heydrich was a man of many talents. He was a linguist, a swordsman, a skier and a horseman. He piloted airplanes, played the violin and competed in pentathlons. When he joined the German Navy as a cadet in 1922 he seemed certain to have a promising career, and he soon established a fine record as a signals officer.

But Heydrich was an austere, harsh man whom fellow sailors detested. In the wardroom his officers shunned him and mocked his reedy voice behind his back. The fact that he was also a ladies' man did nothing to endear him to his colleagues. Heydrich wooed and discarded a succession of women, until his philandering finally got the better of him. He was briefly captivated by the daughter of a well-known Navy officer. When Heydrich abruptly announced he intended to marry someone else, the girl's father was enraged. He brought pressure to bear on the Naval authorities, and Heydrich was discharged. He was jobless and embittered when, in 1931, his fortunes took a new turn.

Through Nazi acquaintances, Heydrich was introduced

Recounting the assassination attempt on Hitler, the Nazi Party newspaper (left) lines up photographs of British intelligence agents Captain S. Payne Best and Major R. Henry Stevens with that of German Communist Georg Elser. The publication praised Major Walter Schellenberg (above) for his apprehension of the two Englishmen. "England threw the bomb so that it could find an escape from the embarrassment caused by its reverses," said the newspaper indignantly.

to Heinrich Himmler, chief of the Schutzstaffel, or SS, Hitler's armed guard. Himmler was impressed by Heydrich's self-assured bearing and nimble mind, and gave him the job of setting up an intelligence and security branch for the SS. The SD was the result.

Heydrich began his new assignment by emulating the British, whom he held in awe. He based the SD on his conception of the British secret service combined with naïve ideas suggested by his reading of detective stories and spy novels. He took to referring to himself as C, and his office was equipped with a rubber stamp bearing the command "Submit to C." Notwithstanding that somewhat fatuous affectation, by degrees he built up an efficient network of informants who reached into every corner of Germany.

Under Heydrich, the SD exuded an air of dark adventure that attracted some of National Socialism's most intellectual and dedicated young men. Yet to Heydrich himself the Nazi ideology mattered little. He cared only for power, and power he got. By 1934 he had become the head of the Gestapo as well as the SD, a major general in the SS and Himmler's second-in-command—a role he still held in 1939, when under his direction the British agents Stevens and Best were kidnapped.

His success made Heydrich the archrival of Admiral Wilhelm Canaris, the head of the Abwehr (pages 30-39). The more thoroughly either man poked into the nation's security, the more inevitably he trespassed on the other's domain. Each official secretly thought that one must eventually eliminate the other. But being spies and naturally discreet, the two remained superficially cooperative, even friendly. They met for lunch and exchanged family visits. Heydrich occasionally played the violin at the musical soirees that Frau Canaris liked to hold. However, the Admiral wrote of his rival as "a violent and fanatical man with whom it will be impossible to work at all closely." Heydrich in turn considered Canaris "an old fox and not to be trusted."

The puzzling world of espionage had few figures slier than Canaris. His snow-white hair, bushy eyebrows, drooping eyes and slight stoop gave him a grandfatherly appearance that concealed a brilliantly cunning mind and a taste for the devious. He dropped hints that his non-German name could be explained by kinship with Admiral Constantine Kanaris, a hero of the Greek war of liberation from the

Ottoman Empire in 1822. In fact, he was the son of a Westphalian industrialist of Italian descent whose forebears had dropped a final vowel from the name. Canaris' adventures as a Naval officer in World War I were legendary. It was rumored that the spy Mata Hari had been his mistress, and that as a war prisoner in Italy, Canaris had strangled the jail's chaplain and escaped in his cassock.

Canaris was an ardent nationalist. He welcomed the advent of Nazism as a movement of national resurgence and the rise of Adolf Hitler as its standard bearer. "Hitler is reasonable," Canaris once told an acquaintance, "and sees your point of view as long as you put it to him properly."

The flag of the OKW—the Armed Forces High Command—flies over the headquarters of the Abwehr, Germany's primary military intelligence agency. The building, which was located in central Berlin, housed departments of communications, sabotage, counterespionage and false documentation. Abwehr officials supervised a worldwide work force of 13,000—almost as many people as there were in an army division.

But little by little, doubts had crept into Canaris' mind. When an Army officer was drummed out of the service on trumped-up charges of homosexuality—just to make room for a more ardent Nazi replacement—Canaris was visibly shocked. As the Nazis intensified their oppression of the Jews, he grew increasingly disturbed by his government's cruelty. His loyalty shaken, he made a number of anti-Nazis welcome in the Abwehr, and even courted a few personal informants in the Gestapo and in Hitler's entourage.

Nevertheless, Canaris was never wholly able to shake off the mesmerizing effect of Hitler's personality. He kept up every appearance of the efficient and dedicated servant of his nation's armed forces, and he supported Hitler's campaigns with all the skill at his command. From his headquarters in a brown stucco building on a fashionable Berlin street, Canaris commanded a vast network of information. He enlisted Germans who were assigned to diplomatic and commercial posts abroad to supply him with information, and through them he also enlisted a number of foreigners in the German cause. At home and in capital cities abroad he even organized deaf-mutes able to read lips, and assigned them to restaurants to watch diplomats and write down what they said.

By 1939 Abwehr spy rings were operating in Latin America, the United States, the Soviet Union, France and the neutral countries of Europe. They were just getting a foothold in England when they ran into trouble. At the very time that Stevens and Best were being kidnapped in the Netherlands, the British were stepping up their own counterespionage. Within a week of the declaration of war in September, all enemy aliens in Britain were ordered to register with the government. Of the 74,000 foreigners who reported, any who aroused even the merest suspicions that they were engaged in espionage were put under surveillance by MI-5. That action severely cramped whatever operations Germany might have been ready to undertake in England; one British intelligence officer boasted that "Germany would go into the War blind."

He was right. Incredibly, the Abwehr did not respond with a full-scale assault on England's counterespionage. Hitler persisted in the notion that Britain would see the futility of resistance and come to terms with Germany. Only when France fell in June 1940 and Britain's determination

to fight alone finally became clear to him did Hitler fully awaken from his dream of collaboration. In July, he ordered the Abwehr to deluge the enemy country with spies. Now Canaris had to make up for lost time, and he swiftly conceived and set into motion Operation *Lena*, a massive effort to train secret agents and insert them into Britain.

Within six weeks, the first two of the new crop of Abwehr agents had been put through a spy school in Hamburg, where they learned the rudiments of radio transmitting and receiving, writing in invisible ink and encoding. Each was given false identification papers and ration coupons, a radio transmitter and £200 spending money, then flown to England and dropped by parachute at night into the countryside. During the autumn, another 25 or more agents followed, some by air and some by sea; most were men and women in their twenties. Soon the radio receivers at the Abwehr's Hamburg control center were crackling with secret messages from inside England. As instructed, the new agents were sending information on the locations of antiaircraft gun emplacements, troop concentrations, hidden airfields and hangars—crucial data for the Luftwaffe, which was now engaged in the Battle of Britain.

Inevitably, the Abwehr lost some of its spies. Radios suddenly went dead, and word filtered back to Germany of executions in British prisons. But to the Abwehr the attrition rate was acceptably low, and all other signs were positive. The flow of information from Britain increased as more spies infiltrated, and Canaris and his staff concluded that their program of espionage, after a belated start, had taken root in Britain and was branching out rapidly.

But the Abwehr's conception of its British operation was grotesquely distorted. In reality, the operation had been a disaster from the beginning and was growing more disastrous by the week. Every single spy dispatched to England had been arrested. The spies who refused to cooperate with the British had been jailed or executed. The rest of them, persuaded by visions of the hangman's noose, had been "turned"; they were now double agents. While pretending to work for their homeland, they were actually working for their captors, and the information they sent to Germany—the data so prized by the Abwehr—offered no more intelligence than the British wanted to release. Without knowing it, the Abwehr had fallen victim to a gigantic deception that would grow even more complex as the War progressed. The British aptly called their hoax the Double Cross.

The Double Cross—which grew to be one of the trickiest government undertakings of the secret war—had its origin in the fickle allegiance of a single spy, Arthur Owens, a Welsh electrical engineer who had contacts in Germany. Owens independently initiated his career as an espionage agent in 1936 by passing along tidbits of information about German shipping to the British Admiralty. Within the year he swung the other way. On a business trip to Germany, he

met Major Nikolaus Ritter, an officer of the Abwehr's Hamburg branch. Ritter took Owens out on the town, wined and dined him, flattered him and succeeded in recruiting him as a German agent with the code name Johnny. Back in London, Owens confessed to MI-5. Somewhat wary, but willing to try anything that might net information, MI-5 gave Owens the code name Snow and put him to work under careful surveillance to deceive the Abwehr.

When war was declared, the British were understandably doubtful of Owens' true allegiance, and they threw him into Wandsworth Prison. When the spy protested that he had indeed been working as Snow—and not Johnny—they brought a radio transmitter to his cell and carefully watched to see what he would do with it. Owens immediately sent a message to Major Ritter in Hamburg. His first words were "Ein Glas Bier"—"a glass of beer"—a phrase that instantly identified him to Ritter; it was the only German Owens knew, and presumably it recalled their night on the town together. Then followed a message telling Ritter in effect that he had arrived and was fine, and asking for instructions.

That was enough to satisfy MI-5. Snow was released from prison, and from that day on he engaged in a flourishing correspondence with the Abwehr—all of it under MI-5's direction. He sent a stream of information about ship movements and deliveries of matériel from the United States—information that MI-5 deemed harmless because German aerial reconnaissance could verify it. In exchange he received instructions and queries that provided MI-5 with valuable clues about the Abwehr. Released from prison, Snow made several trips to the Continent to see Ritter in the autumn of 1939. During one such trip Ritter passed along the names and addresses of three German spies still at large in England: a team of brothers, and a woman who was acting as a paymaster for German agents near Bournemouth. As Johnny, Owens was instructed to contact the three and use them as his subagents. Instead, on returning to England as Snow he gave their names to MI-5, which promptly had them jailed. Apparently Ritter never learned that his man had been responsible for the arrests.

While MI-5's investment in Snow was beginning to pay dividends, the agency was harvesting other German spies with a minimum of effort and a maximum of cooperation from British citizens. The latter, put on guard by the threat of

At Hradschin Castle, the headquarters of the Germans in Prague, General Reinhard Heydrich (front) leads fellow officers in a Nazi salute. Grateful to Heydrich for his work as chief of the Sicherheitsdienst, the intelligence division of the SS, Hitler rewarded him with an appointment as acting governor-general of Czechoslovakia in September 1941.

invasion, were acutely sensitive to suspicious strangers. Most of the agents sent by the Abwehr were spotted and picked up only a few hours, or at most a few days, after they tumbled from the skies or waded onto the beaches.

Some agents gave themselves away by operating their radio transmitters, which the British immediately tracked down with radio direction finders. More often, the agents were betrayed by their lack of experience, their naïveté or their ignorance of British custom. One pair who had arrived by sea were arrested when a shore patrol noticed them sitting on the beach eating German sausages for breakfast. Another would-be spy, thirsty after a trek inland from the beach, knocked on the door of a pub at 9 a.m. and asked for a pint of hard cider—unaware that alcoholic beverages could not, by law, be sold before 10 a.m.

Another German agent was tripped up when he handed over ration coupons—required only at the grocer's—to pay for a meal in a restaurant. Yet another made a fateful mistake at a railway station. When told that his ticket would cost "ten and six"—10 shillings and sixpence—he offered the booking clerk 10 pounds and six shillings. Civilians lost no time in passing on the news of such aberrations to their own authorities. Clearly, the Abwehr had underestimated the alertness of the British population. As for the spies them-

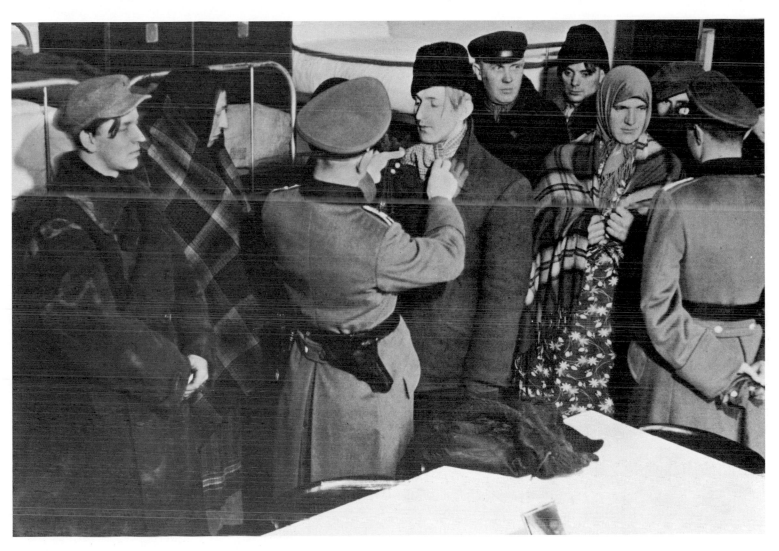

German security police under SS command dress up as Polish peasants in 1941. The masquerade made it possible for the Germans to mingle with partisans, and thus to ferret out and execute resistance leaders.

selves, few of them preferred death to cooperation. Most gave in easily and began new careers as double agents.

Still, the conversion of spies to double agents was no simple undertaking for MI-5 and MI-6. Once turned, the double agent had to be reassured and acclimated before he could be counted on to perform effectively for his new master. He had to be provided with an identity card, ration books, clothing coupons, a place to live and a cover occupation. Each fledgling double agent required a radio operator to monitor and transmit his messages, a housekeeper and cook, day and night guards, sometimes a car and driver, and always a case officer to control and guide him.

The case officer, who was generally an older man, exerted an almost paternal influence over his double agent, exploiting the emotional dependency of the uprooted youth to reshape him into a trusted subordinate. The two were in touch every day and were bound by common interests. To reassure any real German agents who might be observing, and to make sure the recruit would not be tripped up by leading questions from his German contact, the officer made certain that his double agent maintained a spy's routine by lurking around Army posts, dockyards and airfields, so that he appeared to be gathering data.

With the introduction of each new double agent, the Double Cross system grew in personnel and complexity. Inevitably, the larger it grew, the more fragile it became. The greatest potential for disaster lay in communications with Germany. Obviously the double agents had to send back sufficiently accurate information to keep the confidence of the Abwehr. True information had to be harmless to British security; at the same time, false information sent to mislead the Germans had to be subtle—a blatant falsehood could alert the Abwehr to the Double Cross. The more double agents employed by the British, the greater the chances were that they would accidentally send contradictory messages—an error that might kindle German suspicions.

What should be revealed and what kept secret? What lies would be safe? To solve this dilemma, a Double Cross Committee was formed from representatives of MI-5 and MI-6, the armed forces and the Foreign Office. While a branch of MI-5 would continue to handle the double agents, the new directorate would coordinate the flow of messages to the Continent. The directorate was sometimes called the "Twenty Committee"; the name was a play on Double Cross, which was sometimes abbreviated as XX—20 in Roman numerals.

In guiding the Double Cross, the Twenty Committee learned much of value about German plans by simply noting the Abwehr's questions to its spies. When, in the fall of 1940, the double agents were flooded with queries about coastal defenses and the location of food supplies in southeast England, the German intention to invade that area became apparent. But after a time the focus of the questions changed from locations to quantities of foods arriving from the United States and Canada; clearly, the Germans were trying to determine how successfully Allied convoys were eluding German U-boats in the Atlantic.

The Twenty Committee played more than a defensive role. By skillfully shaping answers to many questions, it conspired to influence the plans of the Germans. During the Battle of Britain, when cities all over England were being pulverized at an alarming rate by the Luftwaffe, the Twenty Committee had its double agents plant false information to the effect that certain Royal Air Force bases were noticeably weak in antiaircraft defense. The Germans believed the reports, and shifted the emphasis of their bombing attacks away from the towns and factories to the presumably vulnerable airfields—which actually were stoutly defended. Later in the War, the Abwehr sent one of its agents chilling questions about Britain's ability to defend itself against poison gas attacks. The agent responded with an account of the excellent preparations England had made—and further queries from Germany ceased, suggesting that the Germans had been deterred from whatever plans they may have had for using the gas.

While performing such sleights of hand, the Twenty Committee had to exercise extreme caution. Its vast potential for deception would dissolve instantly if the Germans saw through its lies. "No one can maintain a bluff indefinitely," wrote John C. Masterman, an MI-5 official and participant in the Double Cross. "Sooner or later a blunder or sheer mischance will give it away. If the Germans once gained full knowledge of our procedure in one case, they would inevitably become suspicious of the rest, examine them in every detail, and end by guessing the truth about them all."

Luckily for the Allies, the Germans never did catch on, but the Double Crossers had some uncomfortably close calls. One occurred through a German agent who parachuted into England in September 1940. He was picked up a few hours after landing, turned and given the code name Summer. Summer proved so cooperative and skilled as a double agent that he was installed in a private house near Hinxton, eight miles south of Cambridge. But he was made of sterner stuff than his colleagues: He had only pretended to turn. One day he overcame his guard, tied the fellow up, helped himself to a motorcycle and made off. After traveling some distance, Summer happened upon a canoe, which he lashed to the motorcycle, then continued his flight. Summer hoped to reach Norfolk and from there paddle down a series of inland waterways to the coast and thence into the North Sea. But his luck finally gave out. His machine broke down and he was arrested shy of his goal; he had come, nevertheless, within an ace of wrecking the entire Double Cross system.

For his effort, Summer met the traditional fate of the spy—execution. But of course the Abwehr received an entirely different report of his activities. When Summer's wireless transmitter abruptly went off the air at the end of January 1941, the anxious Germans were informed by Snow that Summer had aroused the suspicions of the police and had used a false set of seaman's papers to flee

In a London suburb, a sentry patrols a detention camp where MI-5 interned captured German spies. MI-5 concealed the camp's purpose from neighborhood residents by spreading the fiction that it was a convalescent home for wounded British officers. Actually it was used as a center for grilling captives and trying to turn them into double agents.

the country by ship. The Abwehr swallowed the story.

Despite his near-escape, Summer was not without benefit to MI-5. Before he made his bid for freedom, he betrayed another German agent who had arrived in England by parachute. After his arrest and breakdown under interrogation, this spy, code-named Tate, underwent an almost religious conversion to the Allied cause. He soon developed into one of the most trusted and productive of Britain's double agents. From October 1940 to the end of the War, Tate transmitted hundreds of messages to his Hamburg spymaster. He was so highly regarded by the Abwehr that it smuggled £20,000 to him. The money, intended to enable Tate to escalate his spying, was confiscated by MI-5.

The Germans, believing that Tate had £20,000 at his disposal—a sum that far exceeded the money a spy would normally have—expected Tate to have unlimited freedom to travel. Suddenly he found himself beset by demands and questions he could not answer. So he cunningly found a way of evading them. He invented a visit from the British police, who, he said, had questioned him about his failure to register for military service. He had therefore taken a job as a farm laborer, work that exempted him from the draft. Unfortunately, he said, such a job curtailed travel; only on weekends could he go to London in search of information.

The Abwehr accepted his fantasy, and Tate then expanded on it. He peopled his imaginary farm in the village of

Wearing a trench coat and fedora, German agent Karl Richter finds himself surrounded by British intelligence officers after parachuting into a Hertfordshire wood on May 13, 1941. Richter was one of the few captured spies who preferred death to collaboration; refusing to bend to his captors, he was hanged seven months after being apprehended.

Radlett, north of London, with appropriate characters. In a snug brick farmhouse at the end of a lane, so Tate's story went, lived a farmer and his attractive daughter. As luck would have it, the daughter had a girl friend who worked for the ciphering department at one of the ministries and visited regularly on weekends. She and Tate became intimate, and in that cozy, bucolic atmosphere the girl soon confided the details of her department's work. She became even more informative after her ministry lent her to an American unit.

Tate's professionalism under trying circumstances impressed the Abwehr, and it was delighted with the treasure trove of intelligence emanating from the little farm in Radlett. So highly was Tate regarded for his misinformation that—he learned by radio message from his controller in Germany—he had been awarded the Iron Cross, Second Class, and then First. In the meantime, Tate was actually working in comparative freedom as a freelance photographer, for the British trusted him too.

The Abwehr, encouraged by the seeming proliferation of its spy network in England, unwittingly fed the flames of its own disaster by sending more and more agents. Without exception, they were either absorbed into the growing Double Cross system, or executed. One agent, who alighted by parachute in January 1940, broke his ankle on landing. His truculent nature and the publicity he received made him useless to British intelligence and ordained his death. Another, a belligerent fellow who descended in May 1941 with a stack of pound notes for Tate, was also executed; the reasons are obscure, but probably he refused to turn.

Though accepted by both the Axis and the Allies, the execution of spies was generally opposed by MI-5. "A live spy," wrote Masterman, "even if he cannot transmit messages, is always of some use as a book of reference; a dead spy is of no sort of use. But some had to perish, both to satisfy the public that the security of the country was being maintained and also to convince the Germans that the others were working properly and were not under control. It would have taxed even German credulity if *all* their agents had apparently overcome the hazards of their landing."

As the Double Cross gathered momentum, it developed that not all of its recruits had to be turned by MI-5; some were willing renegades who had been anti-Nazi all along. A star in that category was Dusko Popov, code-named Tricycle by the British, a Yugoslavian acquainted with wealthy families in both England and Germany. In 1940, when business affairs took him to the German Embassy in Belgrade, a secretary there proposed that his entree into British high society might enable him to do useful undercover work for Germany. Pretending to agree, he consulted a British diplomat who advised him to play along with the Germans. He did, and the Germans sent him to London.

Popov reported at once to MI-5, revealing that he had been furnished the name and address of the most important German agent in England, code-named Giraffe. The information was doubly welcome to MI-5; Giraffe was already a Double Cross agent, having been recruited in Lisbon some time before, and Popov's message showed that the Germans had not caught on to his defection. Rainbow, another anti-Nazi who turned up in England, had been educated in Germany and had worked there until 1938. Careless, a Polish airman, feigned collaboration after being shot down by the Germans, as did Father, a noted Belgian pilot.

Two Norwegians crossed the North Sea by German seaplane and, provided with a radio transmitter, explosives and bicycles, were set adrift in a small boat off the east coast of Scotland. Trained by the Germans as saboteurs, they had instructions to blow up several specified food depots, to establish radio contact and to begin reporting on air-raid damage, troop movements and public morale. As soon as they landed, they turned themselves over to the police and entered the Double Cross, which gave them the code names Mutt and Jeff.

To assure the Germans that Mutt and Jeff were on the job, MI-5 decided to stage a mock sabotage at one of the food depots—no small task, since the British press had to be fooled. "To get full value on the German side," Masterman said, "lurid accounts of the explosion have to appear in the press, but the press very properly will only put in accounts which their reporters can send to them. And if the explosion or wreckage has not been considerable, the reports in the press will, if they appear at all, be correspondingly meager." Furthermore, the fire had to be fierce enough to draw the attention of the press but manageable enough to be extinguished by the local firemen.

"There were many ticklish moments," Masterman recalled, "before the operation was successfully completed. The two aged fire guards at the food store could only with difficulty be roused from slumber and lured away from that part of the premises where the incendiary bomb had been placed. A too-zealous local policeman almost succeeded in arresting our officers." But in the end the bomb went off, the fire burned without injuring anyone or causing severe damage, accounts of the sabotage appeared in British papers, and the Abwehr felt secure in the knowledge that Mutt and Jeff indeed knew their business.

Of all the anti-Nazis who did yeoman service for the British in the twilight world of the Double Cross, perhaps the most famous was a durable, creative and flamboyant Spaniard who went by the code name Garbo.

Garbo was an ardent anti-Nazi who offered his services as a spy to the British early in the War and was rebuffed. Far from encouraging volunteers, MI-5 and MI-6 insisted on doing their own recruiting, the better to keep control over their agents. Undaunted, Garbo wooed the Germans—but with a secret plan percolating in his mind. So plausibly did he present his *bona fides* to the German Embassy in Madrid that officials there agreed to sponsor him on an espionage mission to England, a country he claimed to know well but really did not know at all. Carrying forged papers, invisible ink, money and cover addresses, Garbo bade the Germans farewell in July 1941 and set out for England. He never got there. Instead he stopped in Lisbon, where for the next nine months, aided by a tourist guidebook, a map and an outdated railway timetable, he concocted lengthy and convincing espionage reports on the British Isles. He explained away the Lisbon postmark by telling the Germans that he had the services of a courier, who conveyed his reports from England to Portugal.

Warming to his work, Garbo then created three imaginary subagents who sent information to him from the English West Country, from Glasgow and from Liverpool. He and his nonexistent assistants flooded the Germans with convincing reports on British fortifications, troop concentrations, arms shipments by rail, and shipping. As he intended, his information was close to what the Germans expected to hear, and they were completely taken in.

By 1942, the one-man enterprise had approached the British secret service several times, only to be met with cold official refusals. In February of that year, however, Garbo pulled off a caper that made the British pay attention. From Garbo's imaginary subagent in Liverpool the German Navy received word that a huge convoy was about to sail from that port to relieve the island of Malta, a crucial British outpost in the Mediterranean. Malta-based planes and ships were playing havoc with Axis convoys that carried supplies to the Afrika Korps in the North African desert, and the Germans were trying to eliminate the outpost through blockade and aerial siege. It was therefore crucial that no Allied convoy reach the island. Spurred by Garbo's fictional report, the Axis made elaborate preparations to intercept the imaginary convoy in the Mediterranean. No record survives of how the Germans reacted when they found no convoy, but presumably wild-goose chases were common enough not to throw undue suspicion on Garbo.

When word of Garbo's coup filtered back to London via a neutral diplomat, MI-5 warmed to the freelance spy. "It became clear to us at this stage," Masterman wrote later, "that Garbo was more fitted to be a worthy collaborator than an unconscious competitor." In April, Garbo was smuggled to England—where the Germans thought he had been all along—and there continued his virtuoso performance. "The one-man band of Lisbon developed into an orchestra," Masterman recalled, "and an orchestra which played a more and more ambitious program. Garbo himself turned out to be something of a genius. He was the master of a facile and lurid style in writing; he showed great industry and ingenuity coupled with a passionate and quixotic zeal for his task." In London, Garbo added four more imaginary agents to his ring, some of whom now corresponded directly with the Germans and were sent long lists of queries for which the Twenty Committee provided answers.

Only once did Garbo have to readjust his network to avoid exposure. In the spring of 1942, when the Allies were gearing up for Operation *Torch*, the invasion of North Africa, it became clear to MI-5 that Garbo's imaginary man in Liverpool could not avoid seeing part of the invasion fleet that would be gathering there. If the Germans learned later that Liverpool had been a staging area for *Torch* and yet had not been so informed by Garbo's local agent, they might well conclude that the man was either a traitor or a phony—and that realization could bring Garbo's house of cards tumbling down.

Garbo, the master of fiction, solved the problem by incapacitating his Liverpool agent with a fatal illness. He allowed the man to linger on for a decent interval, then told the Germans he had died. MI-5 added credence to the ruse by placing a false obituary notice in a Liverpool paper. Garbo forwarded the notice to the Abwehr, which, in turn, sent its profound sympathies to the agent's widow.

By the spring of 1944, Garbo had expanded his hypothetical organization to 14 active agents and 11 well-placed contacts, including one in the British Ministry of Information. He had supplied each of them with a personality, a family, a professional background, a prose style and a particular handwriting. Together the team had sent some 400 secret letters and 2,000 radio messages to the Germans, who trusted the senders implicitly. And not one of them existed—except in the fertile imagination of Garbo himself. So indispensable did the Spanish spy appear to both of his employers that in 1944 the British awarded him the Order of the British Empire—at about the same time that he received, in absentia, the Iron Cross from a grateful Germany.

Through the imaginative high jinks of three dozen or more spies like Garbo, the Double Cross system hummed like a well-oiled machine, producing reams of half-truth and subtle falsehood that the Abwehr accepted without complaint.

In return, the German spymasters plied their agents with a mass of questions and instructions that provided the British with an enlightening picture of the Abwehr: its structure, its methods and, most important, its intentions.

By the end of 1942, the nature of the Abwehr correspondence began to indicate that the Germans had recognized a shift in the tide of the War. The panache of 1940 had evaporated. The Luftwaffe had lost the Battle of Britain, and with that defeat the German plan to invade England had been shelved. The Axis powers were being driven out of North Africa and the Mediterranean. Hitler's ill-advised invasion of the Soviet Union had diverted millions of German troops to the East to fight for a victory that was beginning to seem unattainable.

The Abwehr's questions for its agents in Britain now left no doubt that the Germans were on the defensive and anticipating an Allied invasion of Europe. The Abwehr sought information on the arrival of American reinforcements, the concentration and movement of troops, any cancellations of leave, the assemblage of landing craft and equipment, and the appearance of novel weapons, vessels and aircraft that might have been designed for a massive assault. From these myriad clues the Abwehr hoped to find the answer to a burning question: When and where would the Allies invade the Continent?

Indeed, the Allies had already begun long-range planning for such an invasion, and were devising an elaborate scheme to deceive the Germans about its timing and its target. For that ruse the work of the Twenty Committee and the double agents would assume a new urgency and importance, because the agents had the ears of the enemy. The Double Cross, however, would not be the only Allied player in that high-stakes game of deception. In the shadowy arena of the secret war, another contest was simultaneously being waged and an advantage gained. Just as the Allies had bested their opponents in counterespionage, they were gaining the upper hand in the complex craft of devising—and deciphering—coded communications.

GERMANY'S MASTER SPY

Admiral Wilhelm Canaris, chief of German Armed Forces Intelligence, leads his aides on a review of troops specially trained for undercover assignments.

THE ENIGMATIC MAN BEHIND THE ABWEHR

Puckishly wearing an Italian infantry lieutenant's hat with his own Navy overcoat, Wilhelm Canaris casts a suspicious glance over his shoulder.

One day in 1941 Admiral Wilhelm Canaris, head of the Abwehr spy network, was driving down a country road in Spain with a fellow officer when suddenly he braked, sprang from the car and gave a military salute to a shepherd tending a flock by the roadside. "You never can tell when there's a senior officer underneath," Canaris muttered to his astonished colleague.

Few people knew what lay underneath the mask that Canaris presented to the world. He was a staunch authoritarian (he welcomed the rise of Hitler) but disliked wearing a military uniform and usually left his medals in a drawer. He preferred work to his family, and dogs to his fellow workers. His close associate Wilhelm Keitel, Chief of Staff of the German Armed Forces, pronounced him "an enigma and a closed book," and a subordinate found him "contradictory in his instructions, unjust, moody and unpredictable." For all that, Wilhelm Canaris built the Abwehr from an adjunct of the German military establishment into a vast organization that—despite its misfortunes with the British Double Cross—succeeded in gathering intelligence from thousands of spies all over the world.

Though he never served as a foreign agent, Canaris had triumphed in at least one adventure of the sort that fill spies' lives. During World War I, as a Navy lieutenant aboard a cruiser prowling off the coast of Chile, he tangled with three British warships; he and his crew were interned on a sparsely inhabited Chilean isle. Secretly, Canaris slipped off one night in a fisherman's boat and escaped to the mainland. After a two-week trek on horseback over the Andes, he reached Argentina and, with the help of the German Naval Attaché in Buenos Aires, acquired a false passport representing him as Chilean. Canaris booked passage on a Dutch steamer and made his way home to Germany—eluding customs officials when the ship put in at enemy England.

Perhaps Navy Commander Karl Dönitz described Canaris best when he called him a "man with many souls in his breast." Some of the manifestations of those souls appear on the following pages.

Canaris pauses while on a stroll with his dachshunds. He was so fond of the dogs that on trips he used secret radio codes to keep informed about them.

Wilhelm Canaris stands stiffly in the back row, second from right, for a class picture taken in 1905. His superiors at cadet school, which Canaris attended next, said that "despite a certain shyness, he was well liked."

Surrounded by crewmen, Lieutenant Canaris stands aboard the submarine UB-128. He earned command of the vessel for his performance on board a smaller ship, with which he had sunk three British freighters.

34

FROM NAVAL SERVICE TO ESPIONAGE

Canaris spent most of his adult life in the Navy, enlisting in 1905 at the age of 18. Trained at the German Naval Academy, he served as a lieutenant in World War I on a cruiser and several U-boats. In the 1920s he undertook a secret mission to Spain, where he persuaded industrialists to build U-boats for the German Navy.

By 1932 Canaris had risen to the rank of captain. In 1934, the head of the Abwehr resigned and proposed Canaris as his successor. Navy Commander in Chief Admiral Erich Raeder, seeing the advantage to the Navy of having one of its own officers in charge of Armed Forces Intelligence, helped push Canaris into the job.

As a Navy captain, Canaris wears the medals he won during World War I. The lower medal recognizes his service on submarines; the Iron Cross First Class honors a 1916 mission to neutral Spain, where he successfully negotiated for secret supply bases for German U-boats.

Raising a gloved hand, Canaris gives orders aboard the battleship Schlesien in 1934. As commander, he regularly lectured his crew on the virtues of Nazism—a habit that endeared him to officials of the party.

MANEUVERING FOR THE ABWEHR

Canaris relished his job as Abwehr chief, and from the start he worked to establish his department's importance to the Nazi state. He recruited agents by the thousands and dispersed them to sensitive listening posts about the world. Through diplomatic maneuvering he won a set of written accords that guaranteed the autonomy of the Abwehr from the SS in matters of military intelligence. The provisos earned such respect that subordinates dubbed them the Ten Commandments.

Toward the same goal, Canaris subdued his reclusive tendencies and took part in such social events as fox hunts *(below)* and gala dinners, where he might see and be seen by influential people.

On a cobbled street in the outskirts of Berlin, Canaris—wearing a white Naval hat—joins a party of foreign diplomats, German socialites and high-ranking Nazi officials at the start of a fox hunt in 1935.

SS officials and Army officers gather around a table with Canaris in the 1930s. Through such negotiating sessions, Canaris asserted the independence of the Abwehr from the SS.

Canaris meets with SS chief Heinrich Himmler (front left) and Propaganda Minister Joseph Goebbels (rear) in Berlin in 1936. Canaris used amusing small talk to win over his rivals.

At an airfield near Smolensk, Canaris chats with Colonel Franz-Eccard von Bentivegni, assigned to scout the Eastern Front in 1941. Canaris made frequent trips to confer with his agents and to brief military officers.

MISSIONS FOR HITLER AND OTHER EXCURSIONS

As head of the Abwehr, Canaris had agents all over the world to do his bidding, but he liked nothing better than to gather information himself. That predilection suited Hitler, who frequently used Canaris as his eyes and ears.

Sometimes Canaris undertook diplomatic missions of a high order. In 1940 he went to Spain to persuade Fascist dictator Francisco Franco to join the Axis in war against Britain. Franco flirted with the suggestion, then decided against it for want of war matériel.

No matter how sober the mission, Canaris often found time to indulge his fancy for disguises. On a visit to Spain during the 1943 New Year's holiday he dressed as a civilian (right), and amused both himself and the local agents by wearing a chef's hat while he prepared a festive turkey dinner for them.

Festooned in gold braid that identifies him as one of Hitler's staff officers, Admiral Canaris greets General José Moscardó, a Spanish Civil War hero, at a reception in Berlin in 1939. The occasion welcomed the return home of German troops that aided Franco in the Spanish Civil War.

Standing beside a donkey in a Spanish village, Canaris wears a fedora as he travels incognito in early 1943. He made the journey to meet with Franco and to spy firsthand on Allied shipping around Gibraltar.

39

AGENTS IN THE FIELD

Abwehr agent Josef Klein works at the short-wave radio apparatus he built in his New York City apartment, while his German shepherd keeps watch.

POOR ODDS
AND GRIM FATES

For the spy himself and for the Abwehr behind him, espionage was a complicated business that entailed exhaustive preparation and constant watchfulness. Whether he was assigned to cross enemy lines on the battlefield—a task that often devolved to mere boys *(right)*—or to serve in a foreign country, an agent usually had had training at one of some 60 spy schools the Abwehr operated in Hamburg, Berlin and other major cities. There, would-be agents learned such skills as message encoding, radio operation and microphotography to enable them to send their intelligence secretly back to Germany. For many missions, training in physical skills was vital; one group of agents bound for Scotland lost their ground transportation when they failed to prevent their bicycles from sliding off their rubber dinghy into the North Sea.

Once he had made it across enemy lines or into an enemy country, the spy had the contradictory duty of concealing his activity while doing his job. In trying to meet these dual demands, most spies failed; an estimated 95 per cent of those who went in search of military intelligence behind enemy lines were caught and executed or imprisoned. Even where there was no fighting, spying was perilous. Police and spy-conscious citizens pounced at the slightest suspicion. In the United States between 1941 and 1945 the FBI alone arrested some 4,000 suspects, and 94 of them were eventually convicted.

Until that happened the spy mustered all his ingenuity trying to stay hidden as best he could, and the Abwehr lent a hand in getting him started *(following pages)*.

Off the coast of occupied Norway, three Abwehr agents paddle a dinghy toward the shore from a seaplane on a trial run for a mission to Scotland.

Karl Arno Punzeler, a 16-year-old caught spying on U.S. troops in Belgium, hears two American soldiers read him a grim sentence: life imprisonment.

CONVINCING COVERS FOR DOUBLE LIVES

The first thing an agent needed in a foreign land was a cover—some legitimate occupation to justify his presence and cloak his interest in sensitive information.

Many agents came equipped with excellent natural covers of their own. An airline employee in Stockholm used his post to monitor war matériel shipped to England. A German-American automobile executive in Detroit passed on data about American aircraft and diesel engines when U.S. plants converted to war production. In South America, a pro-Nazi priest smuggled messages from Peru to Chile in the prayer book he customarily carried.

The cover could be a real or an imaginary job, but it had to be convincing. One spy in New York City made the mistake of posing as an undersecretary of state in a clumsy attempt to get 50 blank U.S. passports—and gave himself away because the State Department office knew perfectly well that no official of that level would be gathering passports in such number.

SS Captain Johann Siegfried Becker served as a German trade representative in Buenos Aires while masterminding an espionage ring that stretched across South America.

Ernst Weber Drohl, a 60-year-old muscleman who called himself Atlas the Strong, toured Ireland with a wrestling and weight-lifting show and a comely Irish assistant while spying for the Abwehr. He put ashore from a U-boat in February 1940 with a message for the Irish Republican Army and £3,750 to help it sabotage British installations in Northern Ireland.

Colonel Frederick Joubert Duquesne (left), a South Africa-born American citizen who sported medals of honor from Turkey, Bulgaria, Austria-Hungary and Germany, had held a grudge against the British for 40 years, ever since the Boer War. In New York City, he passed as a Wall Street businessman while stealing blueprints of American weapons for the Abwehr. Twenty-seven-year-old Lilly Barbara Stein (below) provided a forwarding address for Duquesne and other German spies in New York while she was running a shop and working as an artist's model.

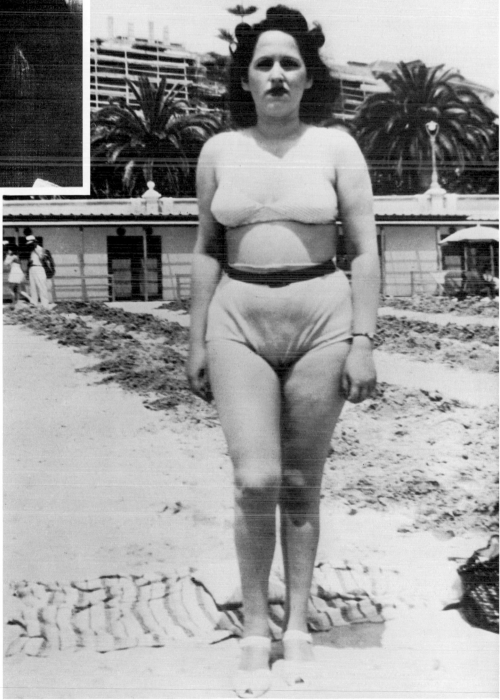

Dr. Hermann Goertz and 19-year-old Marianne Emig, who posed as his niece, photographed RAF bases in England. To explain their travels around the countryside, they pretended to be researching a book on ancient monuments.

The cutter Kyloe (above) sails from France for South Africa under the command of Captain Christian Nissen (right), a veteran yachtsman.

A YACHTING PARTY TO GET UNDER WAY

Most Abwehr spies reached their destinations by U-boat or parachute, two conveyances that could reach enemy territory undetected. But in the spring of 1941, the Abwehr staged a more spectacular expedition for Robey Leibbrandt, a former policeman and heavyweight boxing champion with orders to "stir up as much trouble and carry out as much sabotage as possible" in South Africa, his homeland. He went there from German-occupied France aboard a 60-foot racing yacht called the *Kyloe*.

The journey was a perilous, 67-day run through 8,111 miles of British-controlled seas. To the hazards of war were added the vagaries of nature. "The wind is 10 to 11 knots," wrote one sailor late in the voyage. "The helmsman must lash himself down. Almost three weeks with nothing but wet things next to our bodies."

The athlete-turned-spy was spared that particular discomfort: Leibbrandt spent a large part of the voyage belowdecks suffering from seasickness.

Abwehr spy Robey Leibbrandt practices rowing in the Kyloe's rubber dinghy while a companion focuses a motion-picture camera. Abwehr chief Wilhelm Canaris gave orders that the voyage be documented.

A member of the Kyloe crew undergoes a ritual "baptism" to mark his first crossing of the Equator. Once at sea, the crewmen struck the German flag, doffed their uniforms and postured as an American yachting party.

Captain Christian Nissen (center front) and his crew wear the Iron Crosses they were awarded for the success of the Kyloe's voyage. Chary of tempting fate on the return trip, Nissen prudently brought the racing yacht to port in Spanish Morocco—after 14,128 miles and 110 days at sea—and with his crew returned to Germany by plane.

GERMAN SPY KURT FREDERICK LUDWIG

A SECRET AGENT'S AMERICAN ALBUM

Once at his destination an enemy agent had to see all while trying not to be seen. One spy, Kurt Frederick Ludwig, raced through some 70 aliases while he was traveling the length and breadth of the United States.

Ludwig, who sometimes traveled with a 17-year-old German companion named Lucy Boehmler, was by turns daring and cautious. In Pennsylvania, where he came upon a convoy of Army trucks, he slowed to the convoy's crawl so that Lucy could flirt with the soldiers and find out their destination. But later, on a Midwestern country road where Ludwig was being tailed by FBI agents, he accelerated to 90 miles an hour in an effort to get away. He failed and was captured.

Until then, wherever Ludwig went his camera went along. His snapshots (right) make an interesting record of the kinds of information that struck a German spy as pertinent, from war plants to such harmless signs of American patriotism as a Liberty Bell that ornamented a park.

LAKE ERIE PORT FACILITIES IN CLEVELAND

FLYING BOATS AT A NAVAL AIR BASE

TOPIARY REPLICA OF THE LIBERTY BELL

GAS TANKS AND ELECTRIC WORKS ON NEW YORK'S EAST RIVER

LOWER MANHATTAN WATERFRONT

155MM ARTILLERY PIECE ON PARADE

BRITISH FREIGHTER DOCKED IN NEW YORK

UNDERBELLY OF A UNITED STATES ARMY PLANE

U.S. NAVAL ACADEMY MIDSHIPMEN PARADING IN ANNAPOLIS

PUTTING SPIES
UNDER SURVEILLANCE

In late 1939, when a German-born American citizen named William Sebold made a visit to his homeland, a German intelligence officer thrust upon him the leadership of a ring of Abwehr spies already operating in and around New York. The Abwehr had made a serious blunder. Sebold agreed to cooperate, but only for fear that refusing would result in reprisals against his relatives in Germany. While arranging his passage back to the United States, he surreptitiously tipped off American officials and signaled his wish to work with his adopted land instead.

In New York, Sebold set himself up as a consulting engineer in an office on 42nd Street, a busy thoroughfare in Manhattan. There, with the knowledge and assistance of the FBI, he began to court the spies the Abwehr had told him about. Over a 16-month period beginning in February 1940, he elicited more than 300 reports from the agents. Among his informants was the chef of the liner *America,* who passed on blueprints for turning the vessel into a U.S. Army transport ship. The FBI screened all the information and authorized Sebold to transmit to Germany whatever was harmless or incorrect—in the case of the troopship plans, blurring the gun mounts.

Unbeknownst to the spies, FBI cameramen were on hand in Sebold's office, secretly filming virtually every transaction. By June 1941 they had amassed enough evidence to arrest 33 enemy agents, all of whom were subsequently tried, convicted and sentenced to prison. For the United States the episode represented the biggest spy roundup in American history. For Germany it was fatal. One Abwehr spymaster asserted that it delivered the "death blow" to German espionage in the United States.

American double agent William Sebold (left) talks with German spy Hermann Lang, an inspector at a defense plant. From behind a one-way mirror the FBI took hundreds of still photographs and shot more than 20,000 feet of motion-picture film in recording the spies' visits. Sebold's office was arranged so that a clock and a calendar were visible in the photographs to document the time and date.

A DISASTROUS MISSION OF SABOTAGE

Adolf Hitler was so enraged at the arrests of the spy ring operating under William Sebold that he immediately ordered a new assault on the United States. This time the mission was not to gather information, but to scatter destruction at strategic bridges, railways and factories. A major target was to be the aluminum plants that supplied the American aircraft industry.

Eight men volunteered for the job. They promptly entered several months' training that included reading American newspapers and magazines, and touring German factories and freight yards to learn how best to incapacitate such installations.

In June of 1942 the agents sailed for the United States in two groups aboard German U-boats. One group of four put ashore on Long Island, New York, the other in Florida. Together they carried nearly $200,000 and enough fuses and explosives to keep them busy for two years.

The Long Island group landed at night at Amagansett, on the eastern end of the island. The men had just changed their clothes when a Coastguardsman on patrol stopped them for questioning. They responded with a $260 bribe; the guard took it, then disappeared on his rounds.

Thinking they were out of a tight spot, the four agents buried their supplies for safekeeping and boarded an early morning train to New York City. There they proceeded to amuse themselves by spending the Reich's money at a Fifth Avenue clothier's and in expensive restaurants. But the Coastguardsman had headed straight for his base and reported what he had seen. The supplies had been dug up, and the FBI was already on the trail of the agents.

Suddenly, for reasons not clear, one of the agents, George Dasch (below), blew the whole operation by turning himself in to the FBI. Claiming to be an anti-Nazi leftist, Dasch revealed enough information to fill 254 single-spaced typed pages. Within two weeks the FBI had apprehended his co-conspirators, including the four who had landed in Florida. All were convicted of sabotage. Six were electrocuted; Dasch and Ernest Burger, who also cooperated with the authorities, received prison terms.

The eight German saboteurs stand for their FBI photographs; their names, ages and sentences appear beneath their pictures. "Those poor young fellows, all decent members of the party!" Hitler cried to the Abwehr chief when he heard of their capture. "Next time you can send Jews and criminals."

ERNEST BURGER, 36: Life Imprisonment

GEORGE DASCH, 39: 30 Years' Imprisonment

WERNER THIEL, 35: Death

EDWARD KERLING, 33: Death

Four waterproof cases of equipment buried by the German saboteurs who landed in Florida on June 17, 1942, lie exposed in a pit on the beach near Jacksonville. Among the explosives the saboteurs brought were blocks of TNT, coils of fuses, and bombs that were disguised to look like large pieces of coal (inset).

RICHARD QUIRIN, 34: Death

HEINRICH HEINCK, 35: Death

HERBERT HAUPT, 22: Death

HERMANN NEUBAUER, 32: Death

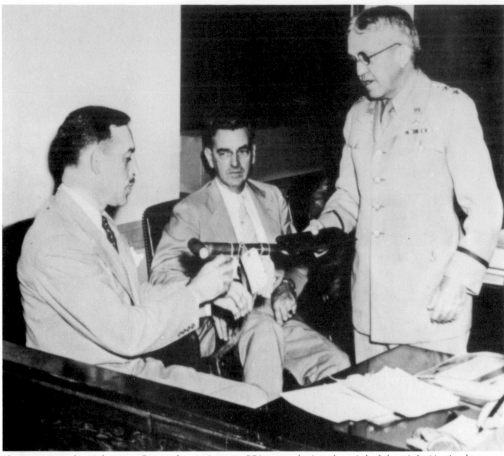

The Army's Judge Advocate General questions an FBI agent during the trial of the eight Nazi saboteurs.

Soldiers escort captured agent Heinrich Heinck through the Justice Department building in Washington.

Onlookers gather in the rain to watch as two

Police wagons carry the eight German agents from the Department of Justice, where they stood trial before a closed military court, to jail to await sentencing.

2

Just past dawn on Sunday, December 7, 1941, at a table in a back room of the stately Japanese Embassy in Washingon, D.C., a code clerk carefully pecked at the keys of an Underwood electric typewriter. From a stack of cable forms at his elbow, he was copying the 14th and final installment of a message that had begun arriving the day before. The radio circuits over which the message had come were those of the Radio Corporation of America and were the same circuits used by the public for ordinary international communication. But the message on the cable forms consisted of five-letter clusters that to the untutored eye looked like garble.

For the clerk at the embassy, the message held no challenge. Every time he tapped the keyboard to copy a letter or a space, an impulse passed into a maze of wires running from his typewriter through a bulky switchboard-like box to a second keyboard, which printed an entirely different letter or a space: The message was transposed electrically into the plain English in which it had been composed by the Japanese Foreign Ministry in Tokyo.

The message contained a litany of complaints. Among them were charges that the United States and Great Britain had "strengthened their military preparations" in Asia, "perfecting an encirclement of Japan" and endangering "the very existence of the Empire"—conditions that the Japanese government asserted it would no longer tolerate. Tokyo intended that the Japanese Ambassador present the message to the U.S. Secretary of State later that day—at 1 p.m. Washington time.

In fact, the opening salvos of the message were already in the hands of U.S. officials, for quite unknown to the Japanese clerk or anyone else at his embassy, another set of machines astonishingly like the apparatus in the Japanese Embassy's code room had been simultaneously clattering out the identical message, installment by installment, under the fingers of a young Naval Reserve lieutenant. He was using the Purple machine (so-called for the Purple cipher, as the Americans designated the code in which Japanese diplomatic messages were exchanged). The machine was a bootlegged reproduction that had been created through the efforts of imaginative American cryptanalyst William F. Friedman *(pages 78-85)* and his staff. And though the purloined message gave no hint that the Japanese were poised to attack Pearl Harbor, it did forewarn the United States that

EAVESDROPPING ON THE ENEMY

the Japanese were ready to break off diplomatic relations.

The need for long-distance communication such as that between the Japanese Foreign Ministry in Tokyo and the Embassy in Washington had brought a new dimension to 20th Century warfare. In every theater of World War II, the fate of many a battle hung on the secrecy—or lack thereof—with which information was transmitted; so, for that matter, did the life line of many a home front.

Most information was communicated long-distance by radio. But anyone with a short-wave radio receiver and a knowledge of Morse code dots and dashes could eavesdrop on radio messages. Indeed, virtually every nation had listening posts throughout the world; the United States had several on Pacific islands even before the opening of hostilities.

In an effort to thwart eavesdropping, most governments also employed dozens, later hundreds, of technicians and savants called cryptographers (from the Greek words for "hidden writing") who devised secret ways of conveying information. Hundreds of cryptanalysts were also employed; they tried to fathom the messages of the enemy and the methods by which he arrived at them. Codes and ciphers, and the making and breaking of them, thus became a major preoccupation of the secret war.

Differentiating between codes and ciphers is complex to say the least, and even the experts have different definitions. Stated simply, a code is any system of symbols (which may be letters or numbers) to which meanings have been assigned. The symbols and their equivalent meanings can be set down in a code book that, like a dictionary, may be used for handy reference. A cipher is the combinations of jumbled letters or numbers in which a message has been rendered by means of substituting one letter or number for another letter or number. The combinations may correspond to meanings recorded in a code book, or they may not—for the combinations may not have been arrived at directly, but by some roundabout mathematical or mechanical process. In theory, enciphering and deciphering can be done with pencil and paper, but in practice the ciphers used by the combatants of World War II required sophisticated machinery to accomplish both tasks.

The machine at the Japanese Embassy in Washington and the American version that eavesdropped on it were just two in a bewildering arsenal of communications devices with which the belligerents tried to inform their allies and betuddle their foes. The devices ranged from simple strips of printed paper, to be shuffled about by hand, to the German Enigma machine, a contrivance so complex that it repeatedly had the Allied cryptanalysts at its mercy.

To the enduring bafflement of those who tried to monitor an enemy's plans, a mere acquaintance with the enemy's equipment was far from sufficient to read an intercepted message. A single cipher machine could generate more letter or number combinations than the human mind could track. Furthermore, the machine's opposite number had to be properly set to unscramble a message.

Every government made the most of that fact and used separate ciphering systems for its separate undertakings—diplomacy, army movements, naval operations, air force plans, espionage, and so on. And virtually every department varied its own systems; the Japanese Navy alone employed more than 25 different systems at a time. The U.S. Purple machine could decipher messages exchanged between Japanese diplomats, but not those between officers of the Japanese Navy. U.S. government officials therefore had no inkling that Japanese aircraft carriers were already preparing for an air strike at Pearl Harbor.

That surprise attack—planned in absolute secrecy by Admiral Isoroku Yamamoto, commander of the Japanese Combined Fleet, and led by Vice Admiral Chuichi Nagumo, commander of the First Carrier Strike Force of 11 vessels and 414 planes—took place at 7:58 a.m. Hawaii time, almost simultaneously with the delivery of the farewell-to-diplomacy message in Washington.

In an hour and three quarters, the attack made a shambles of the United States Navy and Army air bases at Pearl Harbor and crippled the U.S. Pacific Fleet. Two battleships and two destroyers were sunk. Another 13 ships were damaged, among them six battleships, three cruisers and a destroyer. The toll in aircraft was 188 destroyed and 159 damaged.

The strike at Pearl Harbor left the United States at a terrible disadvantage in the opening weeks of the War. Within seven days Japanese planes had wiped out the U.S. Army air bases in the Philippines and struck a blow at the British as well by sinking the only two Royal Navy battleships stationed in the Far East. Within a month Japan ruled an 11,000-mile arc of the Pacific, from the Japanese archipelago to New Guinea. With its air power greatly diminished, the United States was hard put to defend its territories in the Pacific, and mounting an offensive against Japan was unrealistic. Until American industry could restore the balance in matériel, the efforts of Allied cryptanalysts to understand the secret messages of the Japanese were vital to the security of Pearl Harbor—indeed, to the security of the United States.

In the 14th Naval District Administration Building at Pearl Harbor, headquarters of Navy Intelligence for the Pacific, the failure to detect the Japanese plans to attack the base had been dispiriting. But the men of the Combat Intelligence Unit, who labored in two basement rooms sealed off by steel doors, were not allowed to feel sorry for themselves for long. "Forget Pearl Harbor and get on with the job!" exhorted Commander Joseph John Rochefort, who oversaw the efforts of more than two dozen cryptanalysts, radio monitors, traffic analysts and translators.

In the aftermath of Pearl Harbor they were soon working an 84-hour week—12 hours on, 12 hours off, seven days a week—a regimen that gave them red-rimmed, deep-shadowed eyes and pasty complexions, and set them apart from the tanned, robust seamen at the tropical base. Among the men on Rochefort's staff were Japanese-language specialists recalled from sea duty, Naval Reservists from the mainland, and odd lots such as the bandsmen of the battleship *California*, who were jobless because their ship was beached in the Japanese attack. The musicians were a fortunate addition to the staff; they turned out to be particularly adept at cryptanalysis.

Rochefort himself had unbridled enthusiasm and indefatigable energy for the job. His credentials were sound: He was a career man who had spent his adult life in the service of the Navy ashore and afloat. In 1925 he had helped found the Navy's cryptographic unit. In the intervening years he had done a stint at the U.S. Embassy in Tokyo, which had made him fluent in Japanese, and another stint aboard the flagship of the Pacific commander, which had given him valuable insights into fleet movements.

Now, ruling his underground domain at Pearl Harbor with a red smoking jacket belted over his Navy uniform and felt slippers on his feet, Rochefort outdid his men by keeping 16- and 20-hour watches. Occasionally, when the strain

of such long hours overcame him, he flopped onto a cot in the corner for a cat nap—but he was always ready to roll out of the cot at any hour of the day or night to help with a problem or share in the triumph of a breakthrough by a member of his staff. Rochefort left the underground vault only for a haircut, a bath, or a rare conference with his superiors of the Naval District and the staff of Admiral Chester W. Nimitz, the commander in chief of U.S. Naval forces in the Pacific.

Rochefort's deputy, Lieut. Commander Thomas H. Dyer, was at least as dedicated. He might never have left the communications unit at all had not Rochefort ordered him home to Honolulu every three days or so for a square meal and a full night's sleep. Before the War, when prototypical computing machines that could store and sort information by means of perforated cards were introduced for commercial purposes, Dyer had pioneered the application of such card systems to cryptanalysis. Now, as he threw himself into trying to penetrate the Japanese Naval messages, he

Nagao Kita, the Japanese Consul in Honolulu, converses on a telephone. American intelligence agents had secretly tapped the line in the hope of identifying spies on the consulate staff. Despite their efforts, all that the wire tappers overheard was inconsequential gossip.

spent endless hours feeding cards to a battery of machines that stood in one of the Combat Intelligence Unit's subterranean chambers.

A third vital member of the cryptanalysis staff was Lieut. Commander Wesley A. Wright, known to his friends as Ham. An Annapolis graduate, Wright had been drawn into cryptanalysis by amateur cryptograms that the Navy published in a monthly newsletter. At the Combat Intelligence Unit headquarters in Pearl Harbor, he moved with calm courtesy among the cryptanalysts and the clerks, handing out assignments tailored to the men's abilities, and keeping the toughest ones for himself.

Joining these men from time to time was Commander W. J. Holmes, a former submarine commander known to his colleagues as Jasper. He was now serving as liaison between the Combat Intelligence Unit and Admiral Nimitz' intelligence staff.

Few outsiders knew what the men of Rochefort's unit did behind the locked and guarded doors. The unit's main

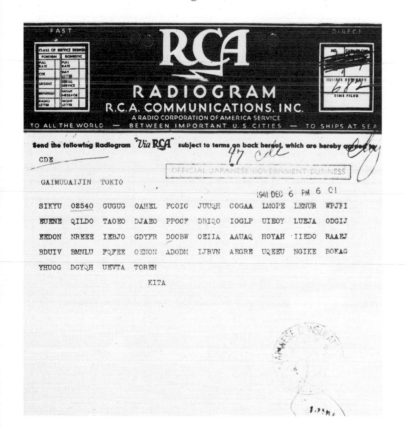

objective was to crack open the complex cipher system that was used by the Japanese Imperial Navy for its ship-to-shore communications.

The Japanese Navy did not depend on the machine used in the Japanese embassies to encipher its messages; that machine had not been mass-produced, and its cost prohibited equipping the entire fleet with it. Instead, the Japanese Navy relied on printed code books and cipher tables that were periodically distributed throughout the fleet.

More than half of the Japanese Navy's radio messages were sent in a form that was known to the men at Pearl Harbor as JN 25—a combination of code and cipher. The code had a five-digit number for virtually every word, phrase and title needed to communicate any conceivable Naval message; more than 30,000 words, phrases, syllables and letters were arranged alphabetically, with their numerical equivalents, in dictionary-like code books, a hypothetical selection from which might be:

attack (ing, ed)	73428
battleship (s)	29781
cruiser (s)	58797
destroyer (s)	36549
enemy	38754

On that basis, the phrase "destroyers attacking enemy cruisers" would be encoded as 36549 73428 38754 58797. Before sending this message, however, a communications officer would first encipher it. To do so, he chose a number from a cipher table, which consisted of columns of random five-digit numbers. If the cipher he chose was, say, 20036, he subtracted 20036 from the code number for "destroyers," 36549, and got the remainder of 16513; he then enciphered the word "destroyers" by writing 16513 on his message form. He subtracted the cipher directly below, say 62115, from the code number 73428—"attacking"—got 11313, and made it the second number in the enciphered message, and so on. In sending the message, he would indicate for the receiving station the page, column and line of the cipher table at which he had begun picking up numbers.

At the receiving station, another communications officer—who was equipped with an identical cipher table—reversed the process in order to decipher the message, add-

Code groups hide the meaning of the last radiogram sent by the Japanese consulate in Honolulu at 6:01 p.m. on December 6, 1941, and signed by Consul Kita. The message was a special agent's report confirming that most of the U.S. Pacific Fleet was still anchored at Pearl Harbor.

ing the first cipher of the message to the first cipher table number, the second to the second, and so on, thus revealing the original code groups. Then he looked up the resulting sums in the code book to find the Japanese words that the numbers stood for.

Because the relationship of the transmitted numbers to the code numbers appeared to be random, the system should have been unbreakable, and the Japanese remained confident that it was. But the system had one serious flaw. The Japanese Navy changed its code books and cipher tables only once in several months. That meant frequent use of the same numbers in the same sequence. The repetition permitted the cryptanalysts, once they had caught onto the system, to tabulate the cipher numbers. When a new message had been intercepted and a single word from it deciphered, they could line up the rest of the message's numbers alongside the appropriate table, add the cipher numbers to the message numbers word by word, find the underlying code groups, and then proceed to reconstruct the meaning of the message.

In addition, the Americans monitoring the Japanese messages had a variety of other clues to help them. One clue was that the location of a ship sending a message could be derived from the angles of its radio beam as measured from two or more American receiving sites. If on a given day the location of several intercepted messages coincided with information reported by the U.S. fleet—for example, on that day at a certain hour five Japanese destroyers had attacked an Allied cruiser—the American cryptanalysts could single out from the day's intercepted messages those that had come from any of the destroyers attacking the cruiser.

Next, a subtle human trait came to the aid of the cryptanalysts in their efforts to narrow the possibilities. The way a radio operator manipulates his telegraph key is as distinctive as his handwriting. Over a period of time the American monitors learned to identify any number of enemy ships by the idiosyncrasies of their radio operators. Of the operator aboard the Japanese flagship *Akagi,* for instance, one of the men at Pearl Harbor said, "He hits the key like he's kicking it with his foot."

Moreover, certain kinds of messages—sighting reports, for example—followed set patterns, and in time the cryptanalysts learned to pick out some vital words. The first two

or three numbers of any message would represent the name of the ship and sometimes the name of her commander (who generally had a three-letter call signal) plus the word "sends." Next there would be a number that was noticeable because it had six digits instead of five. The cryptanalysts discerned that this number combined the date of the month with the time of transmission, and called that part of the message the date-time group. Somewhere in the message would be the ship's location, usually as numbers representing a pair of letters. That separate code was a difficult one to break; to determine the location of a ship, the cryptanalysts usually had to depend on their own direction-finding apparatus.

Using such clues, the cryptanalyst examining an intercepted message could start with certain known elements: the name of the transmitting ship and her commander, the word "sends," a date, a time, and very likely such words as "destroyer," "attacking," "enemy" and "cruiser."

Enough messages intercepted over many weeks enabled Rochefort and his men to make some inspired guesses that yielded a host of basic code groups and their definitions. A small ship that frequently operated with several aircraft carriers could be deduced to be an oil tanker. Each time the carriers summoned the tanker, a few more code groups might be revealed, such as those for the words "refuel" and "rendezvous" and the names of favored refueling locations.

Needless to say, Rochefort's work did not always go smoothly. Yet little by little, the cryptanalysts at Pearl Harbor unraveled the mysteries. As they did so, they began compiling their own "dictionaries" of code groups and tables of cipher numbers. By April 1942 they had figured out perhaps 30 per cent of the Japanese system—a fraction that proved far more decisive than its size would suggest.

In the first few months following Pearl Harbor, when the cryptanalysts of the Combat Intelligence Unit at Pearl Harbor were making stabs at JN 25, the Japanese Navy was running rampant in the Pacific. Admiral Nagumo's Pearl Harbor Strike Force ranged one third of the way around the world—striking at Rabaul in New Guinea, Ambon in the Dutch East Indies, Darwin in Australia, Java in the Indies again, and finally across the Indian Ocean at Ceylon—and then returned in triumph to Japan with all the ships intact.

With the few ships and planes that Admiral Nimitz had under his command in April 1942, he could do little more than make nuisance raids on the Gilberts, the Marshalls and other islands held by the Japanese.

Meanwhile, Yamamoto and his top strategist, Captain Kameto Kuroshima, concocted an elaborate plan intended to destroy the Pacific Fleet and to anchor Japan's forward defense line on the Aleutian Islands off Alaska and on Midway Island in the central Pacific—all in one well-coordinated stroke. The key to the operation would be Midway, a pair of atolls that the U.S. Pacific Fleet was obliged to defend for the security of Pearl Harbor, 1,300 miles to the southeast. The Aleutian Islands would be a secondary target.

In April, in strictest secrecy, Yamamoto and Kuroshima proposed their plan to the Japanese Imperial General Headquarters, and won approval for it on May 5. They asked for 160 ships—the largest combat fleet in modern history—to be divided into 10 task forces. The first force would assault the Aleutian Islands, with a massive air raid on Dutch Harbor on Unalaska Island and troop landings on the islands of Kiska and Attu. This attack might make the Americans believe that Alaska or even the West Coast of the continental United States was the fleet's main objective. Then a four-carrier strike force would attack Midway Island the following morning.

The U.S. Pacific Fleet could be expected to make a dash

AMATEUR CODES TO BEAT THE CENSORS

Not all the codes and ciphers used in World War II were sophisticated and official. Some reflected the efforts of GIs to beat the constraints of censorship.

One typical amateur cryptographer told his family he would let them know where he was by using a different letter for his father's middle initial whenever he wrote home. After he had dispatched five letters bearing the successive middle initials T-U-N-I-S, he received a perplexed inquiry from home asking where Nutsi was. He had forgotten to date the letters, and they had arrived out of order.

More somber was a postcard sent by a U.S. Army lieutenant from a prison camp in Japan to "Mr. F. B. Iers" in Los Angeles. The message eluded the prison-camp censor and reached an alert FBI agent, who recognized it for a null code—a code in which certain words are nulls, or words to be eliminated. It may be doubted that the FBI considered the disclosure compelling, but the lieutenant succeeded in finding an outlet for information he desperately wanted to share with someone.

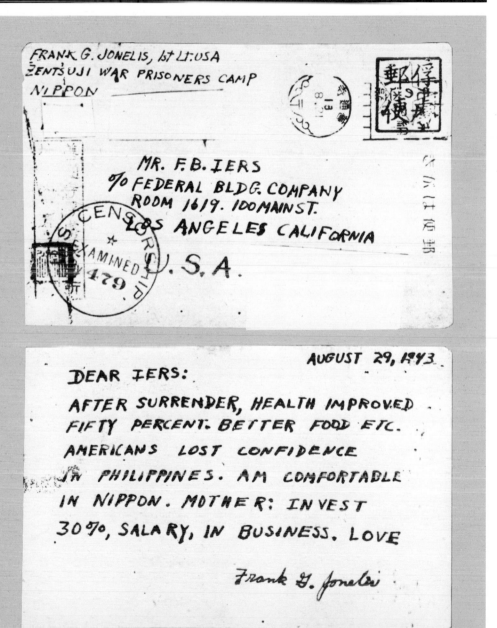

This null-code message was deciphered easily by an FBI agent who, by eliminating all but the first two words in each line, read it to mean: After surrender, 50 per cent Americans lost in Philippines; in Nippon, 30 per cent.

from Pearl Harbor to rescue Midway. En route, the fleet would be waylaid by an advance force of 15 submarine groups, pummeled by aircraft from four carrier groups under the command of Admiral Nagumo and utterly destroyed by the main force—consisting of the 72,500-ton battleship *Yamato,* two smaller battleships and a light carrier—led by Admiral Yamamoto himself. An occupation force would seize Midway and turn it into a Japanese air base for bombing Pearl Harbor—presumably obliterating the U.S. Naval base this time. The Japanese would then head south and isolate Australia and New Zealand—cutting the American and British Naval forces off from each other in the Pacific.

The earliest intimation that the United States received of the plot that the Japanese were hatching came in the first week of May, when the Pacific airwaves began to crackle with the multitudinous radio messages necessary to assemble, refit, refuel and dispatch the ships. Directives, questions and replies shuttled up and down the command channels and back and forth between ships, conveying the appropriate parts of the complex plan to the commanders who would carry them out. Because Yamamoto had no hint that the American codebreakers had made any inroads on JN 25, he fully expected that his plan would surprise and entrap the American fleet.

However, the scant 30 per cent of the JN 25 vocabulary that the Americans had worked out represented the very terms most often used in Japanese fleet operations, and with them Rochefort had figured out by mid-May an astonishing 90 per cent of Yamamoto's plan. If Nimitz' meager forces could be in precisely the right place at precisely the right time, they would have a chance of disrupting Yamamoto's massive assault. But where and when was the blow to fall? In the 10 per cent of the messages that the Americans could not decipher lay hidden the two things Admiral Nimitz needed most to know: the main target of the operation, which was identified only by the letters AF, and the date on which the operation would be launched. In this instance, the date lay embedded in a cipher that eluded every effort of Rochefort and his men to crack it.

One day the team's head translator, Lieut. Commander Joseph Finnegan, noted the presence of the letters AF in a message from a Japanese scout plane that was flying over Midway. Finnegan was a relative newcomer to the team, but he was given to amazingly accurate flights of second sight, and now he guessed that AF might stand for Midway. Rochefort instantly checked the letters against a recently captured Japanese grid map and found that A and F were two coordinates for an area that encompassed Midway.

On that basis alone, Rochefort was inclined to believe that Finnegan's guess was correct, and so was Admiral Nimitz. Persuading the Joint Chiefs of Staff in Washington was harder. The Joint Chiefs saw no reason to conclude that the letters in the cryptic message necessarily coincided with those on the lone map. They thought AF might just as easily stand for New Guinea, the Solomons or even the West Coast of the United States. Consequently, they advised against the withdrawal of ships from these areas in order to guard Midway.

But Rochefort held to his conviction, and with Nimitz' approval, Rochefort devised a scheme that would confirm their hunch. He instructed the commander of the Naval base on Midway to fake a plain-text radio message from Midway reporting that the island's water purifier had broken down. Promptly from the Japanese radio-monitoring station at Wake Island came the intercepted intelligence that AF would soon be out of fresh water.

That was enough for Nimitz. The date of the attack remained unknown, but he acted at once to concentrate his limited assets around Midway. From the Coral Sea he secretly called back the carriers *Enterprise* and *Hornet,* leaving behind a cruiser to imitate the radio messages of the absent carriers so that the Japanese would not notice that they had been moved. From Pearl Harbor he summoned the carrier *Yorktown*—preparing another surprise for the Japanese. The *Yorktown* had been so severely damaged in a battle with the Japanese in the Coral Sea on May 8 that the Japanese believed she had been sunk; under Nimitz' prodding she had been patched up in a record two days at Pearl Harbor. Nimitz planned that the U.S. carriers should run for Midway before the Japanese submarines arrived in neighboring waters to spot them, and then should lie in wait off Midway. To the island he also sent 28 fighter planes and a few B-17 bombers; these planes and their pilots would have to make the first raid on Nagumo's fleet as the U.S. ships moved into position.

In all this deployment of forces Nimitz made one concession to the Joint Chiefs of Staff in Washington, who still remained doubtful that Midway was the main target. He bowed to their concern by sending Rear Admiral Robert A. Theobald with 13 destroyers and five cruisers to guard the western approaches to the Aleutian Islands, which might be used as steppingstones to the West Coast of the continental United States.

By May 23, the U.S. forces were taking up their positions, and only the date of the Japanese strike on Midway remained to be determined. Deductive evidence placed it as late as the 10th of June, as early as the first. Time was running out; on June 1 a new set of Japanese codes and ciphers would go into effect, and then the Americans would have to start all over again to figure out the new system.

Late on the afternoon of May 23, Finnegan approached Ham Wright, who was about to take a supper break after a 12-hour day, and asked him to stay around and lend a hand. Wright went with Finnegan to an empty desk, and together they puzzled over the date ciphers from four messages. One was a new message relating to Midway; the other three had been intercepted earlier. The messages had been virtually decoded except for the date ciphers, which still eluded the men.

While they worked, Wright had an inspiration. He already knew that the Japanese had two alphabets, each one reflecting different combinations of phonetics. Both were used in the coding. Up to now one alphabet had been used in some messages, the second alphabet in others. He had tried to decipher the numbers with reference to each alphabet separately, and had come up with nothing but gibberish. Suddenly it struck him that the elusive ciphers might contain the two alphabets in combination.

To test this new thought, Wright and Finnegan worked out a grid: They arranged the characters of one alphabet horizontally and those of the other alphabet vertically. It took the two men all night to make the grid and match the date ciphers against the 2,209 possible combinations the squares allowed. But the theory worked. The squares turned up syllables that could be read as real words. At 5:30 a.m. they triumphantly roused Rochefort from his cot to tell him that the Japanese planes would strike at Midway on June 4.

Rochefort hurried immediately to the headquarters of Admiral Nimitz to announce the exact date of the Japanese attack on Midway. As the day wore on, Nimitz' intelligence staff pored over all the information they now had, and finally worked out more details. "They'll come in from the northwest on bearing 325 degrees and they will be sighted at about 175 miles from Midway, and the time will be about 0600 Midway time," concluded one of the men on the Nimitz staff.

The information came not a moment too soon. Three days later, on May 27, Admiral Nagumo, commanding the four-carrier strike force from the *Akagi,* signaled through his heavy-handed radio operator, "Sortie as scheduled." Imperial General Order No. 94 blared over the loudspeakers of some 160 ships: "We shall destroy the enemy fleet, which will appear when our operation is under way." And Nagumo smugly recorded in his intelligence summary that "the enemy is not aware of our plans."

Admiral Nimitz monitored the next several days' events through U.S. aerial-reconnaissance reports that were radioed to his command post at Pearl Harbor. On June 4 he noted with a happy sense of vindication that Nagumo had been sighted off Midway at 5:20 a.m. as the sun was rising. The Japanese ships' radios were now silent, as always in the moments before battle. But from the U.S. station on Midway came a terse cable reporting "Air raid Midway," thereby revealing that Nagumo had launched his planes earlier than expected. Would the U.S. aircraft carriers be able to move into position for a fight with Nagumo's carriers before the Japanese planes made a second strike on the island?

For two hours the radios were silent, the tension of waiting broken only by a mournful cabled report from Midway that it had lost all but three of its fighter planes to Japanese Zeroes. Then Rochefort began telephoning Nimitz news that had been picked up piecemeal from Japanese radio reports to Nagumo. The first item indicated that a Japanese reconnaissance plane had sighted the U.S. cruisers and destroyers off Midway. The second said that a carrier appeared to be bringing up the rear of the American formation. A third warned Nagumo: "Ten enemy torpedo planes headed toward you."

Now at last the Japanese fleet broke its radio silence with two long messages. The Rochefort team could not discern

A ONE-MAN COUP AT PEARL HARBOR

In the first stunned days after December 7, 1941, most Americans believed that only a vast underground network of Japanese spies could have provided the information that had made the surprise attack on Pearl Harbor so accurate and so devastating. But in fact, Japanese intelligence on Pearl Harbor came largely from readily available data: Some information was gleaned from published maps *(opposite);* some of it was gathered openly under the noses of tourists and shipboard passengers.

The only Japanese spy at Honolulu was a man named Takeo Yoshikawa, a 25-year-old Navy ensign who was posted to the consulate there in March 1941. His as-

signment was to behave as a diplomat while monitoring the day-to-day activities of the American fleet at Pearl Harbor.

Yoshikawa's method was simplicity itself. By day he sallied out like any tourist, in slacks and an aloha shirt, and usually escorting a pretty companion. Sometimes he taxied around the island; sometimes he cruised the harbor in a sightseeing boat. Once he sprawled on the grass at Wheeler Field to watch an Army air exercise; another time he took an aerial junket around the island, chatting amiably with his companion while snapping photographs of the airfields and naval installations below.

At night Yoshikawa frequented a teahouse on the heights above Pearl Harbor. He flirted with the Japanese waitresses, drinking enough to seem idly relaxed but not so much as to be unpleasant—and all

the while he kept an ear open for loose talk. The proprietor, who did not know Yoshikawa's real purpose, let him sleep off his carousing in a spare room from which he had a view of the harbor.

All these activities looked so innocent and so commonplace that they aroused no suspicion if they were noticed at all. But when Yoshikawa's nightly carousing ended, he made notes and maps from memory. He turned them over to the Consul General, who relayed them weekly to Tokyo. There other Japanese intelligence officers marked maps and constructed three-dimensional mock-ups of the base.

When Japanese pilots attacked Hawaii on December 7, they had in their laps aerial photographs and charts detailing their targets, based on data gathered from available sources—or supplied by Yoshikawa.

Japanese technicians position models of American warships on a detailed replica of Pearl Harbor. In order to prepare for their attack on the base, Japanese pilots made extensive use of three-dimensional mock-ups.

The Japanese liner Taiyo Maru plies Pacific waters between Tokyo and Honolulu. In October of 1941 she traced the course that was being planned for the Pearl Harbor attack force while—unbeknownst to the paying passengers on board—her intelligence officers compiled vital information, such as the absence of other shipping along the route.

A U.S. Hydrographic Office chart is overlaid with Japanese notations that pinpoint targets in and around Pearl Harbor. During the attack, bomber and submarine crews used maps like this one, which could be purchased in Honolulu shops as readily as picture postcards.

their meaning, for they were transmitted in a new cipher. But Rochefort and his colleagues reached one satisfying conclusion. The messages were transmitted with a particularly heavy hand. That meant that the messages came from the flagship *Akagi*.

Many hours after the battle, Nimitz would get a report that clouds had obscured a view of the Japanese fleet from the first wave of 41 U.S. torpedo planes, so that their pilots flew straight to disaster. Without support from the U.S. fighters, they dashed themselves to death against Nagumo's fleet; only six of the torpedo planes and seven of their pilots survived the attack.

By 6 a.m. American dive bombers were on their way toward the Japanese. It was the Americans' turn to break radio silence, but only briefly. Over the airways came the voice of Captain Miles Browning, chief of staff aboard the command ship. "Attack immediately!" he shouted, in response to a bomber pilot's radioed sighting report.

Then the radios fell silent again for such a long period that Nimitz was finally driven to demand irritably whether the U.S. carriers had attacked the *Akagi,* and how the Japanese were reacting. "Not a thing," came the reply. "We've tried every frequency we know they've got." The absence of messages from the Japanese flagship could be a promising sign that she had been hit, and just before noon Rochefort confirmed that she had. A long message bearing call letters they knew to be Nagumo's had been intercepted, and it had been sent not by the key-thumping chief warrant officer of the *Akagi* but by a lighter-fingered operator recognizable as the chief radioman of the cruiser *Nagara*. Nagumo's presence aboard the *Nagara* could mean only one thing. The *Akagi* was no longer in action.

But other Japanese vessels were still fighting hard. At noon came an airborne Japanese flight leader's message to his ship—"We are attacking the enemy carrier"—followed by the chilling order to his wingmen, "Attack! Attack! Attack!" Almost simultaneously came a succinct confirmation in plain English from the *Yorktown:* "Am being attacked by a large number of enemy bombers." Clearly planes were flying from at least one Japanese carrier, and one plane had scored a hit on the *Yorktown*. The Midway battle proved to be her last; she was so badly damaged that she later had to

be taken in tow by another ship and was sunk by a torpedo before she could reach Pearl Harbor for repairs.

Not until after 10 p.m. did Admiral Nimitz receive a comprehensive account of the day's action and the reassuring news that Midway had been held. The battle had ranged over hundreds of miles and had lasted all day. After a midmorning engagement in which many U.S. pilots had been lost but three enemy carriers were set on fire, the planes of the *Enterprise* and *Hornet* had caught up with the retreating Japanese fleet between 5 and 6 p.m. and set alight the fourth carrier and two heavy cruisers. By sundown all four Japanese carriers were dead in the water and burning. Admiral Yamamoto soon turned the main battle fleet toward home and recalled the Midway invasion force.

Only in the minor affair of the Aleutians had Yamamoto's grand strategy worked. Because Admiral Theobald had stationed his cruisers too far out to sea, he had missed sighting the Japanese attack force. The Japanese planes swooped in, bombed Dutch Harbor, and landed troops unopposed on Kiska and Attu. There in the Aleutians the enemy troops would remain until the Japanese Navy returned to take them away in 1943. They were a nagging but isolated and harmless splinter in America's eye. Theobald was subsequently removed from command and assigned to shore duty.

The Battle of Midway proved to be the most crucial naval engagement of the War. General George C. Marshall, who viewed it from Washington, was to call it "the closest squeak and the narrowest victory," and credited it with recapturing America's dominance of the Pacific. The victory at Midway ended the Japanese threat to Hawaii and eventually enabled the United States to mount the reconquest of the Pacific.

At Pearl Harbor, Admiral Nimitz summoned Rochefort on June 6 and, before a gathering of high-ranking Naval officers, gave him and the men of the Combat Intelligence Unit credit for providing the keys that had made the American victory possible. "Had we lacked early information of the Japanese movements, and had we been caught with carrier forces dispersed," he said, "the Battle of Midway would have ended differently."

No other cryptanalytic victory ever held quite as much excitement for the Rochefort team. However, the men performed equally vital, if less spectacular, work in breaking the "maru code." The marus were the Japanese merchant ships—freighters and tankers—that sailed in convoy to supply Japanese island garrisons with men, food and equipment, and to fetch from Borneo the supplies of oil necessary to maintain Japanese ships and planes.

Every day the maru code was used to convey the position that Japanese freighters and tankers in a convoy were expected to reach by 12 noon, the nature of the cargoes they carried and the arrangement of escorting vessels. The code consisted of clusters of only four digits, instead of the JN 25's five digits, which should have made the maru code less difficult to solve. But it eluded the American cryptanalysts until they realized that—because Japanese merchant shipping was controlled by three separate companies, each with a different code book—they were dealing with three different systems. As soon as the Americans reached that conclusion, they were able to break the maru code by the same trial-and-error techniques that had succeeded with the JN 25.

The effect of their codebreaking was dramatic. Jasper Holmes, who had a hand in exploiting the breakthrough on the maru code, later wrote: "There were nights when nearly every American submarine on patrol in the central Pacific was working on the basis of information derived from cryptanalysis." One submarine that sank a whole convoy returned to port with a broom tied to the forward periscope to boast that it was sweeping the Pacific clean of Japanese merchant shipping. By 1945 a total of 1,113 Japanese vessels had been sunk, together with 4,779,902 tons of sup-

plies. Japanese island garrisons were starved, the home-front war effort was strangled, warships were tied up in port, and planes were grounded for lack of fuel.

Meanwhile, the Purple cipher—the one used in Japanese diplomatic messages—was yielding dividends for the Allies in Europe. Baron Hiroshi Oshima, the Japanese Ambassador to Nazi Germany, sent long messages to Tokyo by radio. But the United States had shared the invention of the Purple machine with the British, and copies of the machine had been distributed to key listening posts. Oshima's messages inadvertently provided Allied commanders with quotations from conversations that Oshima had with Adolf Hitler on German strategy. In 1943 Oshima provided meticulous accounts of a guided tour that he and his military attaché made along the Atlantic Wall—the string of steel-and-concrete fortifications that the Germans were building from the coast of Norway all the way south to the coast of Spain.

As a result of those intercepted messages, Allied invasion planners were able to learn such details as the depth of the Cherbourg defense zone—about four and a half miles—and to plot on their maps the numbers and sites of the anti-tank defenses flanking the Normandy beaches. From Oshima's messages, declared no less an authority than General Marshall, the Allies obtained their "main basis of information regarding Hitler's intentions in Europe."

But penetrating the ciphers in which Hitler's armed forces communicated their battle plans was a challenge of a far higher order. The Germans had their own cipher machine, a box that was about one cubic foot in size and appropriately

The stern of the torpedoed freighter Nittsu Maru is framed in the periscope sight of the U.S. submarine Wahoo on the 21st of March, 1943. The vessel was located thanks to the efforts of American cryptanalysts, whose swift and accurate decipherment of Japanese messages made it possible for submarines to zero in on enemy supply ships day after day.

named the Enigma. It was distributed by the thousands among the units of the German Army, Navy, Air Force and intelligence services even before the War began in 1939. No other ciphering machine caused Allied cryptanalysts so much trouble.

The first Enigma had been produced in 1923 by a German engineer, Arthur Scherbius, and marketed by the Cipher Machine Corporation of Berlin at the modest price of $144. It was first promoted as a useful business tool. "The natural inquisitiveness of competitors is at once checkmated by a machine that enables you to keep all your documents, or at least their important parts, entirely secret," said a brochure that advertised it.

The Enigma had a typewriter keyboard from which the message was transmitted into a series of electrically wired rotors, or wheels. Around the inside surface of each rotor

At a Luftwaffe airfield, German authorities treat visiting Japanese officers to an inspection of an infrared aircraft detector. Information about such secret German weapons often reached the Allies via enciphered messages that were intercepted and radioed back to Tokyo by the Japanese, who believed their cipher system was unbroken and unbreakable.

were 26 electrical contacts, each representing a letter of the alphabet. Each contact was wired to a typing key, to some other contact on the rotor, to a contact of the next rotor, and finally to an output device, which consisted of a panel that lit up to show the cipher letter that the mechanical processing system produced.

Each rotor multiplied by 26 the number of possible cipher alphabets the machine could produce. Three rotors—the original complement—would yield 26 by 26 by 26, or 17,576 cipher alphabets. Later models employing four rotors yielded 456,976 alphabets, and additional changing in the wiring and positioning of the rotors increased the possibilities to astronomical numbers.

Deciphering an Enigma message required an identical machine with identically wired rotors. The receiver had to know which rotor to insert, in what order to insert them and at what position to set each one. This required a list of so-called key settings shared by sender and receiver. Without knowing the prescribed key settings, an unauthorized recipient of a cipher message sent by an Enigma using three rotors might have to try as many combinations of rotors and settings as is represented mathematically by the expression 3×10^{18}—a figure of galactic proportions—before the Enigma, operating in reverse, would produce the letters of a plain-text message.

Before reaching the Allied cryptanalysts, the Enigma machine itself traveled a circuitous route. An Enigma machine had been serendipitously dropped in the lap of the Cipher Department of the Polish Intelligence Bureau in 1929. On a Saturday in January of that year, a crate arrived in the Warsaw customs office addressed to a German firm in the Polish capital. Almost immediately an official of the firm arrived to say that the crate contained radio equipment and had to be returned, unopened and immediately, to Germany. A telephone call from the German consul reinforced the request.

The Germans' anxiety aroused the customs officer's suspicions, and he stalled with the excuse that government offices closed at noon on Saturday and nothing could be done until Monday. Then he called in Polish intelligence agents, who took the crate apart and found inside it a cipher machine. With infinite care, they spent the remainder of the weekend probing the machine, photographing its keyboard and rotors, and making diagrams of its wiring. Then they carefully repacked the machine and resealed the crate; on Monday the customs office returned it to Germany.

The diagrams and photographs were duly examined at the Cipher Department—and filed away. No one seems to have given the matter much attention until 1931, when the Polish Intelligence Bureau received reports from its agents in Germany that both the German Army and Navy were using a cipher machine called the Enigma. Then, through a cooperative partner in a Polish electrical firm called AVA, a commercial Enigma was bought from a German supplier and compared with the purloined plans of the machine in which the German consul had betrayed his government's anxious interest two years previously. Examination proved that if the two machines were not twins, they were at least close relatives.

But, as its inventor had intended, possession of an Enigma machine was useless to an owner who did not have the proper key settings for each message transmitted. Therefore, the German officers who had selected the Enigma for use by the armed services had supposed that it would take foreign cryptanalysts almost endless pencil-and-paper calculations to test all the possible rotor combinations in a single message, even if they had access to a comparable machine.

The Germans did not reckon on the Poles. The Polish General Staff had already selected 20 of the nation's most promising students of mathematics and enrolled them in a special course in cryptography at the University of Poznań. Of those, the three most brilliant were assigned to unravel the mysteries of the Enigma.

Meanwhile, French intelligence officers had intercepted enciphered messages being sent on German airwaves and were puzzling over what they could mean. The Frenchmen's job was made easier one day in 1931 when a "walk-in" agent, a German named Hans-Thilo Schmid, presented himself to a French agent in Germany and offered to sell the secrets of the new German cipher system. For a price, he confirmed that the German armed forces had modified the Enigma and were using it as their principal cipher device. For more money, he turned over to Captain Gustave Bertrand, director of cryptanalysis at the French intelligence service, the instruction manual for the military Enigma and some tables currently in use for its key settings.

Common fear of a resurgent Germany had previously induced France and Poland to form a military alliance, and the general staffs of both nations regularly exchanged intelligence. The French therefore knew of the Poles' work in cryptanalysis. Now Bertrand rushed with his bounty to Warsaw, and there the cryptanalysts of both governments pored over the photographs and diagrams of the machine they had pilfered for a weekend two years before. What they saw dismayed them all.

The German military technicians had not only altered the internal wiring of the Enigma; they had added such features as a plugboard that introduced six more variable circuits to the electrical maze, thereby increasing the possible encoding positions to an incredible number with 88 digits.

Nevertheless, the mathematicians set themselves a task that might have seemed impossible: to deduce, by mathematical reasoning, the new internal wiring of the Enigma machine. Using simultaneous equations that permitted them to carry the large number of unknowns represented by the paired contacts of the three rotors, the mathematicians were able to "freeze" two rotors in position while they worked out the permutations of the other. As soon as they had diagramed its wiring pattern, they sent the pattern off to the AVA factory to be reproduced while they tackled the second rotor and then the third.

Next they addressed the problem of the plugboard and its internal circuitry. Although they did not even have a model of the new plugboard to look at, the Polish mathematicians managed to work out its possible combinations.

Now the men tackled the key settings. Mathematics alone would not do; the analysts would have to use tricks they had learned in their cryptography courses and hope for some flaw in a procedure that, they knew, would have to be simple enough to be taught to thousands of German cipher clerks. In the instruction manual and old key settings that the German traitor had provided, the Poles found the answer they needed.

The manual dictated every step an operator must take to establish the Enigma's key settings. First the operator had to invent and transmit a three-letter signal that would tell the receiving operator which letters to use for setting each of the three rotors on his machine for the deciphering sequence. To make sure there was no mistake, the sender was to repeat the three-letter signal. As a result, the first six letters of each message consisted of two identical sets of three letters each. And therein lay a hazard that the Germans had overlooked; this prescribed repetition provided the first clue in solving the mystery of the workings of the Enigma machine.

The second clue, revealed in the messages now being sent by the Germans, was the tendency of the cipher clerks to choose familiar letter combinations—AAA and XYZ, for example—and to use them day after day. From that it followed that the German clerks were repeating the same settings instead of choosing from among the 17,576 letter combinations that random selection would have made possible. With that discovery, the Poles finally cracked the key-setting system during the Christmas holidays of 1932. Immediately thereafter they deciphered their first German Army Enigma message.

On the theory that more machines would enable more cryptanalysts to work simultaneously on the intercepted messages and so speed up deciphering, the Polish government now had the AVA factory turn out another Enigma machine and then another. At this stage the Poles introduced a shortcut: They hooked together the rotors of two Enigmas, thereby creating a new device that doubled the speed with which they could run through rotor combinations to find key settings. For a while the Polish General Staff was reading German Army and Air Force messages on the same day they were intercepted.

That triumph was short-lived, for soon the German engineers made further alterations in their machines, and the Polish interceptions again became meaningless jumbles of letters. Then followed another series of trials and errors, until one of the three Polish mathematicians tried gearing together the rotors of six machines and attaching them to a motor. Soon the rotors were revolving at a speed the eye could not follow, testing all possible key settings. The machines were programed to stop spinning when a match had been found with the setting that had been used for the ciphered message.

The Polish mathematicians dubbed the new monster machine the *bombe,* and by November of 1938 the Cipher Department had acquired six *bombes.* Once again, the

Poles could read what the German armed forces committed to the airwaves.

As the German shadow spread across Poland in the fateful year 1939, the Poles learned from a disaffected Luftwaffe officer that the Germans were providing two more rotors for the machine. The Enigma still operated with three rotors at a time, but it had two spares; all five were interchangeable. The Poles decided they could no longer go it alone. To break this combination would be beyond their material resources. They concluded that the French and the British, as the only two remaining European powers strong enough to take a stand against Germany, must be given all of the Polish cryptographical secrets while there was still time.

On July 24, 1939, two Polish military intelligence offi-cers, Lieut. Colonel Gwido Langer and Major Maksymilian Ciężki, and the three Polish mathematicians met with a delegation of British and French intelligence officers in Warsaw. Among the visitors were the head of Britain's Government Code and Cypher School, Alastair Denniston; Alfred Dillwyn Knox, a brilliant alumnus of Britain's World War I Cryptanalytical Bureau, and a Professor Sandwich—who was actually Stewart Graham Menzies, then deputy head of Britain's MI-6. Menzies used a false name to conceal his identity, lest German intelligence pick up the scent of his trip to Poland and realize that British intelligence was on the trail of important secret information. Captain Bertrand and an aide represented France.

Colonel Langer showed the visitors the Enigma machines

Workers assemble equipment in the AVA radio-manufacturing firm in prewar Warsaw, where copies of the German Enigma machine were made for Polish intelligence. By the time the Germans rolled into Poland in September 1939, at least 15 machines had been clandestinely built.

that the Poles had made for themselves. When a Polish expert explained the mechanism and demonstrated its use, pressing the key of one letter and causing another to light up on the panel, Commander Denniston, grasping the implications in a flash, got so excited that he wanted to call the British Embassy in London at once. Calmer heads persuaded him that there was more to be gained by getting on with the job at hand, and Langer led the visitors to the next room, where an even more astonishing demonstration awaited them. Here stood the six *bombes,* all in a row. As Langer threw the switch, the motors hummed and drums whirled. When the machines stopped, a light flashed, indicating that the key setting of a message had been found. Then Langer showed his amazed guests a message sent

that morning by SS headquarters and already deciphered.

Six *bombes* working in harness could in two hours determine the key setting that would enable the Poles to read a message sent by German armed forces via the Enigma machine. But working against the new five-rotor Enigma, the Poles would need 60 *bombes* operating for 10 hours to accomplish the same task. Langer explained that the Poles, as their contribution to the common cause of resisting Hitler, would turn over everything they had to the British and the French, who had vastly superior facilities. Upon leaving Warsaw, each delegation was promised an Enigma machine along with blueprints for the *bombes.* The Poles made their present just in time. Scarcely a month later, the German Army rolled over the Polish border.

Within months, France was invaded too. But in England a little time remained to build on the foundations laid by the foresighted and inventive Poles, and it was in England that the next offensive would be mounted against the secrets of German intelligence.

In November, Stewart Graham Menzies succeeded to the command of England's secret service and the control of the Government Code and Cypher School at Bletchley Park, a sprawling Victorian estate located halfway between Oxford and Cambridge Universities and about 50 miles northwest of London. To the ornate mansion that stood on the grounds, and to the huts hastily erected around it, were drawn an assortment of brilliant men—mathematicians and philosophy dons, bank officials and museum curators, chess champions and crossword-puzzle experts, electrical engineers and radio specialists. So secret was the intelligence handled there that not only the product, but also the processing of it, came to be known as Ultra—an abbreviation of Ultra Secret. The staff dubbed the grounds BP for Bletchley Park, and themselves the Golf, Cheese and Chess Society, a name which used the initials of the Government Code and Cypher School and indicated common tastes that the staff shared.

From the start, most staff members were young, ferociously precocious, long-haired, oddly clothed in frayed tweeds and rumpled corduroys—in outward appearance a collection of the eccentrics that have played a respected role in English tradition. According to one story—illuminating if

Major Maksymilian Ciężki of the Polish Intelligence Bureau, shown here wearing medals he was awarded for his heroism during World War I, led the team of mathematicians that succeeded in unraveling the secrets of the German Army's Enigma cipher system early in the 1930s.

apocryphal—Winston Churchill, on seeing the staff, is said to have remarked to Alastair Denniston, "I told you to leave no stone unturned in your recruiting. I did not expect you to take me quite so literally."

In May 1940 the cryptanalysts installed in a brick building on the Bletchley grounds their first *bombe*, constructed by the British Tabulating Machine Company. Knowing that the first six letters in any message represented the key setting—a three-letter cluster that was repeated—the cipher clerk fed the first six letters of the ciphered message into the *bombe*. The *bombe* then spun, testing all possible combinations of rotor settings until the six letters of the cipher became a pair of matching three-letter clusters. When the *bombe* stopped spinning, as in the Polish original, the oper-

ator knew that the key setting had been found and that all of the messages using that key could automatically be reproduced. Achieving a "stop" was a personal triumph for the operator and a blow struck toward victory.

Some of the keys were more easily arrived at than others, because the random letters with which clerks had to preface their Enigma messages were handled differently by the various German armed forces and security services. Among the toughest ciphers to break was that of the Army. To arrive at its key settings, the Army ghoulishly took the last three digits of the numbers representing the daily departures, deaths or survivors reported from Hitler's infamous concentration camps. Then, letting the digits from 0 to 9 represent the letters A through J, the cipher clerks translated those digits into

At the Château de Vignolles, outside Paris, French cryptanalyst Captain Gustave Bertrand stands in the back, midway between two potted palms, with Polish Colonel Gwido Langer to his left and their amalgamated teams in front. During the blitzkrieg of Poland, the Poles fled to Paris.

letters. The Navy's system was the most secure and the toughest to crack; the Navy kept adding refinements, and eventually adopted separate key-setting programs for separate types of vessels (surface ships, U-boats and merchantmen) and for separate theaters (the Atlantic, the Mediterranean and the Baltic).

Oddly, the spymasters of the Abwehr had the least secure of all systems; they used old three-rotor Enigmas that lacked plugboards, and their messages provided easy and early pickings. The men of the SD, the security service, who prided themselves on their toughness, carried over a fetish for coarse conversational language into their radio messages, and that predilection provided a startling clue for the British cryptanalysts. No matter what form the three-letter clusters of the key settings might take, they were apt to stand for one obscenity or another.

It was the Luftwaffe operators, however, who proved Bletchley's greatest boon. In their use of the Enigma, they were careless to the point of irresponsibility. One cryptanalyst remembered with fondness a German operator stationed in Italy who, to set up his message cipher, "unchangingly used the initials of his girl friend—to whom he fortunately remained faithful. He did a great deal of harm of which he had not the slightest inkling."

That careless attitude existed even at the top echelons. Reich Marshal Hermann Göring, the commander of the

Luftwaffe, used the radio like a telephone, spewing out verbose, vainglorious and often trivial communications such as instructions to commanding officers that the men he was going to decorate be properly deloused. "Göring's funnies," the British called these messages at Bletchley Park.

Happily for Allied intelligence, the Luftwaffe messages also provided meatier fare. A Luftwaffe liaison officer accompanied every Wehrmacht division to coordinate both close aerial support and the antiaircraft and antitank fire of the Luftwaffe Flak units. The liaison officers were intended to provide information about the movements of the ground troops in order to aid the Luftwaffe in its air attacks. But the messages detailing such movements were intercepted by Ultra and sped to the chiefs of the armed services—giving the Allied commanders the location of the German Flak units and, by extension, the deployment of the German ground forces.

The same information was relayed to Churchill. Whenever he traveled abroad he took care to keep himself informed of Ultra's latest secrets; so did President Roosevelt. And every major field commander had a Special Liaison Unit, or SLU, attached to his outfit. These units, typically consisting of a Royal Air Force officer (of low rank, to make his work seem insignificant) and a couple of sergeants to serve as cipher clerks, hovered at the headquarters of field

commanders in all theaters and kept them abreast of Ultra intelligence.

Few officers owed more to the Ultra information than General Bernard Montgomery, commander of the British Eighth Army in Africa. Montgomery paid close attention to the deciphered versions of the messages that passed between his opponent, Field Marshal Erwin Rommel—the celebrated "Desert Fox" who commanded the Axis forces in Africa—and Rommel's commanding officer, Field Marshal Albert Kesselring. From his headquarters in Italy, Kesselring arranged for the supplies of fuel and ammunition that had to be shipped across the Mediterranean to keep the Afrika Korps in fighting trim. Kesselring also reported to Hitler on Rommel's plans and progress.

The result of deciphering those messages was disaster for the Desert Fox and prestige for his British opponent. In the Mediterranean, British ships, submarines and aircraft were in short supply. Nevertheless the British got the better of the Germans there largely because intercepted messages from Kesselring meticulously advised Rommel of German convoy sailings and thus unwittingly directed British submarines and bombers straight to their targets. Many a British submarine commander raised his periscope at the spot indicated by an Ultra message and found his prey looming in the cross hairs. Bomber pilots often knew not only the exact routes of the convoys, but even which ships contained the most vital supplies. Thanks to Ultra, almost half of the German transports ferrying supplies through the Mediterranean in 1942 were sunk, thus leaving Rommel desperately short.

Montgomery—secretly aware through Ultra of Rommel's predicament and of his preparations for a do-or-die breakthrough to Cairo at Alam Halfa in August 1942—had British tanks, minefields and artillery ready at the moment that Rommel launched the assault intended to drive the British out of the Middle East. The British scored a stunning blow from which Rommel's forces never recovered.

Montgomery methodically built up his forces over the next three months. Throughout that time Ultra kept him supplied with information about German strength and morale, the critical shortage of gasoline, the disposition of enemy forces, and eventually with the information that Rommel was suffering from jaundice. On October 23, when Montgomery was assured he had the advantage, he launched his

attack at El Alamein. Ten days later Rommel radioed Hitler that the Afrika Korps' plight was hopeless. Hitler radioed back, "In your present situation you can do nothing but hold on, not yield a step. Your choice is to lead your troops to victory or to death."

Rommel had to hold on for two more days, and to send a number of additional messages, before he received permission from Hitler for the inevitable retreat. All of these messages were speedily deciphered at Bletchley Park, and on November 4 the chief of the Imperial General Staff, General Sir Alan Brooke, found Prime Minister Churchill in London "busily dictating messages to Roosevelt, Stalin, Dominions, Commanders, etc." with the news that the tide of the War had turned.

The War was far from won, but Churchill's optimism was not unfounded, for Ultra gave the Allies a decisive advantage. During the Italian campaign in 1943, the Special Liaison Unit at General Sir Harold Alexander's command post in Naples kept in constant communication with Bletchley Park. Alexander's War Room, guarded by sentries who barred admission to all but the select few entitled to Ultra information, had maps and charts of every German unit and organization in the battle zone, the movements of reinforcements and reserves, German divisional strengths, and amounts of ammunition, guns and tanks. The thousands of

Ultra signals flooding into Alexander's headquarters made him almost as well informed about the enemy as the Germans were about themselves, even down to such details as officers' postings, promotions and casualties. Several times each day Alexander would enter his War Room to look at the maps and charts that he depended on.

Even in a negative way Ultra could inform. When the Allies were mounting Operation *Torch*—the Anglo-American invasion of North Africa in 1942—they could tell from the lack of signals that the Germans had no intimation of what was coming. The Allies had the advantage of total surprise.

Nowhere was the effectiveness of the work at Bletchley Park more clearly reflected than in the Battle of the Atlantic, the contest that raged between the German U-boats and Allied shipping from 1939 to 1943. Whenever the team at Bletchley Park made a breakthrough in deciphering the German Navy's messages, Allied losses went down; when

the Germans substituted a new key-setting system, they gained the lead for a time.

Bletchley Park received a gift from the sea in May 1941, when the submarine *U-110* was captured. Captain Fritz Julius Lemp, in command of a pack of U-boats that was attacking an Allied convoy off Greenland, lingered too long before making a dash for safety, and then found himself under attack. His U-boat was blown to the surface by a British destroyer's depth charge. Lemp and his men abandoned ship, trusting that scuttling charges they had set would destroy the *U-110* and its contents.

Moments passed, and the charges failed to fire. Watching the scene from aboard the attacking destroyer was David Balme, a young Royal Navy sublieutenant. He lowered a boat and with some of his shipmates rowed to the submarine to board it.

As Balme descended through the conning tower, he had

A tent marked Cypher Office shields a vital arm of Churchill's intelligence entourage from the snow at Yalta in 1945. When the Prime Minister traveled as he did on this occasion to meet with Allied heads of state—cryptanalysts went along to encipher and decipher radio traffic.

every reason to expect that the submarine might still explode—or, failing that, that an armed German might confront him at any moment. But, pistol in hand, he climbed down into the blue-lit, dank interior, with his shipmates following behind him. There he was rewarded. He found the Enigma in its place, and code books and cipher documents strewn about the radio room.

The men formed a human chain. While depth charges thudded in the wake of the departing convoy, Balme's team spent three hours passing documents and equipment up the ladder, along the slippery deck to the boat and then to the destroyer. The captain then set a course for England with the treasure.

At the time, the need to keep Balme's coup a secret was so urgent that the British reported only that the U-boat had been sunk and that its captain had drowned after abandoning ship. Later reports hinted (but the incident was never verified) that in fact Lemp had been shot when he attempted to return to his submarine to save the documents.

Whichever was the case, the treasure trove was delivered to Bletchley Park, without the public—or the Germans—being any the wiser. The results for the Allies were spectacular: For nine months the Royal Navy hunted down and unerringly found and destroyed the Atlantic U-boats and the tankers that supplied them. In the next seven months Allied shipping losses declined from a monthly average of 200,000 tons to 50,000 tons. In the same period the number of destroyed U-boats reached 31.

On February 1, 1942, Admiral Karl Dönitz instituted a new key-setting system for his U-boats in the Atlantic, and the cryptanalysts at Bletchley Park spent another 10 months trying to penetrate it. The shift brought immediate havoc to the Atlantic shipping lanes; in the next six months nearly three million tons of Allied merchant shipping was sunk—and the monthly figure averaged half a million tons for the remainder of the year. Wolf packs totaling 40 U-boats were ranging the seas between England and America, and Germany seemed to be winning the Battle of the Atlantic and with it the battle for Europe.

The new settings were finally deciphered in December—but the team at Bletchley Park had practically no time to enjoy the results of their labors. When the U-boats sortied in March 1943 they carried a new Enigma model, one that had

four rotors operating at a time. The efforts to penetrate the secret messages had to begin all over again. During four days of that dark month, 21 ships totaling 141,000 tons went down, to the loss of only one U-boat; by the end of the month the losses stood at an unendurable 627,377 tons of shipping. Dönitz' great submarine offensive brought to flood tide the German naval endeavor, and for a brief moment gave him the illusion of victory.

Just as quickly, the tide receded. With astonishing speed the Bletchley Park cryptanalysts worked their way through the intricacies of the latest Enigma in less than a month. In April, Dönitz lost 14 U-boats; in May he lost another 39. By the end of August the toll had reached 127. In the same period, only 11 Allied merchantmen were lost. By autumn of 1943 the Battle of the Atlantic was practically over, and to Ultra went a good deal of the credit.

At the outset, Bletchley Park was exclusively a British institution. But as the War proceeded, the fate of Britain grew increasingly bound with that of the United States. In 1943 several dozen American officers were admitted to Bletchley's inner sanctum. For most of them Bletchley Park was a way station before they moved on to become Ultra advisers to U.S. commands. A few remained at Bletchley Park until the War's end—and counted it a privilege to do so. "It was the one place in the military where there was no sense of futility, of useless work or of nonsense," wrote one young officer who was assigned there—Alfred Friendly, later to become managing editor of *The Washington Post*. In addition to the simple pleasure of working out the never-ending supply of puzzles, the cryptanalysts of Bletchley Park had the exhilaration of seeing the results of their work pay off.

One pleasure they did not have was that of basking in the limelight when they succeeded. Unlike the exploits of military heroes on the battlefield, the triumphs of Bletchley Park had to be kept as secret as the methods, for the least clue that the cryptanalysts were deciphering German messages would have robbed the Allies of the advantage of possessing secret knowledge. The men and women who labored at Bletchley Park had to wait until long after the War for public acknowledgment. When that time came, they won a heartfelt encomium from Winston Churchill. He called them "the geese who laid the golden eggs—and never cackled."

A PIONEER IN CRYPTOLOGY

Conveying a secret message, students and staff of the U.S. Army's
cryptographic school in Geneva, Illinois, assemble for a graduation
picture with their director, William F. Friedman (seated at center
right), in February of 1918. Friedman arranged his pupils and colleagues
to form five-element groups that represent letters in a binary cipher
—one using two elements in various combinations, as Morse code uses
dots and dashes. In Friedman's human cipher, those whose heads
face forward are equivalent to dots; those turned sideways represent
dashes. The message reads from left to right, beginning in the back
row, where the letter "K" is enciphered as "dot dash dot dot dash,"
and spells out "Knowledge is power," an aphorism of the 16th Century
English philosopher Francis Bacon. Alas, Friedman had four fewer
people than he needed and had to serve by himself as the final "r."

THE GENIUS WHO BUILT THE PURPLE MACHINE

To the men and women who worked with him, William Friedman's building of the Purple cipher machine to break the Japanese diplomatic code *(pages 56-57)* was no surprise. Since World War I he had been devising and unraveling codes with dazzling insight and a special imaginative flair, as the class picture on the preceding page suggests. While teaching classes of Army officers in 1917-1918, Friedman wrote a series of instruction manuals laying down mathematical principles that transformed cryptology from an intuitive craft into a full-fledged science. As the pre-eminent practitioner of that science, he trained a whole generation of cryptologists in the rigorously analytic techniques that enabled the United States to become the leading nation in the field by the eve of World War II.

Friedman started his career at a time when global rivalries and the advent of radiotelegraphy were increasing the traffic in encoded messages. The 1920s saw the introduction of a variety of electromechanical enciphering systems, most of them involving multiple-rotor machines that produced codes far more complex than any dreamed of before. As chief codebreaker for the Army Signal Corps, Friedman used mathematical inductive reasoning to reconstruct the new machines and crack their codes, thus laying the foundation for solving all modern rotor-machine puzzles.

By the mid-1930s Friedman had become Chief Cryptanalyst of the War Department, charged with directing U.S. Army codebreaking efforts. His chief responsibility quickly became the breaking of the codes that the Japanese introduced in 1934, after the American press had revealed that the United States government was eavesdropping on diplomatic traffic from Tokyo.

When the War came, Friedman's staff outgrew its little office in the War Department and moved into the campus buildings at Arlington Hall, a former girls' school in Virginia. The work that went on there was unknown to the public, but Army Chief of Staff General George C. Marshall called it the determining factor in "the conduct of General Eisenhower's campaign and of all operations in the Pacific."

In a 1924 photograph, Friedman sits at a cipher machine that created random alphabets. Comparable machines were used widely in World War II.

As civilian head of the Signal Security Agency of the U.S. Army, a felt-hatted Friedman arrives to take possession of Arlington Hall for the agency in 1942.

As a Cornell student, Friedman conducts plant-genetics studies in an insect-free hut at a Carnegie Institution experimental station in 1913.

Elizebeth Smith stands beside employer George Fabyan in 1916.

The newly married Friedmans enjoy a country outing in 1917.

FROM PLANT GENETICS TO SECRET CIPHERS

Friedman found his calling indirectly. He set out to be a botanist. But in 1915, as a fledgling scientist, he worked on the Illinois farm of an eccentric millionaire, Colonel George Fabyan. There he met Elizebeth Smith, who was hired to pore over Shakespeare's plays in search of a cipher that the colonel fancied would prove Francis Bacon the real playwright. That was labor lost. But Friedman fell in love with both Miss Smith and cryptology, marrying one and making the other his career.

In 1918 the American Telephone and Telegraph Company introduced a cipher machine that worked on the principle of the binary cipher—using as the two elements the presence or absence of perforations on a tape. Friedman cracked its system in six weeks, making himself famous. Six years later, when the U.S. Army mistook some radio signals for messages from Mars, Friedman was naturally the man the Army consulted to try to figure them out.

Friedman sits at the keyboard of an American Telephone and Telegraph cipher machine in 1919.

Friedman (center) and two colleagues try to decipher radio signals thought to have originated on the planet Mars, which came close to Earth in 1924.

A MASSIVE ASSAULT ON A CIPHER MACHINE

By the 1930s, most industrial nations had some sort of electromechanical enciphering device. Among the most sophisticated of these was the one that from 1937 on transmitted the Japanese diplomatic code, nicknamed Purple by American cryptanalysts. Shortly after the Purple code was put into use, breaking it became William Friedman's top priority.

Supporting him was a superb team that he had started recruiting in 1930 from scholars in such disciplines as mathematics and linguistics. For 18 nerve-racking months, Friedman's team tried to duplicate the Japanese machine.

Instead of being based on rotors, the machine worked on the principle of a telephone switchboard, using plugs to shuffle arrangements of letters. When a replica Purple machine was finally hand-built in August of 1940, the United States had an instrument that enabled it to eavesdrop on such diplomatic fare as Germany's efforts to press Japan into war against Great Britain in March 1941.

The effort to build the machine told on everyone. It was, one cryptanalyst said, like being "engulfed in an interminable polar night." Friedman himself suffered a nervous collapse.

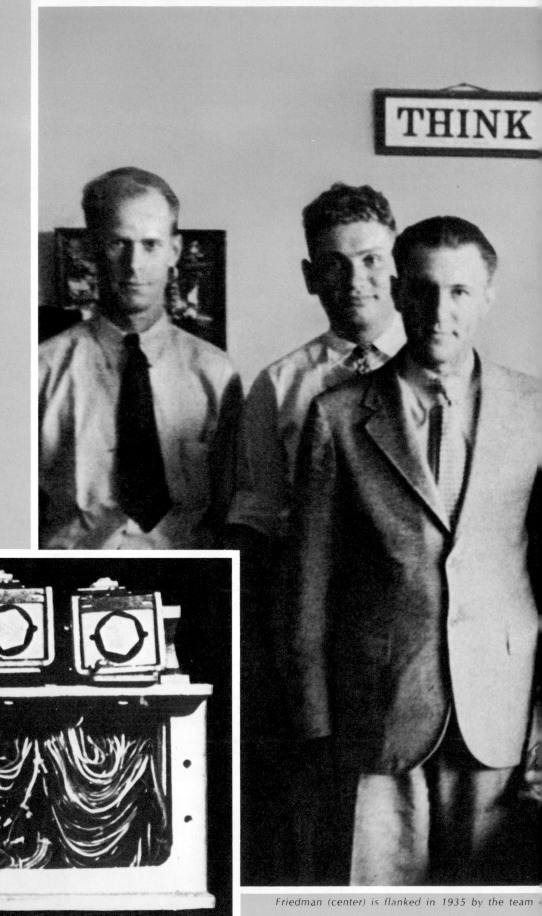

THINK

Friedman (center) is flanked in 1935 by the team

Built from readily available wires and screws, this American machine broke Japan's Purple code.

NO ADMITTANCE

From: Tokyo
To: Washington
7 December 1941
(Purple—Eng)

#902   Part 14 of 14

        (Note: In the forwarding instructions to the
        radio station handling this part, appeared the
        plain English phrase "VERY IMPORTANT")

        7. Obviously it is the intention of the American
Government to conspire with Great Britain and other countries
to obstruct Japan's efforts toward the establishment of
peace through the creation of a New Order in East Asia,
and especially to preserve Anglo-American rights and interests
by keeping Japan and China at war. This intention has
been revealed clearly during the course of the present
negotiations. Thus, the earnest hope of the Japanese
Government to adjust Japanese-American relations and to
preserve and promote the peace of the Pacific through
cooperation with the American Government has finally been
lost.

        The Japanese Government regrets to have to notify
hereby the American Government that in view of the attitude
of the American Government it cannot but consider that it is
impossible to reach an agreement through further negotiations.

JD—1:7143   SECRET   (M) Navy trans. 7 Dec. 1941 (S—TT)

cryptanalysts who helped break the Japanese diplomatic code.

This deciphered message signaled the rupture of U.S.-Japanese relations in 1941.

COMMUNICATING IN THE FIELD

With his left hand poised near an Enigma cipher machine and his attention on a logbook, a German radio operator sits by his equipment aboard a U-boat.

IMAGINATIVE WAYS TO STUMP THE ENEMY

The celebrated Purple and Enigma cipher machines were only two among scores of means the combatants in World War II used to try to obscure their communications from the enemy. One of the most ingenious was a method adopted by the U.S. Marines, who recruited Navajo Indians to man radios in the South Pacific: Navajo was a language so rare that it was understood by barely two dozen non-Navajos in all the world. The Marines got the idea from a Los Angeles civil engineer named Philip Johnson, who had lived as a boy on a reservation where his father was a missionary.

Putting Johnson's suggestion into operation required ingenuity because the Navajo language lacked both technological and geographical terms vital for the belligerents. That did not stump the Navajos; they merely adapted their own descriptive words and phrases to fill the gaps. Australia was called "rolled hat," for the headgear worn by the Australian troops; Britain, "bounded by water"; the Philippines, "floating land"; and America, "our mother." For military terms, the Navajos drew on the natural world of the American Southwest. An observation plane became "owl," bombs became "eggs," and an antitank gun was "tortoise shooter." The improvisations worked; between 1942 and 1945 some 420 Navajos helped the Marines share battle intelligence, and the Japanese never found an interpreter.

For the Navajos themselves, the occupation had an unexpected hazard. In physical appearance they more closely resembled the enemy than their fellow soldiers, and more than one Navajo was captured by Marines and charged with being a Japanese in an American uniform. It took some fast talk—in English, not Navajo—to spare the captive the penalty of execution.

Nonetheless, American Indians were enlisted into communications work elsewhere; members of the Comanche and Chippewa tribes, for example, helped GIs in North Africa and Europe. But there were not enough rare-language speakers. To keep messages secret, the armed forces of all nations had to rely on gadgetry that almost any soldier could master (following pages).

Making sport of the serious need for secrecy, this British cartoon depicts one drastic way to thwart the enemy: An officer eats his code book.

A pair of American Indian Marines in a Pacific island jungle transmit a message in Navajo—a tribal language that no Japanese was able to translate.

EQUIPMENT FOR CIPHERERS ON THE MOVE

The strip cipher, based on one of Thomas Jefferson's contrivances and used by the U.S. Army and Navy in World War II, consisted of a frame and 25 removable paper strips, each numbered and printed with a different scrambling of the alphabet. To encipher a message, the sender slid the strips into slots according to a prearranged order and shifted each strip right or left until the true letters of his message aligned vertically along the central bar. Then he chose at random a vertical column of scrambled letters to send to the recipient. The decipherer put his set of strips into their slots, vertically aligned the letters he had received, then slid the bar across the strips to find the plain-language message.

An American soldier works an M-209 cipher machine in New Guinea in 1944. To keep its method of ciphering secret, every operator had orders to destroy his machine if he was in danger of falling into enemy hands.

The M-209 (shown at left with its mechanism exposed and above, ready for use) worked by means of revolving gears and gear parts. The sender positioned the lettered front wheels to a secret daily setting and turned the knob on the machine's left to the letter he wanted enciphered. When he turned the crank on the right side, the lettered wheels rotated, moving pins and lugs that shifted bars in the cylindrical cage at the back of the machine. The bars acted like cogs in the gear that turned a wheel to print the cipher letter on the roll of tape behind the knob. In order to decipher the message, the recipient repeated the same steps on his own machine.

A KEYBOARD SCRAMBLER CALLED ENIGMA

The German Enigma machine, which resembled a typewriter, enciphered and deciphered messages by illuminating substitute letters in a panel behind the keyboard. Depressing a key started an electrical impulse that traveled along one of billions of possible paths through jack connections in the plugboard at the front of the machine and rotor contacts at the rear. Moving the key also shifted one or more of the rotors so that the machine's internal settings varied from letter to letter.

German soldiers encipher a message on an Enigma, which was compact enough to carry in the field but required two or three men to operate at high speed. Here one soldier presses the keys while a second dictates the illuminated letters to the man with pencil and paper.

To further complicate a cipher, the plugs of a German Uhr machine were substituted for the standard ones at the front of the Enigma. The operator could then alter the paths of electrical impulses passing through the panel of plug connections by simply turning the notched knob on the top of the Uhr machine.

SOME NEW TWISTS
FOR OLD IDEAS

Atop the conning tower of a U-boat, a flagman sends a message while his comrades keep watch (left). The German Navy listed semaphore signals in a code book such as the one below, which also described whistle, light and siren signals. If a U-boat was threatened with capture, code books were thrown overboard; weighted covers made them sink.

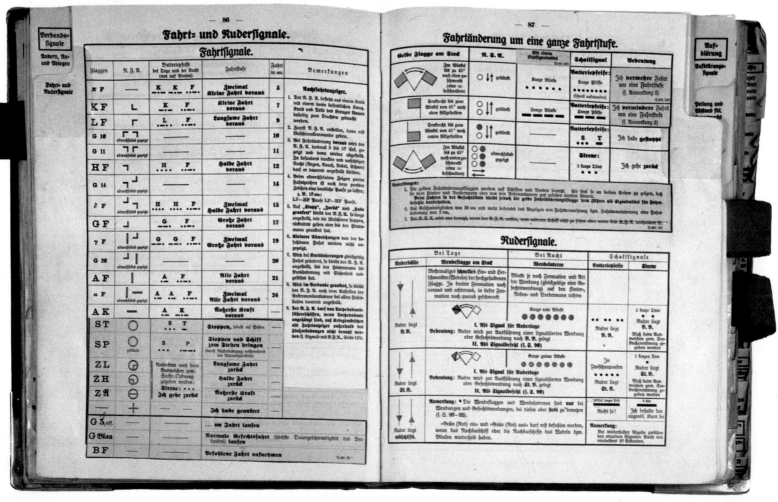

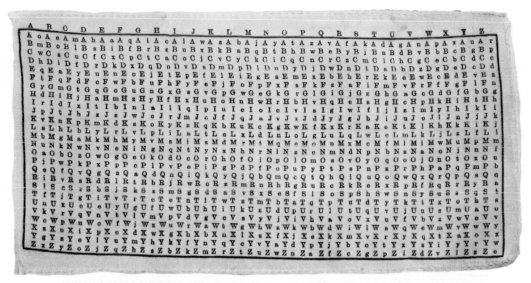

While a dog sits by, two American signalmen outside a mobile pigeon loft prepare birds for flight (below). Carrying holders attached to their legs, pigeons flew as many as 300 miles to deliver messages, some enciphered from tables like the one at left. Senders found each successive cipher letter from a different jumbled alphabet by reading down the columns of standard alphabets in the table; decipherers, knowing the sequence of alphabets used, reversed the process. The dog was the pigeons' security system: It was trained to rescue lost and injured birds.

3

In February 1941, with virtually all of Europe under Axis sway, the United States signed a trade agreement with Vichy France, the part of the Third Republic that Hitler had chosen not to occupy because he was afraid of driving the still-powerful French Navy and French colonies into Great Britain's arms. By the terms of the agreement, the United States was to sell cotton, sugar, petroleum products and other essentials to France's African colonies. There was one stipulation: American observers would supervise distribution of the goods to make sure that the Vichy government did not deliver them into Axis hands.

Accordingly, 12 "food control officers"—all of them former Army or Navy Reserve officers—were given the rank of vice consul and sent to American legations in Oran and Algiers in Algeria; in Tunis, the capital of Tunisia; and in Casablanca, Morocco's largest city. Unbeknownst to the legations, those officers—or the Twelve Disciples, as they came to be called—were under orders to gather intelligence for the War and State Departments in America's first major espionage undertaking for a war it was not yet fighting. American strategists knew that French North Africa could someday serve as an ideally located launching area for an invasion of Axis-held Europe; thus they deemed it vital to know as much as possible about the area.

The Twelve Disciples sent to spy in North Africa were an untrained and oddly assorted lot, including a vintner, an anthropologist and a Harvard librarian. German intelligence in North Africa noted their arrival and—after watching them gad about the countryside shortly after their arrival—concluded that they were agents sent to "pave the way for intended Allied disembarkations next spring." Despite that observation, the Germans dismissed the Disciples as amateurs and paid them little heed. According to one German report, "All their thoughts are centered on their social, sexual or culinary interests; petty quarrels and jealousies are daily incidents with them. We can only congratulate ourselves on the selection of this group of enemy agents who will give us no trouble."

The Disciples soon proved the German agents wrong. Within weeks of taking up their posts that summer, they and a handful of North Africans they had recruited were gathering data on the battle readiness of the 125,000-man French colonial forces and a number of ships of the French Navy

LOW TRICKS FOR HIGH STAKES

that the Germans had confined to port in North Africa. Because the trade agreement gave them unrestricted access to North African ports, the Disciples were able to map harbor facilities and collect details of the defenses there. Every scrap of knowledge they unearthed was passed through Robert D. Murphy, former American Counselor in Vichy and now Consul General in Algiers. Murphy quickly forwarded the information to Washington via cable and in diplomatic pouches.

In December, Japan's attack on Pearl Harbor catapulted the United States into the War and lent new urgency to the Disciples' mission. When Prime Minister Winston Churchill and President Franklin D. Roosevelt met at the White House a few weeks later, they decided that the first major military action undertaken by the new Anglo-American alliance would be the invasion of French North Africa. The invasion, code-named Operation Torch, also was meant to light a fire under the tail of Germany's proud "Desert Fox," General Erwin Rommel, whose Army had by then penetrated some 200 miles into Egypt.

Even before the White House conference, it had been suggested to Roosevelt that American agents infiltrate North Africa "as a concrete example of what can be done" in the field of intelligence. The man who had made that suggestion was William J. Donovan, head of the Office of the Coordinator of War Information (COI), America's first agency established specifically for the purpose of gathering and interpreting foreign intelligence.

With the invasion of French North Africa now a certainty, Donovan's five-month-old COI was ordered to send someone there to work with Murphy and the Disciples and to cultivate local leaders in Spanish Morocco to guard Torch's western flank in the event neutral Spain joined the Axis, as Hitler had long been importuning it to do. Donovan gave the assignment to Marine Colonel William Eddy. His mission, Donovan told him, was to ensure "that the aid of native chiefs be obtained, the loyalty of the inhabitants cultivated, fifth columnists organized and placed, demolition materials cached, and guerrilla bands of bold and daring men organized and installed."

Eddy was the perfect choice for the mission. He had been born in Syria of American parents, had traveled widely through Egypt and Africa, and spoke fluent Arabic. A Marine hero during World War I, Eddy had become a college professor but quit after the Japanese attacked Pearl Harbor, declaring simply, "I am out of love with teaching; I want to be a Marine."

Posted as a Naval attaché, Eddy arrived in Tangier in January and wasted little time in working with the Disciples to set up clandestine radio stations to pass on intelligence to Murphy and, ultimately, to supply information to Torch's planners. Within six months, stations were operating in Casablanca, Algiers and Tunis in French North Africa and in Tangier in neutral Spanish Morocco—only 37 miles away from British Gibraltar. As Eddy expanded his operations, Donovan sent to North Africa several more agents posing as diplomats.

On his own, Eddy increased his numbers by enlisting the support of several local leaders in Spanish and French Morocco. Among his recruits were a Berber adventurer code-named Tassels, whose warriors roamed the mountainous coastal region of Spanish Morocco, and a religious leader code-named Strings. For a fee of about $1,000, Strings turned many of his thousands of followers to the task of gathering information for Eddy. Eddy also cultivated agents in other parts of French North Africa. An Eddy agent who worked as a technician at the airfield in Casablanca, for instance, turned over blueprints detailing several Moroccan landing strips and their defenses, along with their radio-recognition codes.

In August 1942, Eddy was summoned to London to brief a high-level group that included Major General George S. Patton, commander of the Western Task Force of Torch, and Major General George V. Strong, head of Army Intelligence (G-2). There Eddy cut an impressive figure in a room full of impressive figures. When Patton saw the five rows of World War I ribbons on Eddy's chest—two more rows than he himself had won—he commented, "I don't know who he is, but the son of a bitch has sure been shot at enough."

Eddy's facts were as impressive as his ribbons. After listening to Eddy's account of the indigenous forces at his beck and his details on the disposition of French armed forces in North Africa, the impetuous Patton jumped up and declared: "I want Jimmy to hear this." He returned with Lieut. Colonel James H. Doolittle, head of Torch's American air wing, and for the next several hours Doolittle joined Patton and the other military men in pumping Eddy for information. Later Eddy briefed *Torch's* commander, Lieut. General Dwight D. Eisenhower, who told him that the invasion would take place in late October or early November at Casablanca, Oran and Algiers.

Eddy now had two months to prepare for the invasion, and he and Murphy's Disciples made the most of the time. One of Eddy's Berber agents packed grenades in containers marked "sugar" and "tea" and smuggled them from Spanish Morocco into French Morocco on muleback for use by the local resistance. Pistols, rifles and ammunition were shipped under diplomatic pouch from the British armory at Gibraltar to the British legation in Tangier; from there, smugglers in Eddy's employ delivered them to Casablanca.

Eddy also found a ship's pilot to guide the invasion fleet onto the North African beaches. The appointee was René Malavergne, former chief pilot of Port Lyautey, French Morocco, and an authority on the North African coastline, where swirling offshore currents, sunken ships and hidden reefs made landing no easy proposition. Malavergne was hiding out in Casablanca from Vichy authorities because of his pro-Allied sentiments. Two COI agents put Malavergne in the trunk of their decrepit Chevrolet, covered him with an Oriental rug and set out to smuggle him into Spanish Morocco. Hours later, the nearly asphyxiated Malavergne staggered from the trunk in Tangier. From there, he was flown to Gibraltar and then to London.

By late October, the British were mauling Rommel's army at El Alamein, 60 miles west of Alexandria, Egypt. Naturally, rumors of a follow-up Allied invasion somewhere along the African coast ensued, some of them false reports planted by American agents.

Two agents who were most effective in spreading such false information were a pair of anti-Nazi Austrians who had escaped from a Vichy prison and fled to Casablanca. The two men managed to cultivate a high-ranking German diplomat named Theodor Auer by feeding him accurate but inconsequential information about Allied troop movements in Egypt and Libya. Auer dutifully passed the information on to Berlin. When he had swallowed that bait, the two agents sprang their trap: The Allies were indeed planning an invasion, they told Auer, and the destination was Dakar, the

capital of French West Africa, 1,500 miles distant from Casablanca. The Austrians also told Auer—falsely—that the British were sending a massive supply convoy to the island of Malta, which had been under siege by the Germans for nearly two years. Auer promptly cabled the information to the German High Command.

As the invasion fleet—more than 500 ships carrying 107,000 troops, three quarters of them American and the rest British—approached North Africa, the clandestine radio network set up by the Disciples went into action. Its operatives supplied the Allies with up-to-the-minute information on wind and tide conditions, the disposition of French Army and Navy forces, and the manning of coastal batteries along the 1,200-mile stretch of North Africa that was *Torch's* target.

On November 8, 1942, the Allies landed at nine points along the coast of French Morocco and Algeria. At the same time, North Africans in the pay of the COI strong-armed their way into critical public buildings in major cities—post offices, radio stations, utility plants and the like—and cut telephone and telegraph lines; others detonated land mines and removed obstacles from roads leading away from the landing beaches. One agent managed to prevent the French from blowing up the rail tunnel connecting Oran with the port of Mers-el-Kebir; the night before, he had stolen into the tunnel and removed the caps from demolition charges the French had placed there.

In the meanwhile, in response to Auer's intelligence, several German U-boats and warships waited in vain off the coast of French West Africa, while seven squadrons of Sicily-based Luftwaffe planes circled over the Mediterranean at Cape Bon, 300 miles away, in search of the mythical British supply convoy. The two deceptions allowed Allied troops to storm ashore without anyone—German or French—raising an alarm. Only scattered units of the French Navy and Army offered any resistance—many of the other commanders having been persuaded by COI agents not to fight. By November 11, Admiral Jean François Darlan, commanding the French forces, had signed an armistice ending French fighting in North Africa.

Eddy and the Disciples—and the hundreds of locals in their employ—had helped to ignite Operation *Torch*. Just as important, the agents proved the value such work could have. The future of strategic intelligence gathering as a tool of warfare and the creation of America's first centralized intelligence organization—which Donovan had told his fledgling staff might depend on the successful outcome of *Torch*—was no longer in doubt.

Over the next three years, the men and women of the COI—later to become the Office of Strategic Services, or OSS—would range across the world from the cobblestone streets of Bern, Switzerland, to the sodden jungles of Burma and the splendid throne room of the Dalai Lama in Lhasa, Tibet. These agents would carry out thousands of missions of espionage, sabotage and subversion. Taken one by one, the actions were like bee stings: each caused but a moment's pain, yet their cumulative effect slowly and surely helped bring the Axis giant to its knees.

William J. Donovan, creator of America's giant-killing intelligence agency, was a successful Wall Street lawyer, one-time Republican candidate for Governor of New York and longtime friend of Democrat Franklin Delano Roosevelt.

Pearl Harbor had caught most Americans unprepared—but not William Donovan. Nicknamed Wild Bill for his recklessness as a football player at Columbia and for World War I battlefield exploits that had won him the rank of colo-

nel and the Congressional Medal of Honor, Donovan had long been preparing for war. For years, this man—whom Roosevelt admired for his "blend of Wall Street orthodoxy and sophisticated American nationalism"—had served as the President's unofficial eyes and ears, traveling all over the world to meet with its leaders. Donovan hobnobbed with such figures as King Boris of Bulgaria, Prince Paul of Yugoslavia and what one associate called "tons of prime ministers," and he brought back political and military information that he believed would serve his country and his President well in the event of war.

In 1940, traveling at his own expense, Donovan had visited Italy's Fascist dictator Benito Mussolini in Rome. Donovan was curious to see the new Italian Army, he told Mussolini, since he had fought alongside the Italians during World War I. When the Duce refused Donovan's request, Donovan replied casually, "It really doesn't matter. We know the Italians don't have much of an army anyway." Mussolini, his pride wounded by this calculated insult, ordered that Donovan was to be allowed to see whatever he wanted, wherever he wanted. Donovan went to Libya, which had long been an Italian colony, and he saw. He reported back to Roosevelt that, contrary to popular world opinion, Italy's would-be Caesar had assembled what appeared to be a competent fighting force.

Donovan flew on so many missions for the President that political columnist Westbrook Pegler remarked: "Colonel Donovan seems to have a 50-trip ticket on the Clippers, which he must use up in a certain time or forfeit the remainder." Among Donovan's destinations were Bulgaria, Yugoslavia, Turkey, Great Britain, Iraq, Egypt, Palestine, Spain and Portugal.

Donovan gathered useful information everywhere, but his most important stopovers were in London, which he visited in July 1940—less than three weeks after France fell to Hitler—and again in December. Great Britain, now the sole bastion of democracy in Europe, had asked Roosevelt for 50 World War I destroyers to bolster its depleted Navy. But Roosevelt was reluctant to transfer them, lest Great Britain capitulate and the ships fall into German hands. That July, he asked Donovan to assess the situation. For five days, Donovan met with British leaders, among them King George VI and Prime Minister Winston Church-

Lieut. Colonel Ilia Tolstoy (left) and Captain Brooke Dolan (center) pause with their guide before a Buddhist shrine in Tibet. Undertaking an investigative mission for the OSS, the two men trekked 1,500 miles from Siliguri, India, to Lanchow, China, to study the feasibility of building a supply route connecting China and India through Tibet.

ill. The British also made Donovan privy to their most tightly held secrets: the latest radar, the deciphering that was being done on German military codes, even the details of Operation *Double Cross*.

When he returned to Washington, Donovan told the President that the British would not give in to Germany, that Churchill's promise "to fight on unconquerable until the curse of Hitler is lifted from the brow of mankind" was not hollow rhetoric. Donovan recommended that the President transfer the destroyers. Wendell Willkie, Republican candidate for President, agreed not to make a political issue of the transfer, and on September 3, 1940, Roosevelt signed an order giving the British title to the ships for 99 years in exchange for leasing bases in Newfoundland, the Caribbean and Bermuda to the United States.

On Donovan's second trip to London, Sir Frank Nelson, Chief of Special Operations, Executive (SOE), opened his bag of dirty tricks, revealing details of various propaganda, sabotage and subversive operations. When he reported to the President, Donovan described in detail the workings of British intelligence. He had been mightily impressed by its many clever field and spy-catching operations, he told Roosevelt, but he was disturbed by the way the British handled their agents' information. There was no central point where the mass of data they accumulated was being efficiently gathered, sifted, interpreted and condensed. By the summer of 1941, Roosevelt himself had become so inundated by data from several American agencies—among them the Federal Bureau of Investigation, Army and Navy Intelligence and the Secret Service—that he asked Donovan to make specific proposals for one agency to collect and analyze such material.

"It is essential we set up a central enemy-intelligence organization which would collect pertinent information," Donovan told the President in a memorandum. The data, he said, should be "analyzed and interpreted by specialized, trained research officials in scientific fields, including technological, economic, financial and psychological scholars." Donovan also noted the need for "psychological attack against the moral and spiritual defenses" of the Axis through propaganda, an art at which the Germans excelled. Privately, he spoke to Roosevelt also of the desirability of sabotage and guerrilla warfare, but he left any such suggestions out of his official memo because it was felt that the thought of Americans undertaking those measures might distress many politicians and generals.

Roosevelt enthusiastically agreed with Donovan's recommendations, and on July 11, 1941, the COI was established with the 58-year-old Donovan at its head. Its job, said Roosevelt, would be to "collect and analyze all information and data which may bear upon national security and to carry out such supplementary activities as may facilitate the securing of information for national security not now available to the government."

The vague generalities of the Executive Order establishing the COI were deliberate: Roosevelt did not want to antagonize the nation's other intelligence services, most notably G-2 and the FBI. To silence General Strong, who carped that Wild Bill Donovan was too independent to fit in with military intelligence, Roosevelt made the COI a civilian agency in the executive branch of the government—reporting directly to him—and named his own son James, a Marine captain, as a liaison between Donovan and the military. Roosevelt also promised J. Edgar Hoover, cantankerous FBI chief, that Donovan would not conduct espionage operations in the United States; Nelson Rockefeller, head of the State Department's Inter-American Affairs Committee, extracted a similar promise concerning Latin America.

Within a few months of its establishment, the COI, which had started out with Donovan and seven assistants sharing one telephone in the Office of the Budget, numbered several hundred. Still, the COI was an infant in the field of intelligence; to survive, the American agency would need a helping hand from British intelligence. Whatever their shortcomings in coordinating and analyzing information, the British were experienced in espionage.

The COI got that early British help thanks to William Stephenson, a wealthy and influential Canadian industrialist who had accompanied Donovan to London in December 1940. Stephenson, operating under the *nom de guerre* Intrepid, was the head of British intelligence operations in the Americas, working out of a nondescript suite of offices in New York's Rockefeller Center that was marked "British Security Coordination."

As a first step, the British furnished the COI with reams

of material gathered before the War and during its early stages—data that proved especially valuable to Donovan's young force in its formative days, when the COI had little but empty filing cabinets. Stephenson also arranged for the COI to send some of its first recruits to British intelligence's Camp X near Toronto for training as espionage agents.

In December 1941, Stephenson helped put the COI in the propaganda business by giving the organization use of two powerful radio transmitters located in San Francisco and Boston—one to transmit to the Far East, the other to Europe. Donovan's agents promptly put the Boston transmitter to good use. When an American turncoat named Jane Anderson bragged to U.S. audiences via short-wave Radio Berlin about a visit to a German nightspot—"I ate Turkish cookies while my friend ordered great goblets of champagne"—the COI's response was swift and effective. The next evening, the agency beamed her remarks back to Germany, most of whose citizens were making do with a diet considerably less rich. Soon after, reported *Time* in April 1942, "Plain Jane went off the air, has not been heard from since. A technical knockout for Donovan."

By June 1942, the COI's overt propaganda operation—headed by playwright Robert Sherwood—had grown so large that it was split off to become part of an independent agency, the Office of War Information. The rest of the COI was put under the direction of the Joint Chiefs of Staff so its activities could be better coordinated with the military. With that change in command came a new name for Donovan's agency: the Office of Strategic Services. And with the new name came new duties.

Donovan, remarked an aide, possessed "the power to visualize an oak when he saw an acorn." From the first, he

had had big plans for his intelligence agency. The new OSS rapidly branched out as Donovan established divisions to produce studies of every possible strategic area from Tahiti to Timbuktu; to foment dissent and unrest in enemy territory through subversion and covert propaganda; to gather intelligence in enemy territory; and to conduct sabotage and unorthodox warfare behind enemy lines. The mild-mannered scholars and scientists who undertook OSS studies were known as the Choirboys, noted a former intelligence officer, while the field agents came to be characterized as Cowboys because of their wild exploits.

The Research and Analysis (R&A) Division pieced together what Donovan called the raw material of strategy. Started in the early days of the COI, the R&A Division was made up largely of scholars—geographers, cartographers, historians, political scientists, economists, psychologists, linguists, anthropologists—recruited from the universities of America.

These academicians—lampooned by German propagandists as "50 professors, 20 monkeys, 10 goats, 12 guinea pigs and a staff of Jewish scribblers"—worked out of a cluster of nondescript Washington buildings that had in fact once housed the laboratories and guinea pigs of the National Health Institute. There they listened to Axis news broadcasts via short wave and pored over a variety of documents—obscure farm reports, arcane technical journals, village newspapers and the like—seeking to form an accurate picture of the enemy from a jigsaw of data. By studying European farm journals and market figures, for example, R&A statisticians determined that rumors of an impending German food shortage were false, and that Germany would have enough food to keep fighting. Other R&A experts

British intelligence agent William Stephenson tinkers with a transmitter for sending photographs by radio, which he invented and sold worldwide in the 1920s. As an established international businessman, Stephenson had a ready-made cover for espionage; in the 1930s he made tours of industrial plants in Germany, ostensibly representing his own commercial interests but actually gathering details of Hitler's rearmament program.

scanned German newspaper obituary columns and tallied the number of officers killed in action. From those figures—reckoning a constant ratio of enlisted men to officers—they supplied American generals with a remarkably close count of Wehrmacht strength throughout the War.

Ultimately, Donovan's dons turned out tens of thousands of pages of intelligence studies. "Even in purely operational fields such as bomb targets our help was regarded as indispensable," recalled William L. Langer, chief of the R&A Division. "But above all, in the study of the capabilities and intentions of foreign powers, I think we went far beyond anything previously known or previously attempted anywhere else."

The Research and Development (R&D) Division was made up of scientists and inventors whose assignment was to develop unorthodox weapons, plots and schemes of a kind, Donovan remarked wryly, that "no one expects us to originate because they are so un-American." The R&D Division scientists turned their talents to producing counterfeit currency and documents, several kinds of weapons (among them a flashless, virtually silent pistol-submachine gun) and enough varieties of explosives to delight any saboteur. One such explosive device, for example, resembled an ordinary candle; when the candle burned down by one third, the high explosive composing the remainder detonated.

The Morale Operations (MO) Division, with a staff of Madison Avenue copywriters, journalists and Hollywood screenwriters, occupied itself with developing so-called black, or covert, propaganda—described by Donovan as "a judicious mixture of rumor and deception, with truth as a bait, to foster disunity and confusion in support of military operations." Various black-propaganda ploys undertaken by MO to subvert the enemy included distributing phony newspapers throughout Germany and mailing false death notices to the families of enemy soldiers.

The Labor Division was set up and directed by Chicago labor lawyer Arthur Goldberg, who would later become a Supreme Court Justice, and by George Pratt, General Counsel for the National Labor Relations Board. Labor's agents infiltrated numerous socialist and trade-union groups in occupied Europe and Germany to foment subversion and sabotage among men and women forced to work for the Nazis.

These operations were all important. But the heart of the OSS consisted of the Secret Intelligence (SI) and Special Operations (SO) Divisions. SI Division's job was to collect foreign intelligence and its model was England's MI-6; SO Division, modeled on England's SOE, conducted sabotage and guerrilla operations. Donovan recruited men and women from all walks of life to be SI and SO agents. Lieut. Commander Ian Fleming of British Naval Intelligence—later the creator of James Bond, fiction's ultimate secret agent—advised Donovan to pick men in their forties and fifties, possessing "absolute discretion, sobriety, devotion to duty, languages and wide experience." But such staid advice did not suit Wild Bill. He preferred younger men, rakehells who were "calculatingly reckless, of disciplined daring and trained for aggressive action."

Donovan's agents included soldiers and civilians—professors, bankers, lawyers, professional athletes, missionaries, more-or-less reformed gangsters, professional counterfeiters and movie stars. Among the better-known recruits were René Dussaq, an agile Hollywood stuntman nicknamed the Human Fly, who would win a Distinguished Service Cross for his work with the French Resistance; Quentin Roosevelt, a grandson of President Theodore Roosevelt, who served as Donovan's personal representative to Chiang Kai-shek; and John Hamilton, known to movie audiences as actor Sterling Hayden, who ran arms to the partisans in Yugoslavia.

Scions of so many social register families—including Morgans, Mellons, du Ponts and Vanderbilts—volunteered that one newspaper reporter suggested that OSS stood for "Oh, So Social." It might also have meant "Oh, So Socialist," for at the other end of the OSS spectrum were left-wing sympathizers such as Marxist philosopher Herbert Marcuse and several veterans of the Abraham Lincoln Brigade, Americans who had fought with the Republican Loyalists in 1937 and 1938 in the Spanish Civil War. When an aide objected to the inclusion of such radicals, Donovan replied: "I'd put Stalin on the OSS payroll if I thought it would help defeat Hitler."

Whatever their background, SI and SO recruits all were seduced, said Dr. Henry Murray, chief psychologist of the OSS, by "the idea of being a mysterious man with secret knowledge." Another OSS officer recalled that "we were working with an unusual type of individual. Many had natures that fed on danger and excitement. Their appetite for the unconventional and spectacular was far beyond the ordinary. It was not unusual to find a good measure of temperament thrown in."

OSS recruits for overseas assignments were not told what was in store for them. Instead, they were put through a rigorous three-day screening of physical and mental agility tests at a suburban Washington facility known only as Station S. If they passed the tests, they were sent to a training camp for instruction in the techniques of survival, sabotage and espionage. If they failed the tests, they were sent back to their former pursuits with no specific knowledge of why they had been tested.

Donovan's first agents were trained by British, American and Canadian instructors at Camp X outside Toronto and at a former camp for children in Maryland's Catoctin Mountains. Later, other OSS camps were established at Congressional Country Club just outside Washington, at Catalina Island off the coast of California and at eight other sites across the United States. Fledgling American agents learned to send Morse code and to repair radio transmitters; to kill silently with garrote, knife and their bare hands; to parachute into almost any kind of terrain; and to handle Allied and Axis firearms—skills needed to work behind enemy lines.

One veteran British intelligence officer marveled at the speed with which the first OSS agents learned their craft. "They came among us, these aspiring American spymasters,

like innocent girls from a finishing school anxious to learn the seasoned *demimondain* ways of old practitioners," recalled Malcolm Muggeridge, who later became the editor of *Punch*, the British humor magazine. "The first feeling of awe and respect soon evaporated and it turned out that the finishing-school products had learned all the tricks and devices of the old practitioners in no time at all."

Even as the early OSS trainees were beginning to put to practical use their curriculum of unorthodox warfare, one of America's most experienced practitioners of the spy's art, Allen Welsh Dulles, was boarding a train in Vichy France, at Annemasse near the Swiss border. His destination was Bern, where he was ostensibly to serve as a special legal assistant to Ambassador Leland Harrison. Dulles crossed into Switzerland one step ahead of the Germans, who used the Allies' Operation *Torch* as an excuse to occupy Vichy France and seal its borders.

Swiss newspapers announcing Dulles' arrival labeled him "the personal representative of President Roosevelt," but he was neither the President's representative nor Harrison's assistant. He was, in fact, both a master spy and a spymaster. Over the next two and a half years, working from an apartment at 23 Herrengasse—an arcaded street high above the River Aare—Dulles would establish a force that mined the mother lode of German intelligence.

With his tweed jacket, silk bow tie and ever-present briar pipe, Allen Dulles, 49, looked more like a college professor than a spy as he peered at the world from behind rimless glasses. In fact, Dulles was no stranger to the intrigues that swirled around neutral Switzerland's picturesque capital. During World War I he had worked in Bern gathering intelligence for the State Department. At the age of 29 he had headed the Near East Division in the State Department; later he joined a New York law firm as a specialist in international law. Within a month of Pearl Harbor, Dulles had heeded the call of Bill Donovan, an old friend from his Washington days, to join the COI.

Dulles' primary mission in Switzerland was to extract as much information as he could from inside Germany. To do so, he first made contact with Bern's large colony of exiled anti-Nazi German politicians, businessmen, intellectuals and diplomats. His contacts with these expatriates helped

Against a backdrop of the Alps, Allen Welsh Dulles (right) confers with Gero von Gaevernitz, a German-American businessman who managed family interests in Switzerland while spying for the United States. Exploiting prewar acquaintanceships, Gaevernitz provided Dulles with a valuable entree into the circle of anti-Nazi German émigrés in Bern.

Dulles to enlist anti-Hitler Abwehr agents who gave him an accurate picture of conditions in Germany. Possibly his greatest coup was recruiting an obscure Berlin bureaucrat named Fritz Kolbe; over a period of nearly a year, Kolbe delivered to Dulles several file cabinets' worth of top-secret German documents.

Kolbe had joined the German Foreign Service during the 1920s, and he had earned a reputation as a pluperfect civil servant who would plug away at the petty details of day-to-day operations without complaint. His superiors' trust in Kolbe eventually led to his assignment as an assistant to Karl Ritter, Foreign Minister Joachim von Ribbentrop's liaison with the German High Command. It was Kolbe's job to sift through the scores of cables that flowed into Ritter's office every day from German embassies and military posts around the world and to put the most important ones on his chief's desk. It was a position of great trust. And it provided Kolbe, a fervent anti-Nazi, with a golden opportunity to help bring about the downfall of the Third Reich.

On August 23, 1943—after deciding that he could no longer stand by as Germany was ravaged by war—Kolbe arranged to be sent to Bern as a diplomatic courier. There, a businessman named Ernesto Kocherthaler, an old friend who had fled Germany in the 1930s, introduced Kolbe to an attaché at the British Embassy. The meeting was a calamity. Kolbe, a nervous man under the best of circumstances, fussed and fidgeted. When he produced a handful of top-

secret cables, the British diplomat was not impressed. "I don't believe you," he said icily; "and if you are telling the truth, you're a cad."

Shaken by this rebuff, Kocherthaler and Kolbe contacted Gerald Mayer, a Dulles aide who ostensibly worked for the American Office of War Information in Bern. On August 24, Kocherthaler alone visited Mayer at his office. Fearing another rejection, Kocherthaler quickly pulled three cables out of his jacket. One dealt with infiltrating German spies into North Africa; another discussed plans to crush resistance in Czechoslovakia; the third detailed British spy operations in the Balkans.

Mayer, who was fluent in German, was dumfounded by what he read. Where, he asked, had Kocherthaler acquired the papers? From a friend in the German Foreign Service, Kocherthaler answered, a man "willing, indeed eager, to provide this kind of material to you." Mayer took the papers to Dulles. Dulles was impressed. He was concerned by the possibility that the cables might have been concocted by the Abwehr in an effort to infiltrate his operation, but the tidbits of information were too tantalizing to reject. And Dulles, who had declined during World War I to meet with a Russian mystery man named Vladimir Ilyich Ulyanov—known later simply as Lenin—was determined not to be overcautious this time. He arranged to meet with Kolbe and Kocherthaler that night at Mayer's apartment.

Mayer introduced Dulles to the two Germans as his assis-

BOMBARDING GERMANY WITH FAKE PAPERS

One of the sliest of the black-propaganda schemes carried out by MO, the Morale Operations branch of the OSS, was Operation *Cornflakes*. The trick lay not so much in the propaganda itself as in its delivery—which had the unwitting collaboration of German postal authorities.

The propaganda was contained in *Das Neue Deutschland (The New Germany),* a newspaper that purported to speak for a native anti-Nazi underground. MO agents wrote the paper and printed two million copies. They put the copies in envelopes addressed to names listed in German telephone directories, stamped the envelopes with counterfeit postage, then put them into fake German mailbags.

From there, the U.S. Army Air Forces

took over. On bombing runs in January and February of 1945 the Fifteenth Air Force hit Reich railroads in southern Austria. After bombing a mail train, the planes dropped down to 50 feet and deposited the mailbags beside the wreckage. German authorities who salvaged the train forwarded OSS mailbags along with real ones. Some sacks were delivered as far north as the Baltic.

Most of the forged stamps used in *Cornflakes* were made to look authentic. But MO artists also slipped in some wry jokes: On some stamps *(right)* they reworked Hitler's profile into a grinning death's-head, and they changed the legend *Deutsches Reich* (German Empire) to *Futsches Reich* (Collapsed Empire).

tant, "Mr. Douglas." Kolbe, fearful of being shunned again, played his ace immediately, fanning out on the floor 186 pages of cables and other documents that he had smuggled, strapped to his legs, out of the Foreign Office. Kolbe noted the incredulous looks on the faces of the two Americans as they read the papers and he knew he would have to convince them that he was not a double agent. Hitler was ruining Germany, he said. "It is not enough to clench one's fist in one's pocket," he exclaimed. "The fist must be used to strike." Before leaving Mayer's apartment, Kolbe had told the two Americans everything he could about himself, his career and his family.

Mayer and Dulles pored over the documents through the night, summarizing the most significant information for coded radio transmission to Washington. Dulles also asked the OSS counterespionage section to investigate every facet of Kolbe's life. When Washington confirmed that Kolbe's account of himself was genuine, he was assigned the code name by which he would be known for the duration of the War, George Wood.

On his second trip to Bern some two months later, Kolbe delivered 200 pages of cables. For Dulles and his staff—which now included several American fliers who had been forced by battle damage to land their planes in Switzerland and were stranded there—the cables were a treasure trove. Many of them dealt with the minutiae of diplomacy; others, however, contained information that the OSS could turn against the Germans.

One cable from the German mission in Argentina, for example, reported the planned departure date of a large convoy from the east coast of the United States. Dulles notified Washington, the departure date was changed, and the convoy managed to avoid the U-boat wolf pack that had been sent to intercept it.

Another telegram, from the German Embassy in Madrid, read simply: SHIPMENTS OF ORANGES WILL CONTINUE TO ARRIVE ON SCHEDULE. That bit of information led OSS agents to the discovery that Spanish dictator Francisco Franco, breaking his word to the Allies, was shipping tungsten—used to temper high-quality steel—to Germany in orange crates. The Allies retaliated with an oil embargo of Spain.

Over the next several months, Kolbe brought out a wealth of material. Occasionally he even supplied specific information

on request. When Washington badgered Dulles for data on the Japanese Navy, Dulles asked the woman who had been posing as Kolbe's mistress—as an explanation for his frequent visits to Switzerland—to send him an innocuous-sounding postcard. "Perhaps you remember my little son," the woman wrote. "His birthday is coming soon and I wanted to get him some of those clever Japanese toys with which the shops here used to be full, but I can't find any. I wonder if there might be some left in Berlin." Kolbe somehow managed to read between the lines of Dulles' message and obliged on his next visit with a summary of several cables from the German Naval Attaché in Tokyo that gave Dulles the precise battle order of the Imperial Fleet. At times, Kolbe also was able to tip off Dulles when the Abwehr broke an Allied code, enabling cryptographers to switch ciphers before more than a few messages were intercepted.

Eventually, Kolbe began to fear that he would run afoul of the Gestapo if he made too many trips to Bern. Instead, he started using a camera furnished him by Dulles to send long rolls of film to his Swiss "mistress" via diplomatic couriers, who were ignorant of the film's content. Kolbe took most of his snapshots in the basement of a Berlin hospital with the connivance of anti-Nazi friends whom he referred to as "my inner circle." One night, during an air raid, Kolbe was photographing a cable when a confederate passed word that SS chief Heinrich Himmler had asked to see that very document. Kolbe rushed through Berlin's blacked-out streets to his office and pretended to pull the cable out of his files while he actually was taking it from his coat pocket. Despite that scare, Kolbe continued providing film until the end of July, when an attempt on Hitler's life sent the Gestapo sweeping through the highest German circles and forced Kolbe to cease his picture taking.

All told, Kolbe, who escaped to Switzerland in early 1945, brought out more than 1,600 cables. He earned lavish praise from Dulles—who later became head of the Central Intelligence Agency, postwar successor to the OSS—as "an intelligence officer's dream, undoubtedly one of the best secret agents any intelligence service ever had."

The contributions of Fritz Kolbe, who had arrived, unbidden, on the OSS's doorstep, reaffirmed one of Donovan's pet theories: No matter how efficient an organization might be, the successful gathering of secret intelligence was often a matter of chance. Thus Donovan was more than willing to go along with a wildly quixotic scheme proposed to him in the spring of 1943 by a New York businessman named Marcello Girosi. His brother, Girosi told Donovan, was Admiral Massimo Girosi of Italy's General Staff, and—he believed—an ardent, if secret, anti-Fascist. Marcello Girosi volunteered to approach his brother and persuade him to lead a coup against Mussolini. Donovan was so taken with the idea that he immediately formed a special team—code-named, for no special reason, Operation *McGregor*—to get Girosi into Italy. And although the team failed to meet its chief objective, it ended up helping to recover a top-secret naval weapon and to deliver one of Italy's most important scientists into American hands.

Typifying the diversity of men attracted to the OSS, the four-man *McGregor* team Donovan assembled to get Girosi into Italy included Girosi himself, who was given an abbreviated training regimen; Captain John Shaheen, a former Chicago press agent; Lieutenant Michael Burke, a star football player at the University of Pennsylvania and later president of the New York Yankees baseball team; and Lieutenant Henry Ringling North, of the circus family.

The team reached Sicily in mid-August just as the Allies completed their conquest of the island. There, Marcello Girosi put the finishing touches on a letter to his brother. It was within the admiral's power, he wrote, to save their homeland from the bloodshed that would continue to be its lot in partnership with Germany. The highest American authorities had assured him that if Italy overthrew Mussolini and renounced its Axis ties, it would be welcomed with open arms as an ally. If Massimo would meet him, Marcello continued, he would outline a way to redeem the honor of Italy. He signed the letter "Gigi," the brothers' nickname for their childhood governess.

The letter, sewn inside the cover of a book, was to be delivered by an anti-Fascist Italian Army veteran carrying a sick-leave pass that would enable him to travel unquestioned across Italian and German lines. On a cloudy August night, three PT boats—one carrying the *McGregor* team and the other two acting as an escort—set out from Sicily for Calabria, located in the toe of Italy's boot. Just offshore the courier slipped into a rubber dinghy and headed for the beach. The letter was duly delivered, but the mission misfired because its timing was off: By the time Admiral Girosi received his brother's letter, the chief of the Italian General Staff, Marshal Pietro Badoglio, was already negotiating with Eisenhower for an armistice.

Still, the *McGregor* team was on the scene, and the OSS gave it a new assignment: Find Professor Carlos Calosi, inventor of a magnetically activated torpedo that could sink a ship merely by passing underneath the hull.

The *McGregor* team began its search by interrogating several of Marcello Girosi's friends in Naples, which the Allies had taken in October 1943. The friends led them to Admiral Eugenio Minisini, head of the Italian Navy's experimental-weapons division. They found Minisini in a small *pensione* in Naples near the bombed-out ruins of one of the factories used to make the magnetic torpedo. Before he went into hiding, Minisini had been ordered by the General Staff to cooperate with the Allies, and he freely gave the OSS team details of several Italian Navy inventions, including the deadly torpedo and a long-range commando submarine.

Minisini revealed that Calosi was hiding right under the noses of the Germans, in a convent in Rome. Calosi was found, and another OSS team already working behind German lines smuggled him out of the convent and flew him to the United States, where he reconstructed his torpedo for use by the Allies at the Torpedo Station in Newport, Rhode Island.

Even more important, Calosi developed a countermeasure that rendered his torpedo harmless in the hands of the Ger-

A tailor fits an agent with a German Army uniform at an OSS clothing warehouse in London. To supply its agents with clothing authentic enough to pass enemy scrutiny, the OSS confiscated uniforms and other military articles from German prisoners of war; civilian clothes came from European refugees.

mans, who were using it by the thousands against Allied shipping. His new device worked by disrupting the torpedo's magnetic field. To demonstrate it, Calosi installed it on a derelict vessel in Narragansett Bay and then stood confidently on the derelict's bridge while several live magnetic torpedoes were fired at the ship from close range. Calosi's confidence was well founded: Each torpedo exploded before it reached the ship. The Allies quickly installed the device on merchant ships—robbing the German Navy of one of its deadliest weapons.

Few OSS missions produced such lagniappes as the Calosi caper. Nor did Donovan expect them to. Small operations were the meat and potatoes of the OSS, and Donovan relished delivering reports of those missions to the President in a daily summary. A typical report from Donovan usually included extracts of OSS dispatches from several combat zones:

BERLIN: "For months, Berlin has been camouflaging its streets, squares, parks and lakes to confuse Allied fliers," reported Donovan. "All of Unter der Linden is now covered with giant colored nets under which the traffic moves. A simulated village has been erected in the center of a lake, of painted canvas on thin lath. To show contempt for this German effort at camouflage, a single RAF plane flew over the 'village' last night and dropped one wooden bomb."

BURMA: "The mystery of how the Japanese are concealing their fighter aircraft in north Burma was solved by a photograph seized from a captured enemy pilot, showing him standing beside his airplane. An OSS photo technician enlarged the picture and discovered that instead of building revetments, the Japs had dug holes to bury their planes and covered the holes with sod.

"The prisoner admitted that he was based at Meiktila, just south of Mandalay. The Air Force reexamined previous aerial photos of the base and noted 30 suspicious shadows around the perimeter. A few days later, a flight of B-25s bombed and strafed Meiktila, destroying most of the hidden fighters and relieving pressure on our Hump transports"—planes flying supplies from India to China.

FRANCE: "In order to avoid German DF-ing," Donovan reported, with reference to radio direction finding, "a pair of agents hit upon an ingenious device. They secured one of the large hogsheads mounted on wheels that local wine vendors push through town and inserted a partition halfway down the cask. The lower half was filled with wine, which could be drawn from a bung at the bottom, and one of the agents concealed himself in the empty upper half with his short-wave set. The other agent, disguised as a peddler, moved from street to street while his teammate transmitted. If a DF-ing truck approached, the peddler would halt, a signal to stop sending. This team has been operating for months without detection, forwarding intelligence to OSS/London on enemy troop movements and pinpointing bomber targets."

Donovan encouraged the OSS's various divisions—especially Morale Operations and Research and Development—to play any dirty tricks they could think of that would bedevil the enemy. "No project," recalled one OSS officer, "was so implausible, no weapon so outlandish as to be discarded out of hand."

One of the more outlandish schemes Donovan approved was a plot dreamed up by Stanley Lovell, head of R&D, to inject Hitler's vegetables with female sex hormones. "America's top diagnosticians and gland experts agreed with me that he was definitely close to the male-female line," Lovell recalled. "His poor emotional control, his violent passions all led me to feel that a push to the female side might do wonders. The hope was that his mustache might fall off and his voice become soprano."

Lovell's plan called for insinuating an OSS agent or an anti-Nazi German into Berchtesgaden, Hitler's rustic Bavarian retreat, as a gardener. There, he might well be in a position to inject the Führer's carrots, beets and such with the hormones. Lovell supplied the hormones—along with some tranquilizers "for variety's sake"—to an OSS agent, but the plan came to naught. "I can only assume," Lovell noted wryly, "that the gardener took our money and threw the syringes and medications into the nearest thicket. Either that or Hitler had a big turnover in his tasters."

From its bag of devious tricks, the MO devised many plots that were more practical and plausible than the hormone scheme. The simplest involved spreading discomfiting rumors throughout the Reich. According to one rumor, the Allies had perfected a bomb that sucked oxygen out of the air and caused death by suffocation. Another rumor attributed a small outbreak of bubonic plague in German-occupied Rotterdam to germ-carrying enemy rockets.

More complex operations included printing pamphlets to lower the morale of the German fighting man. One MO plot to induce German troops to surrender was inspired by the Germans' own Operation *Scorpion*, which had distributed propaganda leaflets to bolster the spirits of troops battling Allied forces in Western Europe. According to OSS reports, the *Scorpion* leaflets purported "to answer questions asked by frontline soldiers. The answers were given in forthright, dramatic style, calling on the men to show a do-or-die spirit." The OSS leaflets duplicated those of the Germans in style and appearance. But their message was entirely different: They suggested that desertion was becoming easier, that German soldiers and NCOs were shooting their officers and getting away with it, that the High Command intended to scorch every foot of German earth rather than surrender.

In another attempt to spread dissension through the ranks of the Wehrmacht, OSS agents planted phony newspaper clippings in the uniforms of a number of dead German soldiers, then slashed each corpse's wrists and throat to simulate sui-

cide. Anybody finding one of the corpses was likely to read the clipping, which contained an announcement from SS leader Himmler that every German wife who had not had a baby within the past two years must report to an SS-run breeding farm. No one could measure the effect of the phony leaflets and supposed suicides, but one OSS report estimated (perhaps optimistically) that 10,000 Germans deserted because of those and other black-propaganda ploys.

The Germans were not the only targets of OSS mischief. To embarrass the fastidious Japanese, the Research and Development Division came up with a noxious-smelling compound dubbed "Who Me?" which was packaged in collapsible tubes and distributed to children in Japanese-occupied Chinese cities.

"When a Japanese officer came down the sidewalk," re-

called Lovell, "the little Chinese boys and girls would squirt a shot of 'Who Me?' at his trouser seat." The Japanese were horrified by the foul compound, which was virtually impossible to wash out. " 'Who Me?' was no world-shaking new evolvement," recalled Lovell, "but it cost the Japanese a world of face."

The OSS also employed more subtle schemes to distress the enemy. Operatives of the OSS Labor Division, for example, urged skilled workers in Belgium, France, Poland and Norway to go into hiding rather than work for the Germans. Workers who could not avoid the Germans' clutches were encouraged to find ways to throw a monkey wrench into the enemy war machine. In one instance in 1942, a Belgian machinist dumped virtually irreplaceable precision instruments used in airplane production into a freshly poured concrete floor. "That was probably the most expensive floor in Europe," he laughed as he told his tale to friends.

Another machinist, a Frenchman, related an equally destructive sabotage technique. "Let's say that an eccentric cog was to be made," he explained. "The blueprint man would design it with the hole one eighth of an inch from the rim. Then the man who constructed the cog would work the hole even closer to the edge to make sure the cog would break when it was in operation. And the inspector, of course, would always pass the finished products. I know; I was the inspector."

Eventually, Labor Division agents penetrated to the very heart of the Third Reich. A former German trade unionist named Jupp Kapius—known to his controllers in London as Downend—parachuted into the Ruhr, Germany's industrial heartland, in 1944. Within a few months, Downend had organized several cells of factory workers and had made the acquaintance of a local director of the Deutsche Bank and the chief executive of a mining company. All of them supplied him with information and passed on subversive propaganda; the factory workers also helped to foster slowdowns and sabotage in their plants.

"Downend had coverage of all military and industrial developments in the region," according to the official OSS history, "and knew immediately the effect of bombings and frequently could find out the reconstruction plans of damaged factories." Other OSS labor agents were equally successful inside Germany. Some managed to persuade railway workers to misplace shipping orders and delay trains; the resulting bottlenecks often kept supplies far from the front lines when they were needed.

While bottlenecks and bombings took their toll of Hitler's crumbling European empire, OSS agents in Asia were fighting a more elemental kind of battle. Deep in the jungles of Burma, the men of a swashbuckling guerrilla unit known as OSS Detachment 101 were tormenting the Japanese from behind the lines with deadly booby traps and ambushes.

Detachment 101 was the brainchild of Millard Preston Goodfellow, a former Brooklyn newspaper publisher and Boys' Club executive, and now director of special activities for the OSS. Shortly after the United States entered the War, Goodfellow began preparing studies on the possibilities of intelligence and guerrilla operations in Asia for Donovan, who saw that vast area as fertile soil in which his ideas on unorthodox warfare might flourish. In February 1942—with the Japanese Army in Indochina and Thailand and beginning its drive into Burma and Malaya—Goodfellow presented General Joseph W. Stilwell, the recently named American commander of Chinese forces in the China-Burma-India Theater, with plans for an OSS guerrilla unit that would operate behind enemy lines in Asia.

At first the peppery Stilwell, an orthodox military thinker who believed in conventional warfare, rejected the project, ostensibly because of the man that Goodfellow had chosen to head the unit. "That man," snapped Stilwell, "if sent out to blow up a bridge, would blow up a windmill instead and come back with an excuse." After a series of discussions Goodfellow convinced Stilwell of the soundness of the project, and the general gave his reluctant assent—but only on condition that the unit be headed by Captain Carl Eifler, a former U.S. Customs officer who had served under Stilwell in the Army Reserve.

The fortyish Eifler, then serving with the 35th Infantry in Hawaii, was a solid choice to turn the project into a reality. His prewar job along the Mexican border had made him an authority on smuggling and connivance. He was a big man, equally skilled at judo and boxing; he was also an experienced pilot and an expert shot. It was rumored that as a Customs agent he frequently discouraged illegal immigrants from swimming across the Rio Grande into the United

Bundles of supplies float down to an OSS camp behind Japanese lines in northern Burma. To guide the plane to the clearing, OSS guerrillas used strips of light-colored fabric to shape the letters "U" and "S."

States by shooting live bullets within inches of their heads.

Summoned to Washington in February 1942, Eifler was given carte blanche by the War Department to recruit freely among the armed forces. "From the start," Eifler recalled, "men were expected to volunteer blindly. They were advised they likely would be signing their own death warrants. Moreover, if a man indicated he was a hell-raiser or a glory-seeker, he was turned down." By the middle of March, Eifler and seven of his hand-picked recruits were on their way to Camp X in Canada for guerrilla and intelligence training; another 14 men trained at the new American camp in the Catoctin Mountains. Instructors at the two camps deemed the new unit ready for action a few weeks later, but it needed a name. Eifler suggested to an aide of Goodfellow's that it be called Detachment One. "No," replied the aide. "We'll call it Detachment 101; we can't let the British know we have only one unit."

While Eifler and his men had been undergoing training, Stilwell had taken command of a 50,000-man army in Burma, only to be forced into a 200-mile trek to India by the advancing Japanese, who defeated his army with night raids and ambushes—the very tactics Detachment 101 had been mastering.

Eifler and his men seemed to have a tailor-made assignment: Give the Japanese a dose of their own medicine. But when Detachment 101 reached New Delhi in mid-July, there were no orders awaiting it. Finally, in mid-August, an exasperated Eifler, by now a major, wangled a flight to Stilwell's new headquarters in Chungking, China. Stilwell was not expecting Eifler and greeted the OSS man with the kind of tongue-lashing that had earned him the nickname "Vinegar Joe." "I didn't send for you and I don't want you," he barked at Eifler, adding that Detachment 101 did not figure in his plans at the moment.

Eifler, who could be just as obdurate as Stilwell, pressed his argument and finally persuaded the general to let 101 launch an intelligence and guerrilla-warfare operation behind Japanese lines in Burma. Eifler was to set up a base in Assam Province in eastern India; from there, 101 could sabotage the roads and the single rail line leading into Myitkyina, Japan's main air base in north Burma. "All I want to hear," said Stilwell, "is booms from the jungle."

Eifler had been handed a forbidding assignment, one that meant operating in jungles that Churchill had once termed "the most formidable fighting country imaginable." Much of northern Burma was a virtually impenetrable thicket of rain-sodden vegetation. Within that thicket were swamps and mountains, kraits, cobras, man-eating tigers and leopards, wildly chattering monkeys and birds whose weird cries could send shivers down a man's spine. There were giant leeches and swarms of malarial mosquitoes and there was the enemy—hundreds of thousands of jungle-wise Japanese troops.

At Nazira, an Indian tea plantation right on the border with northern Burma, Eifler set up camp to train local recruits for his war against the Japanese. Some men he found in the ragtag remnants of the British Army in Burma; others he plucked from refugee camps. His most important recruits were a fierce tribe of Burmese known as the Kachins. More than any other group of recruits, the Kachins were thirsting to fight the Japanese, who had burned their villages and mutilated their women and children in a miscalculated attempt to intimidate them.

Eifler's recruits learned to send and receive in Morse code, to handle explosives and to use firearms. The Kachins took readily to the explosives and codes but they balked at the complexities of the machine gun. They preferred, they told Eifler, to use a shotgun, a weapon with which they were familiar. Accordingly Eifler wired Washington to send him 500 of the weapons.

Colonel Carl Eifler, the first commander of OSS Detachment 101 in Burma, unflinchingly handles a lethal-looking snake. Eifler, who loved bravado, served in the post from April 1942 until December 1943.

"They said it was an unusual request," recalled Eifler, "and could I justify it?" Annoyed, Eifler wired back sarcastically, "I prefer muzzle-loaders. The natives can make their own black powder and use the nuts and bolts from wrecked vehicles for ammunition." For some reason, that request was not deemed unusual, and Eifler was sent 500 Springfield muzzle-loaders that had never been fired but had been carefully stored, gathering dust, in a warehouse since the American Civil War. The Kachins took an immediate liking to the muzzle-loaders and carried them throughout the Burma campaign.

The Kachins also used their own time-honored killing techniques, which they readily taught to the Americans. One technique was to set a booby trap with a crossbow and trip line. The trap could snare both game and Japanese. Another technique involved hiding sharp bamboo spears

A REWARD PROMPTED BY A MISREAD MESSAGE

Secret codes meant to stump the foe sometimes baffled friend as well. In late 1943 an OSS radio operator received a message from Captain William Wilkinson of Detachment 101 in Burma to relay to Calcutta. In the midst of a request for supplies were the letters CMA, which the operator interpreted as "citation for military assistance." The OSS supply agent in Calcutta accordingly ordered 50 medals cast in silver and hung from an ornate silk ribbon.

Back in Burma, men of OSS Detachment 101 were surprised a few weeks later when these confections arrived. Wilkinson had now been transferred, but his successor passed the medals out to the able Kachins—who wore them thereafter, blissfully unaware that their citation had resulted from a misread message in which CMA stood simply for "comma."

The Kachin Rangers line up, displaying their unexpected decorations.

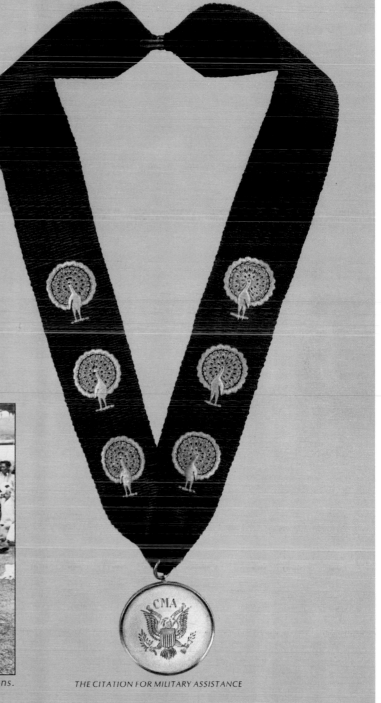

THE CITATION FOR MILITARY ASSISTANCE

on either side of a trail ahead of an approaching enemy patrol. When the patrol was then ambushed, Japanese soldiers diving for shelter would impale themselves on the fire-hardened bamboo.

Detachment 101 came up with a few tricks of its own as well. One was a six-inch hollow spike topped with a .30-caliber cartridge and a pressure detonator. When a soldier stepped on the cartridge, it fired—ripping through his foot and often through his body. The spike, said one OSS officer, "caused untold apprehension among the Japanese. Even when we dropped the use of the device because the enemy was too alert, the threat slowed down the enemy advance."

Four months after he had faced Stilwell in his den, Eifler sent his first patrol out from Nazira, a 12-man unit known as A Group. Its task was to establish a base camp in Japanese territory and to sabotage the rail line into Myitkyina. On January 27, A Group parachuted into a small jungle clearing 100 miles south of Myitkyina, each man carrying food, arms and ammunition and a supply of Composition C, an explosive impervious to rough handling. The group moved swiftly through the jungle, covering 50 miles of rugged terrain to within striking distance of the rail line in two days. Working by moonlight, the men of A Group paired off to set a series of delayed-action charges of Composition C along the railroad. As they stole back into the jungle, the charges began exploding—destroying a total of five miles of track. In other operations, they also demolished one large bridge and several small ones.

Almost five weeks later, after a number of harrowing escapes in which they were doggedly pursued by the Japanese, 11 survivors of the original 12 A Group members reached Nazira. Stilwell had received his "booms" and 101 its baptism by fire.

Detachment 101's next undertaking was not so lucky. A six-man unit known as O Group was sent out in March 1943 to assist Air Transport Command (ATC) crewmen who had been downed in the Lawksawk Valley, 75 miles southeast of Mandalay, while flying from India to Kunming, China. Not far from O Group's drop point were two villages whose inhabitants were suspected by Captain Ray Peers, one of Eifler's top aides, of collusion with the Japanese. "As we made our last pass," recalled Peers, who flew with O Group to the valley, "we could see villagers streaming out from every direction, heading toward the drop zone. I couldn't get it out of my head that they were out to kill." Nevertheless, the drop took place as scheduled. Peers's premonition proved correct. A couple of days later a Tokyo news broadcast announced that six British spies had been dropped behind the Japanese lines in Burma. Three had been killed by villagers, the others captured and delivered to the Japanese authorities.

Despite the failure of O Group, Detachment 101 would

eventually rescue more than 200 ATC airmen downed in the jungles of Burma. In one instance, 101's Kachins saved an airman facing death from his own crewmates. The man, a sergeant, parachuted into the boughs of a towering mahogany tree, breaking both arms in the fall. Dangling upside down and bleeding profusely, he regained consciousness just in time to hear three of the crew from his C-87 transport discussing his fate. They had been unable to climb the tree and were drawing straws to determine who would shoot him to put him out of his misery. One of the men had just drawn back the hammer on his .45-caliber automatic when a group of OSS Kachins appeared. They quickly felled a smaller tree against the mahogany tree to serve as a ladder and scampered 100 feet to rescue the sergeant. The next day, he and his crewmates were on their way to Nazira.

By December 1943, rescues and assorted acts of sabotage against the Japanese had become practically routine. Detachment 101 could be said to be flourishing, as Eifler—who had been promoted to colonel two months earlier—proudly pointed out in a cable to Washington. He now had 29 field stations in operation in India and Burma and had recruited nearly 200 Kachin agents and trainees. Even the British, who initially had been cool to the unit's presence, were impressed, and asked Eifler's help in infiltrating agents of their own into Burma.

When Donovan read Eifler's cable, he decided to see for himself the effect his unorthodox warriors were having on the Japanese. He arrived on December 7—with no advance notice—at Nazira. The next morning, the 250-pound Eifler and the 240-pound Donovan boarded the only available craft, a tiny L-5 liaison plane, for the 275-mile journey to Nawbum, an OSS base 150 miles behind enemy lines. "That damned plane will have a double hernia if it gets off the ground," cracked one of the mechanics who serviced the fragile two-seater. Somehow, Eifler managed to get the plane airborne and all the way to Nawbum. Donovan's daring impromptu visit inside enemy territory gave an immediate boost to the detachment's morale. Before he returned to Washington, he cheered the 101 further by increasing the unit's monthly budget from $50,000 to $100,000. Donovan also approved delivery of 10 new planes to supplant the

L-5—effectively answering Eifler's pithy plea for "more horsepower on the nose." Furthermore, Donovan ordered reinforcements for 101's depleted American contingent.

The increase of men and money enabled 101 to recruit more Burmese and intensify its harassment of the Japanese—blowing up supply depots, ambushing patrols and disrupting communications even farther behind the enemy's lines. Furthermore, 101's Kachins supplied vital information to the Tenth Air Force, stationed in Assam, India, for its bombing runs over Burma. According to Tenth Air Force records, the Kachins contributed 85 per cent of its intelligence on likely targets.

One Tenth Air Force report, dated August 14, 1944, noted that 1,000 Japanese "with considerable stores were located in Moda, a Burmese town that had been disregarded and never photographed" by aerial-surveillance planes. "Fighters loaded with demolition and incendiary bombs," the report went on, "attacked the town at once. Subsequently, 101 radioed that enemy casualties totaled 200 killed and a dump filled with ammunition and arms had been completely destroyed."

Eventually, 10,000 Kachins and more than 500 Americans would swell the ranks of Detachment 101 far beyond the most ambitious dreams of Preston Goodfellow. The Kachins accounted for 5,447 Japanese dead and another 10,000 missing or wounded while losing only 184 of their own number and 18 of their American officers.

Even Stilwell was impressed by the accomplishments of the doughty jungle-fighting unit, but he tended to be skeptical of the Kachins' tally of enemy dead. One day, he asked a Kachin how his people could keep such accurate records. The answer shocked him. The warrior answered by opening a bamboo tube tied around his waist and emptying it in front of the general to display a number of nondescript objects that resembled blackened dried fruit. "What are they?" Stilwell asked. "Japanese ears," replied the Kachin. "Divide by two and you know how many you've killed."

Stilwell never again questioned the Kachins' mathematics. And he never again questioned the value of the unorthodox warfare espoused by Wild Bill Donovan and practiced so well by Detachment 101 of the OSS.

General Joseph W. Stilwell (left), commander in chief of the U.S. Army in the China-Burma-India Theater, confers at a jungle camp in northern Burma with Colonel William R. Peers, who became head of OSS Detachment 101 in December 1943 and served in that capacity until the theater was safely in Allied hands in the summer of 1945.

AN AMERICAN COVERT FORCE

Crouched warily at the controls of his radio, OSS agent Fima Haimson prepares to transmit his report from a secret jungle camp in Japanese-occupied Burma.

THE OSS AND ITS WAR OF NERVES

The speaker, an Army captain, asked the question straight: "Would you be willing to jump from a plane behind enemy lines if you knew in advance you would be tortured to death if caught?" That question—or a variation of it—was put to thousands of American GIs during World War II by recruiters for General William "Wild Bill" Donovan's Office of Strategic Services. The recruiters' job was as difficult, if not as deadly, as the one they recruited for: The combination of cool nerves, good physical condition and linguistic flair they sought was so rare that of 4,000 volunteers who signed up in one recruiting drive, only 50 were acceptable.

The winnowing of would-be agents began with security checks, psychological exams and timed exercises designed to gauge the candidate's ability to think and act under pressure. One test required him to carry a heavy load across a deep creek with nothing to use for a bridge but short planks—all the while enduring harassment from a crew of heckling bystanders. Those who passed that screening went on to attend secret OSS training camps run by experts in everything from camouflage to the art of silent killing—with still more advanced training to follow for those who took up such specialties as sabotage and communications.

All of the screening and training paid off handsomely in the field. OSS agents generated more than 500,000 items of intelligence in 1944 alone, many of them immediately useful in selecting targets and planning troop movements. Agents also mobilized local guerrillas to rescue downed pilots, harass enemy troops, and sabotage both enemy installations and enemy morale. "It became a war of nerves," wrote the OSS commander who organized and led a force of 10,000 Kachins, a people who lived in the hills of northern Burma. "The threat of guerrilla ambush made the Japanese taut and tense, slow, cautious and finally paranoiac. Several Japanese prisoners volunteered the opinion," he went on, "that they rated one Kachin equal to 10 Japanese." Actually, those prisoners thought too well of themselves: The OSS reported that the Kachin guerrillas killed not 10 but 25 of the enemy for every casualty of their own.

William J. Donovan returns from Europe in August 1940. The outcome of his journey was a U.S. intelligence agency modeled after England's.

An OSS agent gives orders to Kachin tribesmen. These Burmese guerrillas were characterized by a "rugged staunchness," one OSS commander recalled.

PUTTING RECRUITS THROUGH THE PACES

Basic OSS training was an unbroken succession of 21 eighteen-hour days of code work, interrogation exercises and memory tests—all designed, according to the official OSS *War Report,* "to prepare the trainees psychologically for the fact that the life of an agent is a constant and continuing gamble with detection." Recruits zealously guarded their own secret covers during training. Each recruit was watched unremittingly; even the party at the end of the course was an evaluation session.

Later courses toughened recruits for special operations. They learned to live off the land, and to fight and kill with their hands. By the time they were through studying techniques as varied as parachuting, blowing up bridges, operating radios, lockpicking, setting booby traps and forging signatures, they were ready for the field. And perhaps they were ready for other things, too: "Had any of us lacked for a profession after the War," one agent joked, "we would have made perfect gangsters."

OSS recruits skin a wild goat during survival training on Catalina Island off the California coast.

OSS instructor William "Dangerous Dan" Fairbairn demonstrates how to kill a man silently—almost casually—with a scalpel-thin commando dagger.

Agents get in shape for sabotaging bridges and power lines in France by scrambling up an adult-sized jungle gym.

Helmeted agent John Niles issues last-minute orders to French partisans before sending them through German lines. In 1944 more than 500 OSS agents operated in France.

TEAMING UP WITH FREEDOM FIGHTERS

OSS agents relied on teamwork and cooperation with local resistance groups to accomplish their missions behind enemy lines. The resistance groups provided the know-how for survival. And the OSS men (who adopted local dress and behavior to blend in with their collaborators) provided equipment and matériel.

The OSS smuggled some 20,000 tons of supplies into occupied Europe in 1944 alone. In Greece, the OSS furnished not only medical supplies but a mobile hospital, which was hauled from village to village by a packtrain of 134 mules. And American and British arms, dropped into France, sparked the largest resistance uprising in history: It involved 300,000 freedom fighters, their raids closely coordinated with the Allied advance by OSS agents.

The resistance gave back as good as it got. French guerrillas smuggled agents into Brest in wine casks and down the Loire River under wire chicken crates. Some 300 Yugoslavians helped a three-man OSS team construct a 600-yard-long airstrip, used to evacuate more than 400 downed American airmen. Most important, guerrillas tied down Axis troops: In Italy they sidetracked no fewer than 200,000 Germans after the 1943 Allied invasion.

Burmese guerrillas follow an OSS agent along a jungle stream. "We weren't far removed from pioneer times," remembered one Texan who served in Burma. "We had the same love of courage, the same rugged spirit, and the pleasure in doing manly things."

A team of OSS agents and observers model the homespun suits given to them by Chinese guerrillas.

Italian partisans listen to a premission briefing by their commander and their OSS liaison officer.

Two guerrillas working with an OSS mission in Indochina fire on a Japanese garrison in the town of Thai Nguyen. The OSS agents adopted local garb and subsisted on the sparse guerrilla diet while training an elite force of some 200 Indochinese in the use of modern weapons.

Outside a stone hut on a rocky Greek mountainside, OSS operatives, British Commandos and Greek guerrillas gather around a patchwork flag that proclaims their individual nationalities as well as their esprit de corps. In the upper right-hand corner of the flag are initials that stand for Royal Special Reserves (the official designation of the Commandos) and United States Operational Group (an OSS designation).

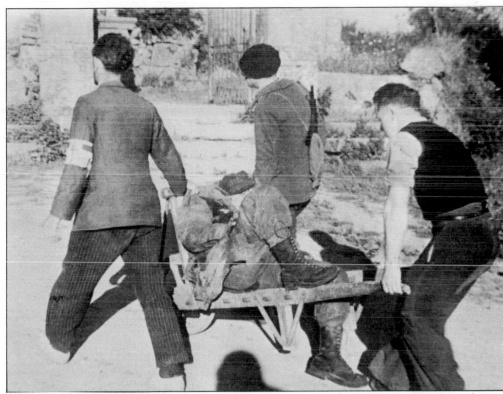

OSS-armed French freedom fighters wheel away a German casualty in Brittany in August of 1944.

DOING A BANG-UP JOB AROUND THE GLOBE

The German troop train sped through occupied Belgium toward a bridge that it would never cross: The OSS had arrived first. "When the train reached the halfway point," an agent later wrote, "a splash of flame erupted. It was the last thing the two German soldiers operating the locomotive were to see in this life."

OSS saboteurs liked to combine targets —to knock out a train and a bridge, pull down power lines and block river traffic all in one blast. To help them, OSS scientists developed such deadly marvels as the "Mole," which exploded as soon as the train it was attached to entered a tunnel.

With other explosives disguised as coal, manure and flour, OSS saboteurs could hit any target they were able to get near. Operation *Smashem* in Greece ambushed 14 trains, blew up 15 bridges and destroyed 61 trucks. Within a week of D-Day in France, the Allied-backed Resistance sabotaged some 800 similar targets.

A bridge sabotaged by the OSS stands on end about 100 miles north of Mandalay. All told, the 566 OSS operatives in Burma and their 10,000-man guerrilla army destroyed 51 bridges and 277 military vehicles.

Outside Oslo harbor the German troopship Donau lies half-sunk—victim of a combined OSS, British and Norwegian operation designed to keep German troops in Norway from getting to the Battle of the Bulge.

An experimental curiosity, this hand weapon could silently send a dart some 200 yards. Rubber bands, now frayed with age, powered the linen-cord bowstring.

NOVEL WEAPONS FOR NOVEL WORK

More than any other combatants engaged in fighting the War, secret agents needed weapons and equipment that were easy to carry, easy to hide and easy to use. Allied scientists and inventors showed a truly prodigious ingenuity in obliging them; researchers came up with more than 26,000 items for the OSS alone. Some were imaginative new creations, others were modifications of old ideas.

Among the agents' favorites were guns that were silent and flashless. OSS scientists muffled 90 per cent of the noise of the standard .22-caliber pistol by merely adding a baffle of wire mesh to the barrel, thereby slowing the escape of gas released in the firing. That particular innovation so pleased OSS director William Donovan that on a visit to President Roosevelt in the Oval Office he gave an unscheduled demonstration of its effectiveness: While the unsuspecting President was dictating a letter, Donovan fired 10 rounds into a sandbag.

The OSS scientists who devised new weapons went about their work in the same ebullient spirit as their boss—an enthusiasm that was reflected in the names they bestowed on their creations. One concoction, a device for igniting oil, was called the "Paul Revere" because it worked equally well for oil tanks on land and oil slicks at sea. Another was a firecracker that simulated the noise of an exploding bomb, making it possible for agents to escape in crowds; the firecracker was named the "Hedy" for movie actress Hedy Lamarr because, the inventor wrote, "lusty young officers said she created a panic wherever she went." The Bushmaster was a tube eight and a half inches long; clipped to the branch of a shrub and set to fire a bullet at a specified moment, it could provoke the enemy into betraying his position by returning fire.

Some zany ideas literally backfired: A project to employ bats as arsonists by attaching walnut-sized bombs to their wings was scrapped after several buildings burned down in the testing. But to hundreds of other inventions, such as those shown here and on the following pages, the agents owed countless successes and even their lives.

An OSS agent prepares to test-fire the "William Tell," a crossbow that was intended for eliminating Japanese sentries and watchdogs in the Pacific.

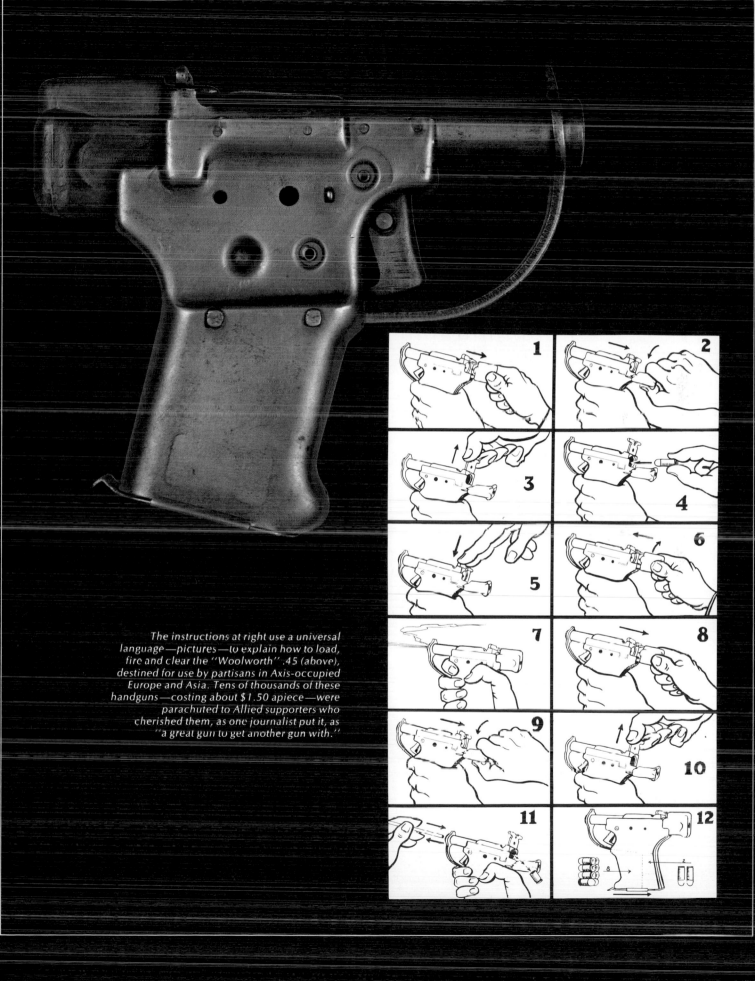

The instructions at right use a universal language—pictures—to explain how to load, fire and clear the "Woolworth" .45 (above), destined for use by partisans in Axis-occupied Europe and Asia. Tens of thousands of these handguns—costing about $1.50 apiece—were parachuted to Allied supporters who cherished them, as one journalist put it, as "a great gun to get another gun with."

STEALTHY MEANS FOR BRINGING DEATH

The knife—one of the oldest tools known to mankind—remained among the most versatile of weapons that were included in the arsenal of the secret agent. Lightweight and unobtrusive, knives came in all shapes and sizes, from scarcely three inches to a foot and a half long. They could slash anything from human flesh to tough cable.

Furthermore, blades had the advantage of being able to do their work in the silence that was essential to many of the secret agent's operations.

But occasionally silence was not the main concern of the agents. They might have to bludgeon their way out of a tight spot, or—while keeping themselves at a safe distance—halt an unexpected intruder or blow up enemy property. For these jobs they had a wide variety of alternative weapons *(pages 132-133).*

The Smatchet combined a solid metal pommel—suitable for bludgeoning—with a machete-like blade of high-tempered steel.

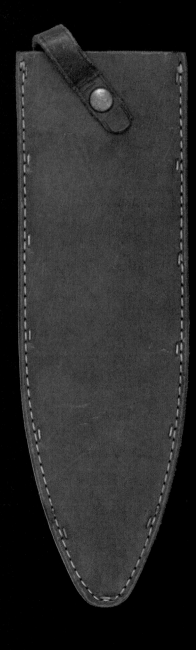

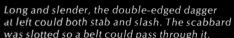

Long and slender, the double-edged dagger at left could both stab and slash. The scabbard was slotted so a belt could pass through it.

The lapel knife at top right had a ridged finger grip and came with a leather sheath to be sewn into clothing. The British gravity knife at bottom right snapped open with a flick of the wrist. The pocket knife below left contained in its heel a beak-shaped blade to puncture a tire, and the British escape knife below right combined a lockbreaker, a knife, three hacksaw blades and wire cutters.

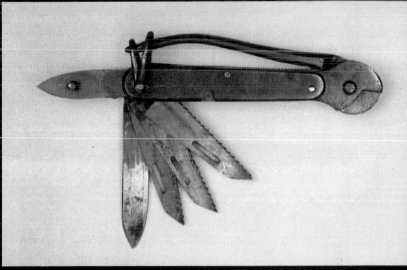

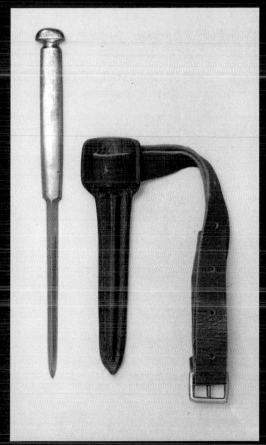

This spike could kill if accurately thrust into an eye or an ear. When not in use, it could be strapped to the arm under clothing.

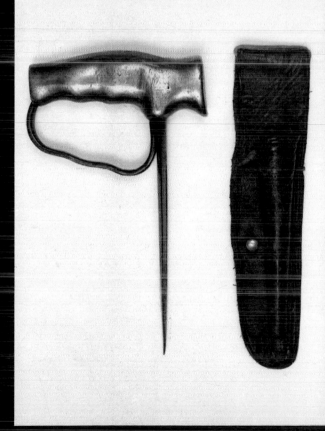

A British dagger for use by women agents combined a picklike blade with a contoured handgrip that added power to the thrust.

131

When the pen clip was depressed and released, this "fountain pen" fired a steel dart no bigger than a record-player needle. The range was 40 feet.

A gadget appearing to be an old-fashioned wooden penholder (top) in fact hides a steel dagger within, as revealed in an X-ray photograph (bottom).

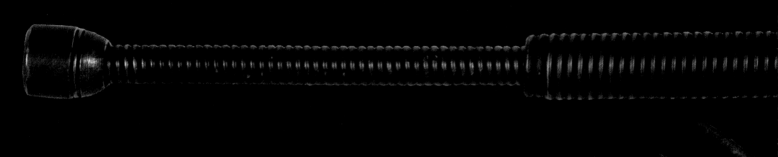

The U.S. Navy's Fist Gun—a .38-caliber pistol that was riveted to a heavy leather glove— fired a single shot when the user clenched his fist and punched his enemy's body.

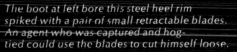
The boot at left bore this steel heel rim spiked with a pair of small retractable blades. An agent who was captured and hog-tied could use the blades to cut himself loose.

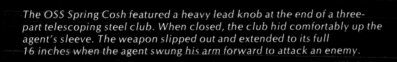
The OSS Spring Cosh featured a heavy lead knob at the end of a three-part telescoping steel club. When closed, the club hid comfortably up the agent's sleeve. The weapon slipped out and extended to its full 16 inches when the agent swung his arm forward to attack an enemy.

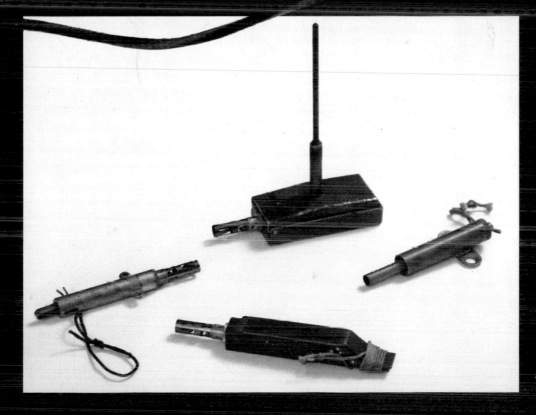
Four little devices set off some big bangs. The pull-firers at left and right, attached to a wire laid inconspicuously across a path, were activated when the enemy tripped. The pressure-firer at center top—hidden under a bed, stairs or railroad track—detonated when its adjustable antenna was depressed. The release-firer at bottom was wedged in a door or under a wheel; when the door or wheel moved, the weapon's snout snapped open and fired.

INGENIOUS DEVICES FOR PASSING THE WORD

After survival itself, perhaps the biggest challenge confronting agents was the rapid collection and secret transmission of intelligence. To help them conceal these activities, scientists developed such miniature tools as the Matchbox camera, a device that could be concealed inside a penny matchbox and hidden in the palm of an agent's hand.

Contrivances of all sorts helped agents communicate both with headquarters and among themselves. One device allowed agents to use the enemy's own telephone lines to relay secret messages by Morse code; the telegraph signal operated at the same frequency as the human voice, so as long as two agents kept talking, the signal could not be detected by the enemy.

Ultraviolet lights guided airplanes and boats to night rendezvous with agents, and a high-pitched whistle attached to supplies dropped by parachute helped agents locate them after they landed.

A camouflaged direction finder enabled agents to scan for both enemy and friendly radios. Its antenna, when pushed down, appeared to be the head of a bolt on the surface of an otherwise innocent-looking suitcase.

The latchkey above carried microfilm messages between Britain and German-occupied Denmark—eluding Nazi border sentries. The microfilm (seen on a microscope slide) was sealed inside a hole in the key's oval handle.

The OSS 16mm Matchbox camera—shown above with its film spool detached— came either plain or disguised with Japanese or Swedish labels. The hole at center is the lens; the button on the side is the shutter release.

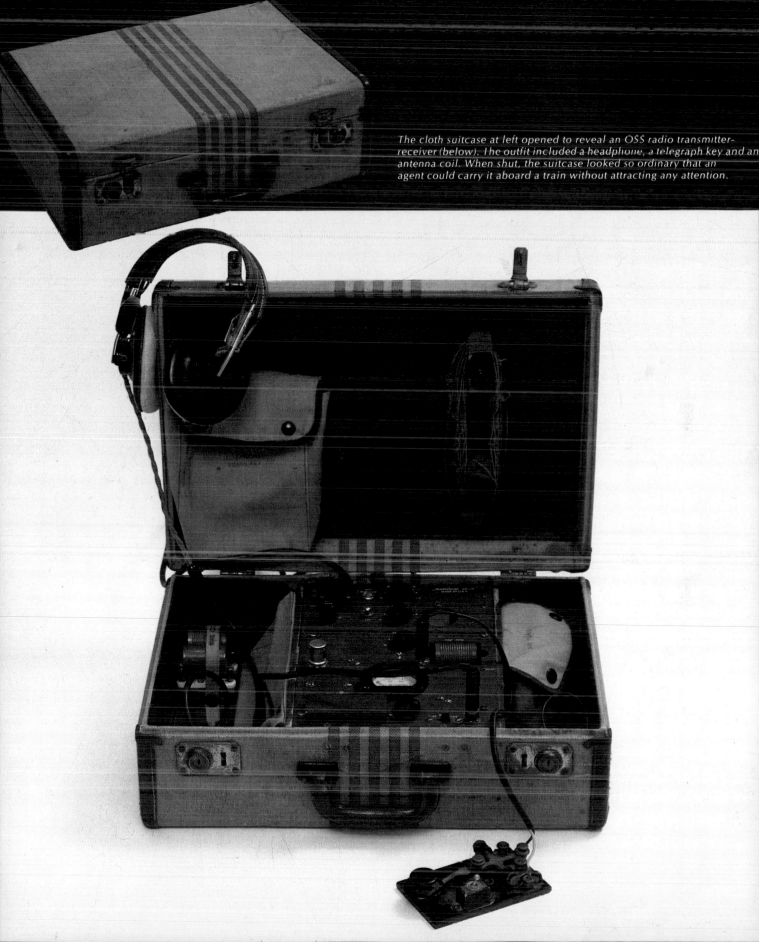

The cloth suitcase at left opened to reveal an OSS radio transmitter-receiver (below). The outfit included a headphone, a telegraph key and an antenna coil. When shut, the suitcase looked so ordinary that an agent could carry it aboard a train without attracting any attention.

4

On the morning of November 4, 1939, when the War was barely two months old, the Naval Attaché at the British Embassy in Oslo, Norway, found an unexpected package in his mail. Inside a plain wrapper he found several handwritten pages in German describing what appeared to be weapons. There was no explanation except for a simple cover note: "From a well-wishing German scientist." The attaché urgently forwarded the document by diplomatic courier to London, where it was scrutinized by the science experts at the various military ministries.

The Oslo Report, as the document came to be known, contained some startling revelations. Buttressed by a wealth of technical data, it described secret German weapons far in advance of any the British had developed. The revelations included the existence of electronic systems that could guide bombers to their targets, and of long-range missiles being launched experimentally from an island in the Baltic Sea. Such futuristic weapons—if they were real—foreshadowed a new and frightening dimension in warfare.

But in those early days of the War, the British intelligence community remained skeptical. There was not a shred of evidence to verify the contents of the Oslo Report. And most who read the report refused to believe that a single German scientist, "well-wishing" or not, could have access to so many vital secrets. They concluded that the document was probably a hoax—a scare tactic invented by German espionage.

They could not have been more wrong. Future events proved the accuracy of the Oslo Report down to the last detail. Its author, who remained anonymous, had sounded the first warning that a war of secret technology was under way. That contest was being waged not by soldiers, but by physicists and chemists, technologists and engineers.

Both the Allies and the Axis had long been girding for such a confrontation. As the clouds of war grew darker over the European landscape, the elite of the scientific establishments in the hostile countries laid aside their peacetime endeavors at universities and in industry and lent their genius to their governments. In hidden laboratories and clandestine workshops far from prying eyes, they strove to invent new weapons that would give their country an edge over the enemy.

In Great Britain, this effort concentrated initially on the

THE WIZARDS' WAR

development of radar, the still-new device that bounced radio waves off a distant object to determine its location, altitude and speed. Beginning in the mid-1930s, the British had erected a series of radar stations along the coasts of England and Scotland to provide early warning of air attack. As the War approached, a team of experts led by the Scottish physicist Robert Watson-Watt worked feverishly to improve the accuracy and range of British radar, and by 1940 the stations of the Chain Home Radar, as the network was called, could detect aircraft 150 miles away.

The Germans, for their part, had largely neglected to make use of radar as a defensive weapon. Bolstered by visions of a quick victory, German scientists had turned their attention to inventing a welter of offensive tools. Among them were advanced and ingenious systems of radio-beam navigation that would direct Luftwaffe bomber pilots to their targets.

One of these systems the Germans called *Knickebein,* or "crooked leg." Two widely separated radio transmitters in Germany emitted narrow beams that intersected over a target in England. A bomber pilot would fly down one beam, which sounded a continuous tone in his headphone. If the aircraft drifted either to the left or to the right, the tone signal would change to dots or dashes, depending upon the direction of the error. This change would warn the pilot that he must correct his course to bring the bomber back on the beam. A drop in the pitch of the tone alerted the pilot that he was crossing the second beam; at that point he knew he was over his target and released his bombs.

Knickebein was far in advance of British bomber navigation, which still depended on the traditional mariner's method of finding a position by compass, map and sextant. The Royal Air Force had not even considered the possibility of radio-beam flying in combat. And when the Luftwaffe began using the system in early 1940 for random flights to probe British defenses, British scientific intelligence did not know it existed. The struggle to understand the German beams, and then to neutralize them, constituted the opening skirmish in the war of secret technology.

The first concrete evidence of the German system came in the spring of 1940, when a search of two downed German bombers yielded scraps of paper that mentioned the word *Knickebein* in the context of radio navigation. Then in March a German prisoner hinted under interrogation that *Knickebein* was a bomb-dropping device.

Such evidence was paltry, but it was enough to convince one British scientist that the Germans possessed a sinister, sophisticated tool of some sort. Reginald V. Jones, a young physicist and astronomer serving as a science officer for the Air Ministry and as an adviser to MI-6, had been one of the few scientists who considered the Oslo Report authentic. Jones remembered a mention there of a navigational aid for bombers, but he had to have more clues. All he could do was wait.

The Germans themselves inadvertently came to his assistance. At Bletchley Park on the 8th of June, 1940, British cryptographers intercepted and decoded a Luftwaffe radio message that read: "*Knickebein,* Cleves, is adjusted to position 53°, 24' north and 1° west." The message was mystifying to everyone who read it but Jones. To him, its meaning was crystal clear: At the German town of Cleves a transmitter called *Knickebein* was sending a radio beam through the geographic position mentioned—a position that was quickly identified as a point on England's Great North Road near the town of Derby. Within days of the receipt of that message, another clue dropped into Jones's lap and helped him fill out the picture of the elusive radio beams: A highly sensitive receiver, disguised as a piece of ordinary radio equipment, was recovered from a German bomber that had been shot down. And on the 14th of the month another German prisoner of war confirmed that *Knickebein* was indeed a bomb-dropping device.

Jones was now convinced that his theory was correct, but when he presented it to other scientists working as consultants to the military, he met with surprising disagreement. Professor Frederick A. Lindemann, Winston Churchill's personal science adviser, maintained that such beams could not exist. Because of the physical properties of radio waves, he argued, a beam as narrow as the one Jones mentioned would necessarily be composed of quite short waves. And according to prevailing theory, short waves would not reach England from Germany because they would not follow the curvature of the earth. To a degree, that theory was correct. But the British scientists failed to take into account that the German beams would not have to follow the earth's curve exactly to be received by German bombers flying at high altitudes.

Despite opposition to his theory, Jones was ordered to appear before Churchill and the Air Ministry Staff on the 21st of June to present his case for the existence of the new threat. He spoke for 20 minutes, methodically laying out the evidence that pointed to the use of the beams. Churchill believed him, and was concerned. The implications of Jones's conjecture were sinister indeed. The beams would enable the Luftwaffe to attack at night and in foul weather, for the German bomber pilots would not actually have to see their targets. In addition, British defenses against night attacks were inadequate. Although the Chain Home Radar stations provided early warning of enemy sorties, British fighter pilots still had to rely on their own eyesight to find the hostile bombers in the air.

To make matters worse, the War was entering a new and alarming phase. In the past months the Luftwaffe had been fully occupied in supporting the Wehrmacht in its blitzkrieg of Western Europe. Luftwaffe operations against England, a secondary target, had been sporadic. But now the German conquest of Western Europe was complete. On June 22, the day after Jones warned Churchill of the beams, France formally surrendered. The Luftwaffe was now free to turn its full fury on England, and possession of the beams gave it an enormous and perhaps fateful edge.

After hearing Jones, Churchill immediately issued orders to neutralize the ominous threat. But before that could be accomplished, the beams had to be located. Specially equipped aircraft were sent to search the skies for them. When two such missions found nothing, Jones began to doubt himself. "Had I, after all," he wrote later, "made a fool of myself? Had I jumped to false conclusions? Had I fallen for a great hoax by the Germans?" The third search flight allayed his fears. The plane crossed the beam, which registered a continuous tone on a receiver aboard. Later the pilot flew through a second beam aimed to intersect the first at a point directly over Derby.

Jones was vindicated. It was for him a moment of fierce joy. Eager to thwart the Germans, he set to work with experts from the Air Ministry's Telecommunications Research Establishment (TRE) to develop countermeasures. The beams were code-named Headaches. An antidote ar-

rived just in the nick of time—at the end of August 1940, when the Germans began to add massive night attacks to their already heavy daytime raids. For their first countermeasures the British employed hospital diathermy sets ordinarily used for cauterization. Adjusted to the frequencies of the German beams and placed in mobile vans and country police stations, the diathermy sets emitted a cacophony of noise that drowned out the beam sound in the Luftwaffe pilots' headphones. High-frequency radio sets, adjusted to produce a signal transmitted on top of the beam, proved to be an even more effective measure against Headaches (and were accordingly code-named Aspirin). Hearing the new sound, a bomber pilot would mistakenly assume that he had drifted off course and in trying to compensate he would steer his plane out of the beam—in many cases never to find it, or Germany, again.

The success of Aspirin was soon confirmed by the number of German bombs that fell relatively harmlessly in the English countryside, much to the puzzlement of the farmers,

British physicist R. V. Jones experiments with electromagnetic radiation as a way to measure distance. Jones had great enthusiasm for his role as scientific-intelligence chief for air defense. When he was offered the job in 1939 he joked, "A man in that position could lose the War—I'll take it."

who could not imagine why their crops were important enough to be Luftwaffe targets. And missing a target was just the beginning of problems for more than one German bomber crew. The Luftwaffe, having anticipated raiding mainly in daylight, had neglected to train pilots in the difficult skills of navigating at night by star sighting, map and compass. Many pilots, upon losing their beam, had trouble getting home again. The total confusion of one crew whose plane was lured off course by Aspirin turned to panic and then to disaster. The crewmen became convinced that since their beams were not functioning properly all of their electronic gear had gone haywire. In the pitch-black night, the disoriented and frightened pilot could not even keep the craft flying on a level course. His bombardier and wireless operator bailed out; he and the gunner rode with the careering aircraft down to oblivion. Aspirin had proved to be as effective as well-aimed antiaircraft fire.

Once they realized that the British had neutralized their *Knickebein,* the Germans turned to an alternative beam system called X-apparatus. Like *Knickebein,* the new system used a main directional beam that guided a bomber to a target in England. But the X-apparatus added cross beams that worked in conjunction with a radio receiver combined with a clocklike computer device to drop the bombs automatically. Each of the cross beams was transmitted at a different frequency—if only one or two of the beams were jammed, the system would still function—and they were in a range higher than the British had encountered before; the wizards of TRE would have to devise new, higher-powered transmitters to combat the cross beams.

Throughout the autumn of 1940, German raiders guided by the X-apparatus bombed with comparative impunity. On the night of November 14 the beams led the Luftwaffe unerringly to the Midlands city of Coventry, where the German planes carried out a raid that killed 400 people, injured 800 and destroyed more than 50,000 homes and commercial buildings. Not until December did Jones's countermeasures team manage to thwart the X-apparatus with their new transmitters (which they code-named Bromide). By the end of the year the accuracy of the X-apparatus had been curtailed so dramatically that German bombs were once more falling in the countryside, and the Luftwaffe aircrews had lost confidence in the system.

Germany still had one electronic ace up its sleeve and now proceeded to play it. The ace was the Y-apparatus, a system that used a single main beam to guide a bomber to its target. There were no cross beams. Instead, the same ground station that emitted the beam radiated another signal, which was received by a device in the aircraft and sent back to the station. Ground operators were then able to determine the distance of the aircraft from the ground station and radio the pilot at the moment when he should drop his bombs.

But Jones and his wizards were well prepared to combat the Y-apparatus. Tipped off by the Oslo Report, which mentioned an identical system (and which was now being taken seriously), they had developed a jamming device for both the single beam and the ranging signal. The Y-apparatus was disrupted on the very first night it was used, to the bewilderment of the Luftwaffe.

"The success of our efforts," Churchill wrote, "was manifest from the acrimonious remarks heard passing between the aircraft and their controlling ground stations. The faith of the enemy aircrews in their new device was thus shattered at the outset." During the first two weeks of March 1941, German bombers equipped with the Y-apparatus flew 89 sorties over Britain. In all but 14 of them the British jamming so thoroughly confused the German pilots and ground controllers that the planes returned to base without having been ordered to drop their bombs.

By the end of that month the German night attacks on England were on the wane. The tenacious RAF, though outnumbered from the start, had proved increasingly adept at night fighting and was exacting a devastating toll on enemy bombers. British ground defenses as well had sharpened their rough edges. The Battle of Britain had swung decisively in favor of the British.

Then in May, to the puzzlement of the British, the night attacks all but ceased, thanks in part to a decision made by Adolf Hitler. Throughout Western Europe, German Air Force units were being transferred to the east to begin Operation *Barbarossa,* the invasion of the Soviet Union. Never again would the Führer's mighty Luftwaffe prove a serious threat to England.

The frustration of the German radio-beam systems had

played a vital role in Britain's survival. Though the Germans had been able to bomb large targets such as London indiscriminately, without the beams they had been denied the pinpoint accuracy required to knock out their primary targets: the aircraft factories, airfields and warplanes without which Britain might not have survived.

Having stymied the Luftwaffe in the Battle of Britain and having dashed Hitler's hopes for a cross-Channel invasion, Britain gradually turned to the offensive. Sporadic attempts by the RAF early in the War to bomb Germany during daylight hours had taught the British the same lesson that the Germans had learned: Daytime raids against a determined air and ground defense were costly.

In May 1940 the British switched to night bombing. Although this provided a measure of protection for the bombers, it played havoc with their accuracy. Darkness obscured the landmarks that enabled a navigator to find the targets. And the RAF used no radio beams to guide the planes down an invisible path to their destination. The map, compass and sextant that the British bomber crews still relied on proved woefully inadequate for pinpointing a target in the darkness. During the summer of 1941, photographs taken by RAF reconnaissance planes of German targets after raids showed that 90 per cent of the British bombs were falling off target. Clearly, British bombers needed some sort of radio-navigation device if they were ever to achieve worthwhile results with the night offensive.

Fortunately for the RAF, such a device had reached the final testing stages by the summer of 1941. It was called Gee (for grid), and it was based on three widely separated transmitters in England. Each of these stations emitted a signal that was picked up by a special receiver on board an aircraft. By measuring the time intervals between the signals and the order of their reception, a navigator was able to plot his position on a special map of Europe overlaid with a color-coded grid that represented his distance from the transmitting stations.

Just when it seemed that Gee promised a solution to the problem of night navigation, an accident threatened to render it useless. On the night of the 13th of August, 1941, a Royal Air Force bomber carrying experimental Gee equipment crashed in Germany. If the Gee set survived the crash,

German scientific intelligence would figure out how it worked and would soon produce a jamming device. Because Gee would not be ready for wide-scale use for at least six months, the Germans would have ample time to develop a countermeasure.

The dilemma was passed to R. V. Jones. Working on the assumption that the Germans now at least suspected the existence of a new radio aid, Jones concocted an elaborate hoax to lead them down the wrong path. He would trick the Germans into thinking that Gee was something else.

Jones later described his scheme as "the culmination of all my prewar efforts in practical joking, with virtually as much of the national resources at my disposal as I wished." To begin with, he abolished all references to the word "Gee" to ensure that the Germans would get no further clues. Then the Gee transmitters already built in England were disguised, by means of additional tall masts, to look like ordinary radar transmitters. The serial numbers on Gee mounting equipment being installed in the bombers were changed to make them coincide with the numbers on ordinary radiotelephone equipment.

Having eliminated all traces of Gee, Jones provided the Germans with fresh bait to lure them away from the scent. He devised a decoy system based on the old *Knickebein*. "What better than to flatter them by letting them think that we had copied their beams?" he wrote after the War. "And so we invented the Jay beams and actually set up some Jay-beam transmitters on our East Coast."

To plant word of the decoy Jay beams, Jones sought help from MI-5's Double Cross operation. At his instigation, one of the double agents concocted for the Abwehr a fictitious conversation, and claimed that he had overheard it in London, at the Savoy Hotel. According to the double agent's story, a Royal Air Force officer was irate that a superior had received a high award for his work on a new radio directional system. "All he has done," the officer sputtered, "is to copy the German beams—and a year late at that." His companion, also an RAF officer, took a more generous view. "But," he said, "you must admit that at any rate we now have the Jay beams to get us to our targets. They worked okay on Brest, and soon we shall have them over Germany."

Another double agent supposedly with RAF contacts sent

the Abwehr another false clue. He had been informed, he reported, that some RAF units were receiving special lectures describing the new "Jerry" radio directional system. "I left it to my German opposite number to work out whether 'Jerry' stood for 'Jay' or for 'German,' " Jones wrote. "The agents were enthusiastically thanked by their German masters for their very valuable information."

The seeds of Jones's chicanery sprouted and took root. When the Jay beams were turned on, the Germans promptly jammed them. But when the real system, Gee, was first used on a big scale in a raid on the industrial city of Essen on the 8th of March, 1942, the Germans took no radio countermeasures. Jones's ruse had worked and would be even more effective than he had envisioned. He had counted on gaining three months of jam-free bombing with the new device; as it happened, German scientific intelligence did not discover Gee for seven months and was unable to devise an effective countermeasure until early 1943. In the meantime, German interrogators were pumping captured airmen for information about a radio system called Jay—a tribute to Jones's "practical joke," one of the more successful hoaxes of the War.

The thrust and parry of the electronics war, as it came to be known, evolved into a distinct pattern. Whenever either side put a secret new blind-bombing or electronic navigation aid into use, it was only a matter of time before the opposing forces of scientific intelligence responded with a countermeasure. Along with Gee the British scientists invented a blind-bombing device called Oboe, which was based on two converted radar transmitters. Pulses from one station kept a bomber on track to its target; a signal from the second station told the bombardier when to release his payload. Oboe was perfected in February of 1943, and it kept British bombers on target until the following October, when, inevitably, the Germans developed an effective jamming device.

In the meantime, the British had added another weapon to their electronic arsenal. This was H2S, an airborne radar scanner so sensitive that it provided a pilot with a rough facsimile of the terrain below, including the target cities. The Germans responded with a device that enabled their night fighters to home in on the H2S signal and intercept the British bombers.

To produce such countermeasures, the forces of scientific intelligence first had to find out how the new weapon worked, most often a painstaking, step-by-step process of collecting and sifting clues until the puzzle pieces fell into place. One of the most enduring, and to the Allies most devastating, of German secrets was the Luftwaffe's network of defensive radar.

Although before the War the Germans had concentrated their scientific genius on offensive radio beams such as *Knickebein,* they did erect a few early-warning radar stations along the French coast in 1940. Then the defeat of the Luftwaffe in the Battle of Britain and the increasingly effective British bombing attacks pushed the Germans deeper into radar development.

Belatedly, the Luftwaffe began to construct a chain of radar stations around Germany in order to provide advance

A Y-beam transmitter, intended to direct German planes to targets in England, crowns a coastal hill in German-occupied Norway. The Germans had no sooner put the instrument into operation than R. V. Jones and his staff detected its transmissions and jammed them.

warning of British aerial attacks. By the autumn of 1941, a formidable radar barrier stretched around the western edge of the Reich from the Alsace region of France all the way to Denmark.

The radar belt was known to the British as the Kammhuber Line for its developer, Major General Josef Kammhuber, the commander of the Luftwaffe's night defenses. It consisted of a series of adjacent zones that were each approximately 20 miles long by 20 miles wide. Each zone had a radar set called a Freya, two other radar sets known as Würzburgs, and a night fighter to intercept the enemy. The Freya set provided an early warning of an approaching foe. As the enemy bomber flew into the zone of defense, one of the Würzburg radars picked it up and tracked it. The other Würzburg tracked the path of the German interceptor. In the ground control station, the two planes were projected as dots on a glass screen. A controller, his eyes focused on the pair of dots, radioed directions to guide the interceptor to the enemy bomber.

The Kammhuber Line functioned with ruthless efficiency. British losses mounted at an alarming rate. In November, during one raid on German cities of the Ruhr region, a staggering 21 per cent of the British bombers failed to return to England, prompting Prime Minister Churchill to curtail sorties for the coming winter.

Clearly something had to be done to confound Kammhuber's formidable defenses. But before the British could take countermeasures, they had to know exactly what they confronted: what the German radar looked like, how the different sets worked, and how they were coordinated with ground control and night fighters.

The task of unraveling the mysteries of German radar fell to R. V. Jones and his team of scientific sleuths. They began their quest in almost total darkness, and two years passed before they could see the light. As had happened with other German secrets, the first clue about the existence of the German radar came to Jones from the Oslo Report, which mentioned an aircraft-detection system that had a range of approximately 75 miles.

Then in July of 1940, Ultra intercepts of Luftwaffe radio traffic provided Jones with more evidence. The overheard messages referred to Freya as a warning system and revealed that one of the Freya stations was located on the coast of Brittany. Jones was intrigued by the choice of the code name Freya, the Norse goddess of beauty, and curiosity led him to research its mythological origins. He discovered that Freya's most prized possession was a necklace known as Brisingamen, which was guarded by Heimdall, the watchman of the gods. Heimdall's eyesight was so sharp that he was able to see 100 miles in any direction, day or night. Without a doubt, Heimdall was the personification of the German radar. His name would have been a much better code word than Freya, Jones reasoned, but it would have been entirely too obvious.

Jones now knew that the Germans had a radar called

Booklets like this one were distributed monthly to Allied junior officers and enlisted men to provide them with tactical information gleaned from prisoner interrogations and equipment analysis. Among the subjects covered were ways to deal with enemy booby traps and smoke screens.

Freya, but he had no evidence of its location. Not until the 22nd of February, 1941, did a reconnaissance plane, flying a mission over the Cap de la Hague 15 miles northwest of Cherbourg, return with a photograph that showed, near the village of Auderville, two squarish aerials shaped like the heating elements of an electric toaster. These, presumably, were radar antennas.

On the same day, a listening station in southern England detected inexplicable high-frequency radar signals from across the Channel. Bearings of the pulses indicated that they were emanating from a site close to the village of Auderville. The search for Freya was over.

Signals from other Freya stations betrayed their locations, and Jones was able to compile a complete dossier on Freyas along the French coast. "This is all very pretty," a colleague from the Telecommunications Research Establishment remarked to him, "but what good is it?" "Some day," Jones told him, "we're going back, and we shall need to deal with those stations if we are going to land successfully."

But Freya was not the whole story of German radar. From what Jones could hazard about its characteristics, Freya could detect the range and bearing of a British bomber but was incapable of detecting the plane's altitude—essential information for directing fighters to enemy aircraft at night. Freya was limited. Lurking behind it was undoubtedly another radar system.

The first hint of such an auxiliary system came in an intercept, forwarded from Bletchley Park, reporting that Freyas were being sent to Rumania along with other equipment called Würzburgs. What sort of device was the Würzburg? If it could determine the altitude as well as the bearing and range of an aircraft, it could furnish the missing link in the night-fighting system that the Germans were developing for the defense of the Reich.

In May 1941 a Wellington bomber specially equipped with a sensitive receiver flew over Brittany and intercepted short-wave radar signals. Jones figured these must be coming from the Würzburg, wherever it was.

Then, in August 1941, Jones and his associates edged closer to a glimpse of the Würzburg—almost by accident. The revelation came when British reconnaissance planes flew a routine mission over the Freya station at Cap d'An-

tifer, a chalk headland 12 miles north of Le Havre, where two by-now-familiar Freya antennas perched on top of a 400-foot cliff. The photographs that the planes brought back showed a track running from the antennas several hundred yards to a villa near the village of Bruneval. A close inspection of the prints revealed that the track ended in a loop a short distance from the villa. Inside the loop was a speck so small that photographic interpreters at first thought it might be dust on the negative. Closer examination proved that the speck was not dust, and Jones was intrigued; it might be the Würzburg, the key that scientific intelligence had been searching for.

Word of the mysterious speck reached a reconnaissance pilot, Flight Lieutenant Tony Hill, who privately resolved to get a proper picture that would solve the puzzle. On December 5, 1942, acting entirely on his own, Hill took off in a Spitfire and headed for Bruneval. At an altitude of 300 feet and a speed close to 350 miles per hour, he zipped over the radar site, his camera churning; he was gone before the startled antiaircraft defenders below knew what had happened. Hill returned with two of the most important photographs of the War. There, in the clearest detail, was the bowl-shaped Würzburg. From its size and shape, Jones was certain that the new radar was the source of the short-wave transmissions detected back in May.

Jones spied something else interesting in Tony Hill's photographs. Though the Würzburg stood near the cliff's edge, the ground sloped down from there to a small beach a few hundred yards away. Jones stared at the beach. "Look," he said finally to his assistant Charles Frank, "we could get in there!" He was envisioning a Commando raid to seize the German radar and bring it back to England, where its lingering mysteries might finally be resolved.

Passed up the chain of command, Jones's idea soon became reality. On the night of the 27th of March, 120 British paratroopers floated down and seized the radar site, encountering only light resistance from the Germans. A skilled RAF radar technician dismantled the Würzburg, and the raiding party withdrew across the beach to British boats, which ferried them back across the Channel. At a cost of two men dead and four wounded, Jones had his Würzburg.

"So what had we gained?" Jones wrote later. "A firsthand knowledge of the state of German technology. We now knew the extreme limits of wave length to which the Würzburg could be tuned, and that it had no built-in counter either to jamming or spurious reflectors." But Jones and the scientists at TRE also noticed something about the Würzburg that was not so heartening. Although it had no antijamming devices, it could be tuned to a wide range of frequencies, a feature that made it very difficult to jam electronically.

In fact the British did possess the means to jam the Würzburg—to throw any radar in existence into turmoil, for that matter. It was thought to be the ultimate electronic weapon of the time, a tool so devastating that its use became a topic of raging controversy in the British War Cabinet. Yet the device was so simple in concept and construction that it could be fashioned by a child with a pair of scissors. It was a bundle of tin-foil strips.

Jones himself had suggested as far back as 1937 that a piece of metal floating through the air would produce an echo on a radar screen. Tests conducted early in 1942 by Joan Curran, a TRE scientist, showed that a bundle of 240 foil strips, each eight and a half inches long by five and a half inches wide, produced a radar blip that resembled that of a British Blenheim bomber. Ten such bundles loosed in the air would generate a chaotic cloud of blips that would obscure the real planes. She also discovered a chilling fact: The strips worked best on the ground radar that provided Britain's first line of defense.

Thus argument arose against the use of the strips, which were code-named Window. If the British dropped the Window, its secret would be revealed and the Germans would copy it immediately and use it against the Chain Home Radar during their own bombing attacks. On these grounds, the physicist Watson-Watt and Professor Lindemann were dead set against employing Window, despite indications that it would save the lives of countless British aircrews. Until an antidote to Window could be developed, their argument ran, its secret should remain inviolate.

In fact Window was no secret at all. The Germans had it too, but they were afraid to use it for fear the British would reciprocate. In 1942 the Luftwaffe had made its own tests of foil strips, which they called Düppel. When a report on its effects reached Reich Marshal Hermann Göring, he was aghast; he ordered that the report be destroyed and all ex-

periments with Düppel cease immediately, lest the British get wind of it.

"We dared not experiment with the little beasts," General Wolfgang Martini, head of Luftwaffe Signals Intelligence, later said, "for fear of their being discovered. Had the wind blown when we dropped the metal strips, people would have picked them up, talked about them, and our secret would have been betrayed."

Finally, in the spring of 1943, the British arguments against employing Window began to slacken. American scientists had by then developed an airborne radar that was immune to Window's effect. More important, the loss of British bombers to the Kammhuber Line now demanded a countermeasure to Würzburg—and to a newly developed airborne radar called Lichtenstein SN-2 being used by Luftwaffe night interceptors. Churchill put an end to the controversy that spring by decreeing: "Very well, let us open the Window!"

The elementary but awesome weapon was unveiled on the night of July 24, 1943, in a mammoth raid on the German port of Hamburg. As 746 Allied bombers approached the sector of the Kammhuber Line protecting the city, aircrews loosed 40 tons—92 million strips—of tin foil. And as the foil spread and billowed through the night sky, it

Scientists of the Telecommunications Research Establishment, which studied the uses of radio waves, gather for a weekly meeting with Royal Air Force officers. University scientists were conscripted from all over Britain to help out in the war effort. Because scientists were traditionally regarded as impractical, they faced resistance from the military; one group was even called "Winston Churchill's toyshop."

magnified the Allied aircraft into an imaginary aerial armada of some 11,000 bombers on the German Würzburg screens. The shimmering false echoes were so thick that they completely obscured the bombers. "It is impossible," one German ground controller was heard to exclaim. "Too many hostiles!"

The night interceptor crews circling in fighters waited in vain for directions to the enemy aircraft. "I cannot control you," exclaimed a controller to his fighter crew. "Try without your ground control." On the ground, the radar-controlled searchlights that were supposed to pinpoint attacking planes scanned the sky fruitlessly; the antiaircraft batteries aimed by radar fired wildly at targets that were not there. On board the night fighters, the Lichtenstein SN-2 radar had also run amok, its screens blotched by the drifting clouds of foil. For the fighter crews the night became surreal. Their radar led them to huge formations that turned out not to exist. One German pilot aloft that night later described the bizarre effects of Window on his plane's radar. The pilot was flying at about 16,000 feet when his radar operator, whose first name was Facius, reported an enemy target on the radar screen.

"I was delighted," the pilot recalled. "I swung round on the bearing, and then Facius proceeded to report three or four targets on his screen. I hoped that I should have enough ammunition to deal with them. Facius shouted: 'Tommy flying toward us at great speed. Distance decreasing . . . 2,000 meters . . . 1,500 . . . 1,000 . . . 500.' "

But no British bomber appeared. "I was speechless," the pilot continued. "Facius already had another target. It was not long before he shouted again: 'Bomber coming for us at a hell of a speed. 2,000 . . . 1,000 . . . 500 . . . He's gone!'

" 'You're crackers, Facius,' I said jokingly. But soon I had lost my sense of humor, for this crazy performance was repeated a score of times."

Window crippled Hamburg's defenses, enabling the RAF raiders to devastate the city at a cost of just 12 planes. Over the next nine nights, British bombers protected by the tin foil returned to Hamburg four times, destroying or damaging half of the city's buildings and killing some 50,000 of its inhabitants.

Early in August, General Martini admitted in a report that Window had been catastrophic. "The technical success of this action must be assessed as absolute. By these means the enemy has delivered the long-awaited blow at our radar sets both on the ground and in the air." Field Marshal Erhard Milch, the Luftwaffe armaments chief, put it differently. "I am beginning to think that we are sitting on a limb," he said, "and the British are sawing that limb off."

In time, the Germans would develop radar that was impervious to Window. But they never would retaliate on a significant scale with their own version of the tin-foil miracle weapon. By 1943 the Luftwaffe no longer possessed the strength to mount a major bombing campaign against England; since 1940 the Germans had lost 6,172 bombers over Britain and the Soviet Union, and production was not replacing the losses.

Adolf Hitler instead chose another means of retaliation. After the Hamburg raid, the infuriated Führer turned his attention to the secret weapons that he envisioned as the ultimate saviors of Germany: the *Vergeltungswaffen,* or "vengeance weapons"—rockets and flying bombs intended to rain destruction on Britain.

In the predawn hours of June 13, 1944, a tiny aircraft with stubby wings flew across the English Channel at high speed, heading for London. It made a raspy, popping noise like a motorcycle without a muffler, and fire shot from its tail. When it reached London it suddenly nosed over, and the engine stopped. The craft went into a dive, and crashed with an earsplitting explosion in the Bethnal Green area. Six people were killed and a number of houses were destroyed. When rescue workers had finished providing first aid for the wounded, they poked around in the wreckage to locate the crew of the unfortunate airplane. To their amazement, they could find no one. No crew existed. The first of the Führer's V-1s, winged bombs propelled by jet engines, had arrived to torment London. Within three months, the city would be subjected to another diabolical device, the V-2 rocket.

The vengeance weapons astounded the English civilians, who had no inkling of their existence. But the British government was not surprised. Though the V-weapons were among the Germans' most precious and closely guarded secrets, the British government had known for nearly a year before the first V-1 fell that German scientific genius was preparing to unleash a startling new achievement.

The first clue about the German V-weapons program had been provided by the Oslo Report, which mentioned in a sketchy manner an experimental program in rocketry under way at a place called Peenemünde. But the Oslo Report had been widely considered a hoax, and the British had ignored that first warning sign. Had they had any idea of the extent of the German experiments, the scientific establishment of Britain would doubtless have been appalled.

The Germans had grasped the military implications of guided bombs and rockets long before the War. The German rocket program dated from 1929, when the Army Weapons Office created a special department to experiment with liquid-fuel rockets. By 1939 the testing grounds for what the Germans called their *Wunderwaffen,* or "wonder weapons," had been established at the village of Peenemünde on the remote island of Usedom, in the Baltic Sea. The western side of the island was reserved for the Luftwaffe and its V-1s, while on the opposite shore a large staff of scientists, engineers and technicians—under the direction of Army Major General Walter Dornberger and his brilliant assistant, a young scientist named Wernher von Braun—developed and tested various rocket models, the last of which was designated V-2.

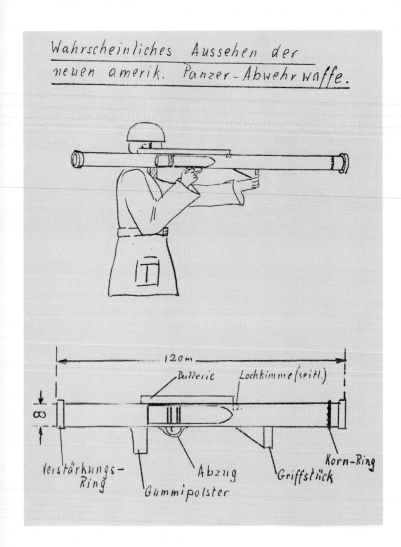

The progress of the experiments on both sides of Usedom was erratic, largely because of the ambivalent attitude of Adolf Hitler, whose reaction toward the wonder weapons alternated between warm and cold but was mostly cold. Hitler tended to be a military traditionalist whose concepts were fixed by his experiences in World War I, and he distrusted innovations. His attitude toward the V-weapons was displayed on a cold, rainy day in March 1939, when he was persuaded to attend a rocket-firing demonstration at Kummersdorf, a test site near Berlin. He arrived in a bad mood, stood morosely in the downpour and watched silently as several fixed rocket engines were fired. To the disappointment of Dornberger and Braun, the Führer maintained his moody silence at a luncheon in his honor, toying with his salad and sipping mineral water. Only at the end of the lunch did he offer the ambiguous comment: "That was powerful indeed."

Despite Hitler's lack of enthusiasm, the V-weapons had their champions in the high ranks of the Wehrmacht and Hitler's inner circle. Chief among them was the astute Albert Speer, Minister for Munitions and War Production. Recognizing the potential of the rockets, Speer determined to speed up tests of the prototype and begin mass production of the weapons. His position enabled him to channel funds to the V-weapons program surreptitiously, thereby fostering the work at Usedom.

On the island there was little contact between the scientists and engineers of the Luftwaffe and those of the Army. Interservice rivalry and professional jealousy kept them from sharing the results of their experiments. In fact the weapons they were developing had little in common, except that both had an internal guidance system and carried a one-ton warhead. The V-1 was essentially an aerial torpedo with a jet engine on its back and stubby fins to keep it steady in flight. It was launched by steam catapult from a long, inclined ramp aimed in the direction of the target. As a weapon the V-1 had several inherent disadvantages. At a top speed of 400 miles per hour, it was too slow to outrun the newer British fighter planes or escape well-aimed antiaircraft fire. It also flew at a low altitude, where it could be easily detected by radar, thus increasing its vulnerability. Finally, it was not particularly accurate.

On the other hand the V-2, a liquid-fuel rocket with stabi-

This German-made sketch of the new American antitank rocket launcher, dubbed a bazooka by GIs, was based on facts that were pried from an American soldier who had been captured in North Africa. The drawing was distributed to panzer troops along with a plea for more information so German tank technicians could take effective countermeasures.

lizing rear fins, could be launched vertically from a flat concrete pad or a mobile platform. Its top speed of 3,400 miles per hour made it invulnerable to fighter planes and to ground fire, and it was much more accurate than the V-1. There was no defense against it, and no warning of its arrival. But the V-2 had one glaring drawback: It cost 10 times as much to produce as the V-1, a deficit that would prove telling as the increasing Allied air offensive diminished Germany's industrial capacity.

The full-scale mass production of the vengeance weapons still required Hitler's imprimatur, which was late in coming. Not until Germany's fortunes took an inexorable turn for the worse did the Führer awaken to the possibilities of the V-1 and the V-2. The devastating Allied air attacks in the spring and summer of 1943, aided by the new weapon Window, and the severe reverses on the Russian front that summer combined to drive Hitler to desperation. On July 7, 1943, he summoned Dornberger and Braun to the Wolf's Lair, his headquarters in East Prussia.

Dornberger was shocked by Hitler's appearance. The once-robust Führer was now haggard and sallow, with trembling hands and an unsteady gait. He watched in si-

Smoke and flames spew from three of 23 Allied ships hit by the Luftwaffe raid on Bari harbor. One of the bombed ships carried a top-secret carg

lence as the two scientists presented a dramatic film showing the progression of a V-2 from hangar to launching site and then to takeoff through surging flames. Braun provided a narration and Dornberger tacked on a persuasive conclusion to sell the V-2. When Dornberger finished, Hitler stood up and impetuously seized his hand. "I thank you," he said. "Why was it I could not believe in the success of your work? If we had had those rockets in 1939, we should never have had this war." And as Dornberger left, Hitler apologized for his neglect, adding that this was only the second time in his life that he had ever apologized to anyone.

To Hitler, the rockets now seemed the key to the victory that had eluded him. That day he ordered Speer to give the V-2 project top priority. Later in the day he remarked that the rocket was the decisive weapon of the War. That night he went to bed at an early hour and for the first time in months slept soundly.

While Hitler was asleep in his Wolf's Lair, untroubled by dreams, a nightmare was brewing for him and his rocket program. The Germans had hoped that the remoteness of Usedom and the stringent security maintained there would protect the secret of the V-2. The scientists and workers liv-

A GRISLY ACCIDENT, A HIDDEN BENEFIT

On the evening of December 2, 1943, as darkness was cloaking the Adriatic coast of Italy, more than 100 Luftwaffe Ju-88s swept over the port of Bari and dropped a load of bombs. In moments the harbor was ablaze with burning ships and the air was thick with acrid smoke. Hundreds of sailors jumped overboard to swim for the docks or clutch flotsam and wait in the chill water for rescue.

As the survivors came ashore, the Bari hospitals began to fill with waterlogged sailors who seemed to suffer from nothing more unusual than burns, shock and exposure. But within 18 hours men were dying. In a month 83 had died, and 540 had been beset by eye irritation and skin lesions. After some initial bafflement, an Army medical expert in chemical warfare diagnosed the cause as mustard gas, a dire weapon that the Allies had pronounced too sinister for use by civilized nations.

Ultimately, the grim incident had a be-

nign side effect. Autopsies revealed that the mustard-gas poison had done its work by attacking the white blood cells. By a coincidence, an Army doctor in Bari knew of work being done at Yale University to combat leukemia, which is caused by the presence of too many white cells in the blood. He sent his colleagues there a report of the Bari findings. The report gave the Yale researchers evidence that mustard gas could be used to fight cancer cells.

But the immediate question was how mustard gas had appeared in Bari harbor. Had the German bombs carried it? They had not. The *John Harvey*, one of the American merchant ships berthed in Bari harbor on that fateful night, had a secret cargo of 2,000 mustard-gas bombs in her hold, and the vessel had exploded under the German fire, turning her malevolent cargo against the Allies themselves.

Such information was not only controversial but embarrassing. So not until 1959 did the United States government declassify the information and confess to the dark secret that in 1943 it had been storing poison gas in Italy.

ing on the island had become accustomed to the distant rumble of Allied bombers passing over their domain on their way to raid the German cities beyond. No bomb had ever fallen on Usedom, even by accident. But attack was merely a matter of time, for British scientific intelligence was aware of the activity on Usedom and would soon demonstrate to the Germans, in dramatic fashion, that their secret was no longer safe.

One of the first positive indications that the Germans were experimenting with rockets had been received in December of 1942, when a Danish chemical engineer forwarded information about the testing of a large rocket. A similar report, obtained from a Swedish source in January of 1943, mentioned the village of Peenemünde as a testing ground for rockets.

Suspicions about the veracity of these reports were laid to rest in March, when the rockets' existence was confirmed by an unimpeachable source: the captive General Ritter von Thoma of the Afrika Korps. At a London detention center, in a room that British intelligence had wired for eavesdropping on prisoners, General von Thoma remarked to another captured general of the Afrika Korps that "no progress whatsoever can have been made in this rocket business. I saw it once at a special ground. The major there was full of hope. He said, 'Wait till next year and the fun will start!' " Thoma concluded that since he had heard no explosions since his arrival in London, the German rocket program must have faltered.

The generals' recorded conversation, added to the other evidence, spurred the British to action. Churchill appointed his son-in-law, Duncan Sandys, to head an intelligence inquiry into the German rockets; Jones conducted a parallel investigation. An intense campaign of aerial photography of Peenemünde was launched. And Jones, examining one of the photographs taken on June 12, finally identified the rocket, a cylinder about 38 feet long with tail fins.

Obviously it was only a matter of time before the rockets descended on Britain. On June 29 Churchill reacted to the threat by ordering an all-out attack on Peenemünde. Because Sandys considered the German scientists to be the greatest menace, their living area was designated the top-priority target. Second in line would be the rocket factory,

and third the development works and administration offices. August 17 was set as the date.

A full moon shone that night through wisps of drifting clouds. The Peenemünde settlement was quiet. The workers had returned to their barracks after their 12-hour day. On the horizon the air began to vibrate with the roar of Allied planes on their way to bomb the charred cities of the Reich, so common an evening occurrence by now that the sentries on duty scarcely bothered to look up. When they did, they saw the blue-black sky above them suddenly starred with hundreds of red lights like Japanese lanterns that floated down to earth to mark the targets for the approaching bombers. Then incendiaries and high explosives rained down on the island. Peenemünde was almost undefended, a decoy raid on Berlin having enticed away most of the German fighter planes. Only toward the end of the raid did the absent fighters return, and by then much of Peenemünde lay in ruins.

When the sirens finally sounded the all clear, Dornberger emerged from an air-raid shelter to survey his domain. His first impression was of a smoking devastation, pitted like a lunar landscape. Although the laboratories and test facilities had not been destroyed, the housing enclave of the scientific workers was leveled. Sewers and power lines had been destroyed, water mains ruptured, railroad tracks twisted into spaghetti shapes. Some of his closest friends, Dornberger discovered, were buried in the rubble. How had the enemy managed to get such precise information? He asked himself the question over and over. How had they known so exactly what targets to bomb? Who had told them? His questions would go unanswered until after the War. In England, Sandys waited all night for the planes to return. At daybreak he telephoned Churchill to give him the news of the bombers' great success.

The attack on Peenemünde was crippling, but not fatal. It set back the V-2 program for several months at most. The V-2 test-firing was transferred to the burned-out village of Blizna in occupied Poland. There Russian prisoners were forced to construct new laboratories and launching pads, and around them they erected cardboard cottages and buildings, arranging dummies of men, women and children throughout to give the illusion from the air of an insignificant village not worth bombing. Rocket manufacture was shifted to the Harz Mountains in the interior of Germany, where a large network of tunnels, originally dug as mines, was expanded to create a vast subterranean workshop and labor camp.

The attack on Peenemünde had little effect on the V-1 program. Even before the raid, flying-bomb production had begun in factories in Germany.

In the meantime, the British were receiving ominous intimations that the rocket was not Germany's only new aerial weapon. In October 1943 a member of the French underground reported that the Germans had built six unexplainable "secret-weapons sites" in a woods northeast of Abbeville. Aerial photography revealed that the sites were identical in make-up: Beside a series of long, low buildings, which obviously could be used to store and arm a weapon of some sort, was a long, gently arcing concrete ramp with a metal track on top. The ramps had one immediately apparent and particularly disturbing feature—they were all aimed toward London.

But what was their purpose? Apparently for launching something, the interpreters reasoned, but surely not a rocket; the rockets photographed at Peenemünde had launching pads, not inclined ramps.

The question of the mysterious ramps was answered at the end of November by a sharp-eyed interpreter of photographs, Flight Officer Constance Babington-Smith, while she was studying a picture of a Luftwaffe airfield. There, at the edge of the sea, three strange structures had been erected. In earlier photographs of the same site, the structures

had been dismissed as part of a dredging operation. But Flight Officer Babington-Smith looked closer and spotted something that her colleagues had missed. Atop one of the structures was a tiny aircraft with stubby wings and no cockpit. It was sitting on its ramp, poised for flight.

Flight Officer Babington-Smith had seen a V-1. Her discovery led to intensified aerial reconnaissance of northern France, the most likely area from which the Germans would launch their flying bombs. In a short time, new photographs revealed an alarming development: The ramps seemed to be multiplying. No fewer than 96 launching sites were discovered, all of their ramps aimed at London.

Galvanized by the new threat, the British Chiefs of Staff ordered massive bombing attacks to obliterate the flying-bomb launching sites. The raids began on December 19, 1943, and lasted through January 1944. In 1,053 sorties American and British planes dropped 23,000 tons of explosives on the sites. By February none of the original 96 sites remained intact, and from all evidences the Germans had abandoned every one. The British began to breathe more easily; the threat had apparently been wiped out.

In reality, as the British discovered later in the spring, the Germans had responded not with resignation but with ingenuity. Though they had abandoned the original sites, they had fashioned new ones with prefabricated ramps that could be assembled within days. Some of the ramps were cleverly concealed in orchards or woods; others were close by French villages, where the Allies would have to risk killing civilians if they bombed. By June the Germans had erected 50 new launching sites and were making the final, hurried preparations to attack.

The British braced themselves for the worst. The War Cabinet drew up what it called the Black Plan for the evacuation to the countryside of the military chiefs of staff, the entire Parliament and some 16,000 government officials.

While continuing to attack the launch sites whenever possible, the British arranged defenses against the flying bombs in belts: fighter planes on the coast and antiaircraft batteries inland. Around London, barrage balloons were sent aloft on long steel cables that could knock the V-1s out of the sky.

On June 13 the first V-1 swooshed up its launching ramp in a cloud of steam generated by its catapult; its jet engine

Carrying a sack containing his personal belongings, German General Ritter von Thoma of the Afrika Korps walks in front of his British guards in Cairo. Thoma was captured in November 1942—the highest-ranking officer yet taken prisoner by the Allies. Unwittingly he later gave his captors prized information; left with a fellow general in a London room —and unaware that microphones had been hidden there—he spoke freely of German rocketry, confirming facts the Allies had only suspected.

ignited and with a roar it climbed upward, headed for London. Ten more V-1s followed that night, and by the end of the month 2,000 had been launched. During the month of July 3,000 V-1s were sent to destroy London.

However, less than 25 per cent of the V-1s reached their targets. Many of the flying bombs exploded on the launching ramps, or veered off course to land—comparatively harmlessly—in the Channel or the English countryside. And the British defenses, which at first had faced an unknown weapon, honed their skills through trial and error and

gradually proved more than a match for the flying bombs. By the end of August, fighter planes, antiaircraft guns and barrage balloons were claiming 83 per cent of the V-1s that reached the coast of England. With relief, the British shelved their Black Plan.

For the British fighter pilots, intercepting the weird missile was a dangerous and eerie experience. The flying bombs were almost too fast to catch, and if a pilot got close enough to fire on one there was a good chance that he and his plane would blow up along with it. "We first of all started opening

Hell-Dogs over England!

For two years Allied bombers tried to wipe out one German city after the other, killing or wounding millions of innocent women and children. In spite of all German warnings and the confession by responsible Anglo-American authorities, that German industries could not be stopped to increase their output steadily, the massacre was continued.

Now it's our turn!

Since midnight June 15th/16th a new German long-range weapon of most terrible explosive effect is continuously engaged in massed large-scale raids over London and South-East England. We hate this war against the defenceless population, but you have forced this fight upon us.

These raids will be continued until a decisive military goal is reached.

Statement of an American radio-reporter, broadcasted on June 16th from U. S. A. :

" The new German secret weapon is, there is no doubt about it, the beginning of a new aera in war-history of the world."

S W 18.

Leaflets like this, lobbed by German artillery in Normandy in 1944, were designed to demoralize Allied soldiers. Trying to justify the rocket campaign against England, the writer exaggerated casualties inflicted by Allied bombers on German civilians; the real toll was below 300,000.

fire on them from about 400 yards, for safety," recalled Wing Commander Roland Beaumont, a Hawker Tempest pilot. "They were a tiny target and we used to miss them rather consistently, so we halved the range. At that range you'd have no time to avoid the explosion—as soon as you saw it you were in it. You'd go through the center of the fireball. And come out upside down. It was some time before we could figure this one out.

"But in fact," Beaumont continued, "you were going through a partial vacuum as you went through the explosion. And the enormous torque of the propeller had the effect of twisting the plane over. It was rather extraordinary."

On the ground, the accuracy of the antiaircraft gunners was immeasurably increased by the introduction in the summer of 1944 of a new, American-manufactured secret weapon, the proximity fuse. Actually a miniature radar set in an explosive shell, the proximity fuse sensed a nearby target and triggered the detonation whether or not the shell actually hit the target.

The formidable defenses combined to slow the influx of V-1s to a trickle. On August 28, for example, only four flying bombs reached London—although 94 had been launched successfully by the Germans. Antiaircraft fire downed 65 of the V-1s, fighter planes claimed 23, and the barrage balloons protecting the city got two.

Still, as many as 12 flying bombs managed to make their way to London daily, and for the city's residents the new menace was as threatening as the German bombings of two years earlier. Because of its speed and because London's buildings made it impossible to see from the ground, an approaching V-1 was seldom sighted. But it was always heard, and Londoners learned to dread the sound. First came the guttural roar of the jet engine, a frightening noise that grew deafening as the V-1 drew nearer. Then, as an internal timer caused the weapon to dive, its fuel supply was interrupted and the engine cut off, creating a few seconds of eerie silence before the flying bomb struck home and a shattering explosion rent the air.

That sequence of sounds became a daily and unnerving experience for Londoners, so much a part of city life that the London *Daily Express* printed a cartoon depicting a typical Londoner with one grossly enlarged ear, abnormally developed by constant listening for the so-called buzz bombs.

Occasionally a bomb would score a devastating strike. On the 18th of June, one dived squarely into the Royal Military Chapel at the Wellington Barracks, where a crowd of worshippers had gathered for the Sunday service. The blast killed 121 military officers and civilians and injured scores of others.

Another sizable gathering in London barely escaped a similar fate. Poetry lovers were attending a reading by Edith—later Dame Edith—Sitwell when the air-raid siren began to wail, signaling the approach of a flying bomb. One of the audience, a Canadian officer stationed in London, later recalled the scene as Miss Sitwell read: "Above her voice, above the sirens, we could now hear the stuttering reverberation of the flying bomb. It was a sound we had all been hardened to. No one stirred. Edith continued in her resonant yet restrained voice.

"Air-raid wardens on the roof had begun to blow their whistles—that meant that a direct hit was imminent. People were getting down on the floor, trying to shield their heads with chairs. Edith kept on reading without the slightest change of voice or expression. No one was listening to her. No one could.

"The flying bomb must have all but skimmed the roof. Then the roar of its motor began to fade and some seconds later there was a dullish boom. All the windows rattled and several of them cracked. Edith read on until the end. Then, barely perceptibly, she winked at us."

In the course of the summer it became increasingly apparent to the Germans that the V-1 assault was not living up to Hitler's fantasies of destruction, that British countermeasures had reduced it from a menace to a nuisance. The flying bombs continued to buzz over London like hornets, but rarely did they deliver a fatal sting. Allied ground forces, in the meantime, were sweeping through France, overrunning and capturing the V-1 launching sites in the Pas-de-Calais area. By late summer the German flying-bomb campaign had been crippled.

However, the Germans still had their venerated but untried rocket, the V-2. By September the German Army had produced some 600 V-2s. It had prepared concealed launching sites in the Low Countries and was almost ready to bombard London.

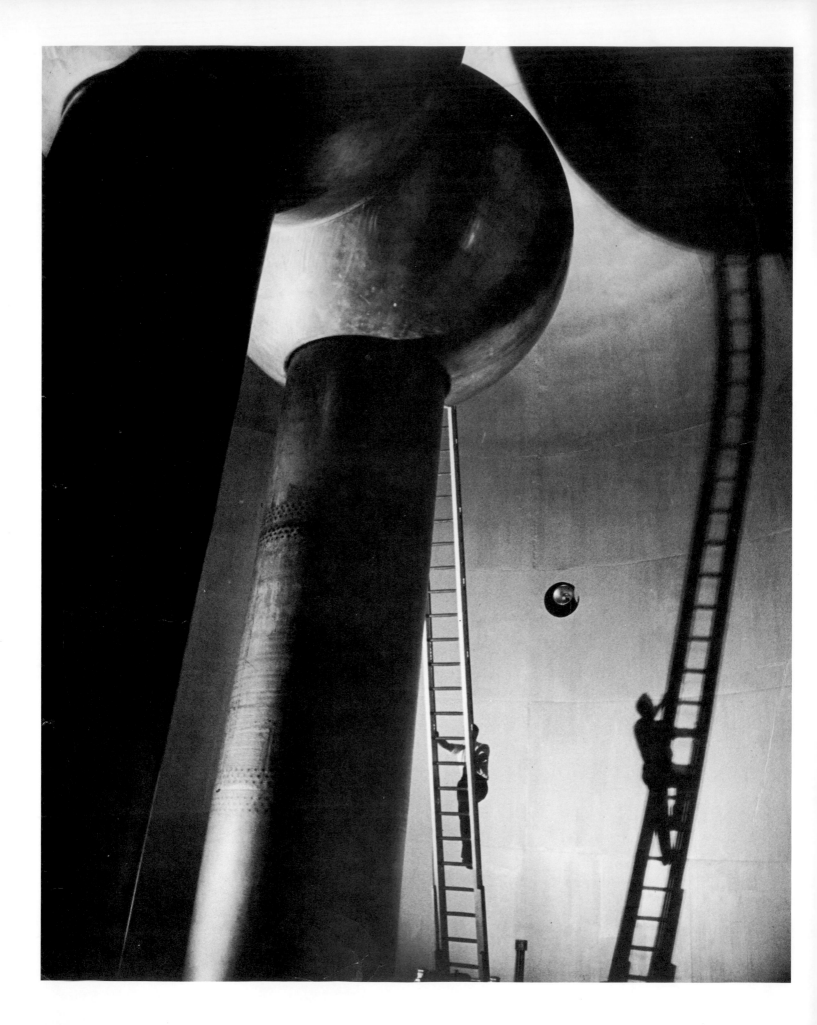

The British were girding for the rocket attacks. They had received ample warning from underground informants in occupied Europe; in fact they had even laid hands on the rocket itself. In May an experimental V-2 launched from Blizna had gone awry and crashed on a bank of the Bug River in Poland. Members of the Polish Home Army hurriedly dismantled it and secreted many of its parts. In July a British Dakota transport flew from Brindisi, Italy, to an abandoned airstrip in Poland. The V-2 parts were placed aboard and flown to England. And in June, pieces of a V-2 that had accidentally crashed in Sweden were swapped to the British for some radar sets.

From these pieces British scientists were able to reconstruct a partial V-2, and in the process learn much about its performance. They soon realized that the rocket was a complex and sophisticated machine, an astounding scientific achievement, and their inquiry led them to an inescapable and dismaying conclusion: There was no defense against the V-2. It flew too high and too fast to be intercepted by either fighter plane or ground fire. The best the Allies could do was destroy the supply depots and launching sites—no mean feat since the sites were small and well concealed—and hope that in time the Allied armies would overrun and capture the installations. The British War Cabinet began preparations to evacuate one million Londoners and make room in the city's hospitals for the multitudes of expected V-2 casualties.

On the evening of September 8 a blast pierced the clear night sky over West London and was followed by a rumbling ground explosion. Several houses were reduced to rubble, three people were killed and 10 were severely wounded. The V-2 had arrived. Twenty-two more V-2s landed on the city that month, followed by 85 in October and 154 in November.

Yet for all their invincibility, the rockets failed to arrive in the droves necessary to bring the city to its knees. The V-2 was less punishing than the V-1 because it had a tendency to bury itself in the ground before its warhead exploded. Moreover, the rocket did not engender the hysteria that Hitler had anticipated. The dread induced by the sound of an approaching buzz bomb was missing with the V-2, which gave no warning of its arrival—a psychological advantage for Londoners. They came to endure the daily rocket blasts with fortitude, knowing that the odds favored survival; some were even able to joke. To avert panic, the government at first did not officially recognize the rocket's existence, and explained away the strange blasts as explosions in underground gas mains. "Another gasworks!" Londoners would exclaim wryly, knowing better, as the echo of a rocket blast reverberated in the city.

By the time the aerial assault was over, 10,611 V-1s and nearly 1,000 V-2s had struck England, killing 8,588 people and injuring 46,838 others. In military terms, the vaunted secret terror weapons had achieved little. With conventional bombers the Germans had managed to kill some 52,000 British civilians from 1940 to 1943. And the Allies, for their part, claimed 35,000 lives in just one raid on the city of Dresden in the winter of 1945.

In the end, the Führer's visions of epic destruction and ultimate victory through the terror weapons had turned to dust, along with the fortunes of the Third Reich. For all their brilliance and technological achievements, German scientists had produced too little too late to stave off defeat. And they had fallen far behind the Allies in the crucial scientific inquiry of World War II. Germany had only just begun to probe the edges of the most awesome frontier of science—atomic energy.

By contrast, Allied scientists and engineers—many of whom had become refugees from Europe as a result of Hitler's policies—were beginning to solve the mysteries of matter and energy. In secret laboratories and testing grounds in the United States, hidden from the public eye, these geniuses were harnessing the power that fuels the sun. From their efforts would come the ultimate secret weapon, the atomic bomb.

Inside the reflecting steel walls of a Massachusetts Institute of Technology laboratory, the 22½-foot stems and 15-foot spheres of an electrostatic generator dwarf the figure of a man climbing a ladder for inspection. The machine, built in the 1930s, enabled American physicists to study the atom's structure, and ultimately it led to the generating of atomic energy.

VENGEANCE FROM HITLER

A noisy V-1 buzz bomb plummets toward London in June 1944. Over a nine-month period, 2,420 of these missiles hit the city, killing more than 6,000 civilians.

THE RACE AGAINST A PLAGUE IN THE SKY

In 1942, British intelligence began receiving reports from agents in Denmark and Sweden about mysterious flying objects that were appearing over the Baltic Sea, streaking noisily toward the east, and falling with a bang into the sea. Taken together the reports brought the first confirmation that the Germans actually had long-range missiles ready for use.

Those disquieting reports were followed in December by data from a Danish chemist describing the test launch of a giant rocket at Swinemünde, on Poland's Baltic coast. By the spring of 1943, so much corroborating information had come in that the armed forces chiefs of staff appointed a special intelligence committee to track the German missile program with the aid of intensive air reconnaissance.

A grim race began as the Germans worked feverishly to manufacture and deploy their *Vergeltungswaffen,* or "ven-geance weapons," which Hitler called "the decisive weapons of the War." The British worked just as feverishly to detect and destroy them. In the deadly maneuvering that ensued, the British relied not only on aerial detection but on the cloak-and-dagger operations of conventional espionage and on saturation bombing of missile factories and launching sites. The Germans, for their part, made every effort to conceal what they were up to.

So artful were the camouflage experts that not until the fall of 1943 did the British realize they were threatened by two distinct missiles—the V-1 flying, or buzz, bomb and the V-2 supersonic rocket. In June 1944—when the first buzz bombs came snarling over London as "impersonal as a plague," in the words of novelist Evelyn Waugh—the British devised new aerial defenses and intelligence ruses to blunt the attack. But the V-2 was a different story: Too fast for interception, it could be combated only by destroying its supply depots and launch sites. It continued to pose a threat until the last of the launching pads in Belgium were overrun by Allied armies in the spring of 1945.

A steam catapult launches a V-1 flying bomb at a German test site on a Baltic island. The clock s... the picture was taken 1.8 seconds after firing

A BALTIC HIDEAWAY FOR BUILDING MISSILES

When Germany's rocket wizard, Werner von Braun, was searching for a missile test area in 1936, his mother recalled that his grandfather had hunted ducks near Peenemünde, a fishing village on a remote island in the Baltic Sea.

Within three years, Peenemünde had become the world's foremost rocket center—a complex of test stands, laboratories, hangars, liquid-oxygen plants, supersonic wind tunnels and huge workshops capable of assembling anything from flap valves to advanced electronic equipment.

In a compound on the beach lived nearly 3,700 German scientists and engineers. Nearby were camps of foreign workers and prisoners of war who provided Peenemünde's unskilled manpower.

Amazingly, the Germans were able to hide their activities at Peenemünde from the Allies for more than three years. New construction was artfully dispersed in the oak, beech and pine forests, while camouflaged rockets were exposed on launch pads only during the four to six hours of launch preparations.

Rail lines to transport construction materials snake into the rising shell of a Peenemünde hangar.

Workbenches, spare V-2 engines and overhead hoists fill the spacious Peenemünde engine plant where more than 500 V-2 rockets were assembled.

G
20

Rauchen verboten.

11/W 4156
37

11/W 4171

Peenemünde hangar. V-2s, painted in camouflage olive, dark green and gray, stand ready for launching. A sign warns that smoking is prohibited.

Interpreter Constance Babington-Smith examines an aerial-reconnaissance photograph with a magnifying glass. Sometimes twin prints were studied through a stereoscopic lens to increase the viewer's depth perception.

An RAF photograph taken on the 23rd of June, 1943, provides a view of two V-2 rockets lying side by side (A) within the elliptical earthworks at Peenemünde, where the missiles were tested. Also visible are giant cranes (B) and the missile storage building (C).

HUNTING OUT MISSILES WITH AN AERIAL EYE

In the spring of 1943, after agents tipped off the British to the German experiments at Peenemünde, the Royal Air Force started sending twice-weekly photographic reconnaissance missions over the island village. At the same time, the RAF kept a close watch on a chain of mysterious concrete structures that had begun to appear around Calais.

The breakthrough for aerial intelligence came in June, when the RAF's scientific director spotted in a Peenemünde photograph "what seemed to be the outline of a rocket." Under a full moon on August 17, the RAF and the U.S. Army Air Forces struck Peenemünde and set back the rocket program two months.

But in the fall of 1943, the French Resistance alerted the British to yet another potential threat: curious inclined ramps scattered through coastal areas with their axes pointed directly at London. Their use became clear when Constance Babington-Smith, the RAF's photographic interpreter, started poring over a picture of a Luftwaffe airfield on the Baltic. Feeling herself virtually "on the ground," as she later recalled, she followed a path to the sea and discovered a small cruciform aircraft sitting on one of the mysterious ramps. It was the first Allied glimpse of a V-1 flying bomb.

Subsequent Allied bombing destroyed virtually every one of the 96 V-1 launching ramps, but the Germans quickly developed prefabricated ramps, which they concealed in woods and orchards.

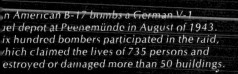

An American B-17 bombs a German V-1 fuel depot at Peenemünde in August of 1943. Six hundred bombers participated in the raid, which claimed the lives of 735 persons and destroyed or damaged more than 50 buildings.

A MOUNTAIN TUNNEL FOR SOARING WEAPONS

Seeking to escape devastating Allied air attacks, the Germans in the late summer of 1943 shifted V-1 and V-2 production to the Mittelwerke (Central Works), a cavernous underground factory complex carved out of the flank of Mount Kohnstein in the Harz Mountains. There, away from the prying eyes of Allied reconnaissance planes, an enormous grid of galleries and mile-long tunnels was built with the slave labor of some 13,000 concentration-camp prisoners. Eventually the complex turned out 30,000 V-1s, and 6,000 V-2s at a rate of 630 missiles a month.

Although they could not see inside, the Allies knew about the Central Works by August of 1944 and bombed the area. The bombing had little effect on production, but it knocked out the transportation system around the factory, stalling the test-firing of missiles that was done at Blizna, Poland, a week's rail journey away.

The Central Works' Mount Kohnstein entrance (inset) gives little hint of the complex inside, where V-2 casings wait on the assembly line (below) to be fitted with fuel tanks and propulsion and nose assemblies.

In a bombproof railroad tunnel, two German mechanics assemble a trailer used to transport V-2s to a launching site.

During a test run, a Heinkel-111 bomber (photographed from inside the nose of another) releases a V-1 buzz bomb.

WELL-TIMED HELP FROM THE UNDERGROUND

Although they could sometimes conceal their missile activities from aerial reconnaissance, the Germans were unable to escape the eyes of informers on the ground.

Reports were sent to London from fishermen, captains of coastal vessels, agents who had parachuted into occupied Europe, and non-Germans mobilized into the Wehrmacht. Perhaps the most dramatic intelligence coup was scored by the Polish underground on May 20, 1944, when it salvaged from the Bug River near Warsaw the engine of a V-2 rocket (opposite) fired from the proving ground at Blizna.

Equally valuable was the intelligence obtained by two Danish agents after a V-1 fell into a turnip field on the Baltic Sea island of Bornholm on August 22, 1943. The agents were able to photograph and sketch the V-1 before a German patrol arrived.

In occupied France, agents repeatedly risked their lives to alert Allied bombers to missile-launching sites. One master agent who was captured was Polish-born Wladyslaw Wazny (opposite). Gunned down as he tried to flee a village hideaway, Wazny died before the Germans could interrogate him.

To provide scale, a Danish police officer stands by a V-1 that crashed on the island of Bornholm. Both the photograph and the sketch at right, made minutes before the Germans arrived, were forwarded to London.

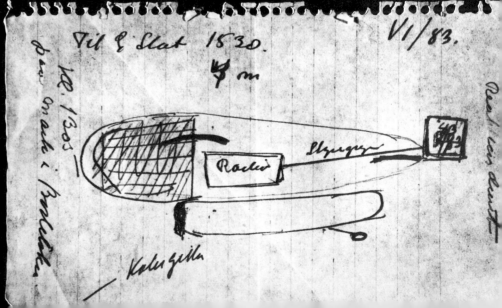

Members of the Polish underground recover the engine of a malfunctioning V-2 rocket that crashed in the Bug River in 1944. Later the men secreted its parts in a barn, and eventually Polish agents were able to send reports describing the components to London.

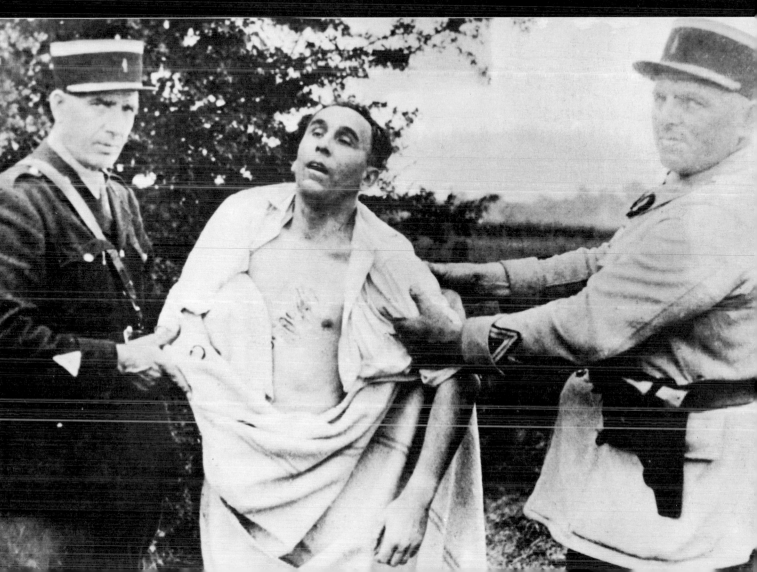

Dying Allied agent Wladyslaw Wazny is kept on his feet by a pair of French policemen moments after being shot by the Germans. While he lived, Wazny was one of the top spies of the War; he located more than 100 V-1 launching sites for British intelligence.

BATTLING THE V-WEAPONS OVER ENGLAND

Realizing they could only delay, and not stop, the German missile offensive, British experts set up around London three defense measures: barrage balloons, antiaircraft batteries and fighters.

Although these defenses were not effective against the 1,837 supersonic V-2s that were fired at England beginning in September of 1944, they had great success against the V-1 flying bombs. Some British pilots learned how to climb above the V-1s, dive to overtake them and either explode them with gunfire or tilt them over with a wingtip so they crashed.

Of the nearly 11,000 V-1s that crossed the coast of England starting on June 13, 1944, more than one third were destroyed before they could reach their targets. Of those that reached the target area, two thirds undershot because of falsified targeting information supplied to the Germans by double agents in England.

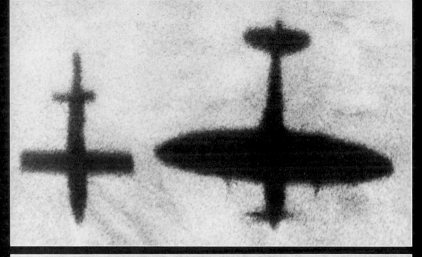

An RAF Spitfire edges into position beside a diminutive V-1 flying bomb (top) and slides a wingtip under one of the flying bomb's wings (bottom) in an effort to tilt it into a crash.

English barrage balloons fill the skies in the flight path of German V-1 buzz bombs. The concentration of 2,000 balloons was the largest ever put in the air

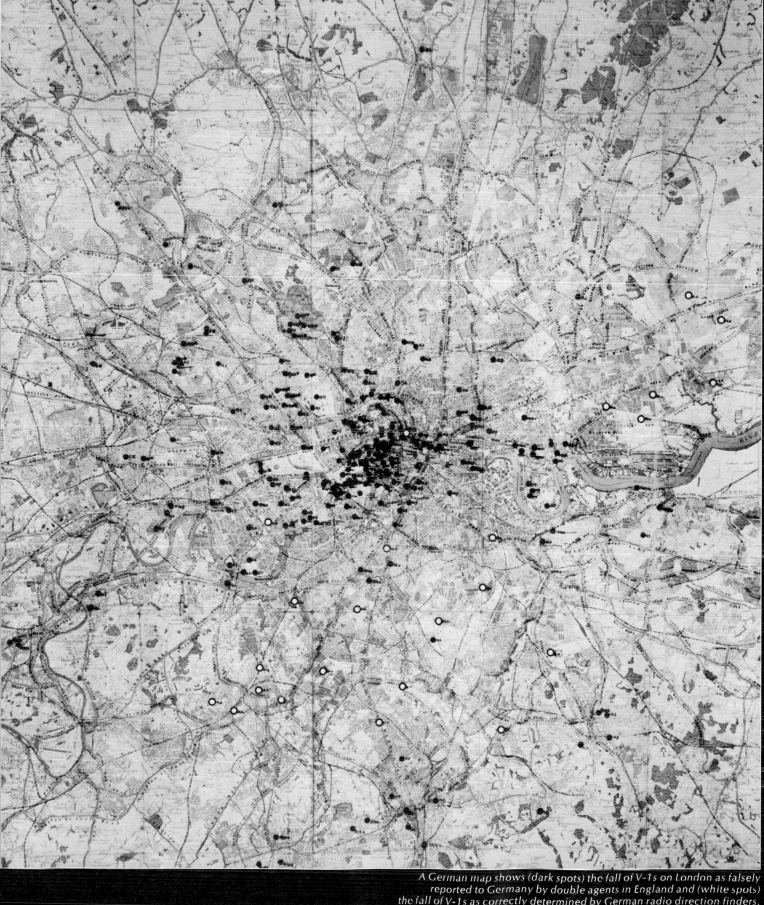

A German map shows (dark spots) the fall of V-1s on London as falsely
reported to Germany by double agents in England and (white spots)
the fall of V-1s as correctly determined by German radio direction finders.
The Germans took the agents' word that the V-1s were overshooting.
Acting on the erroneous information, German missile teams unwittingly
aimed most of their fire at the countryside to the southeast of London.

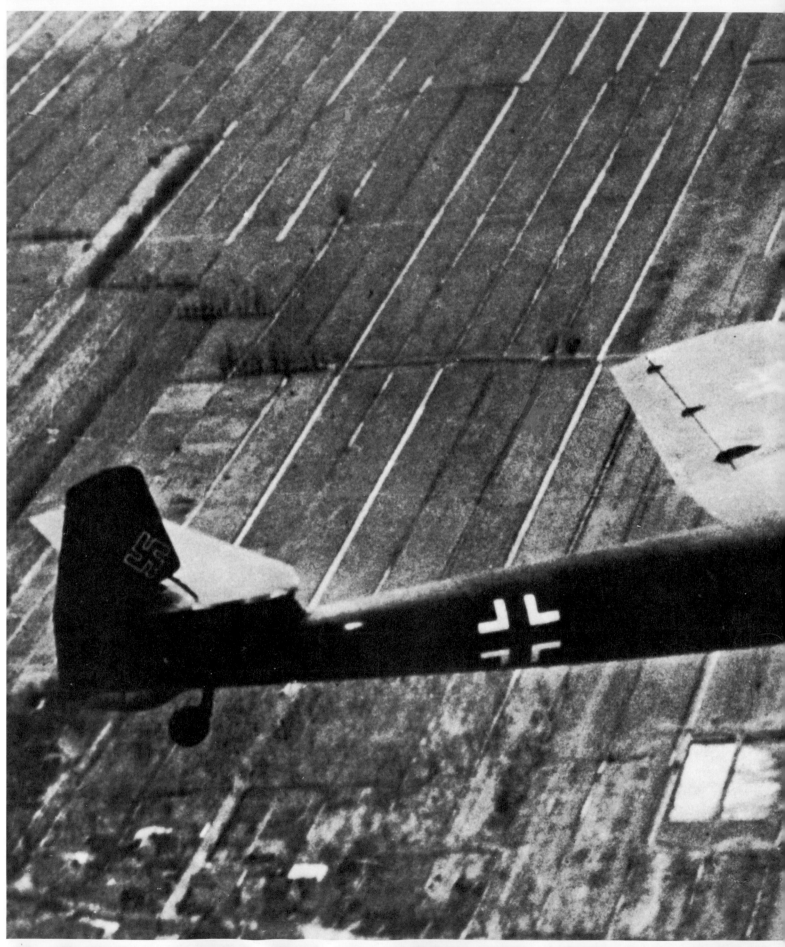

A GALLERY OF WONDER WEAPONS

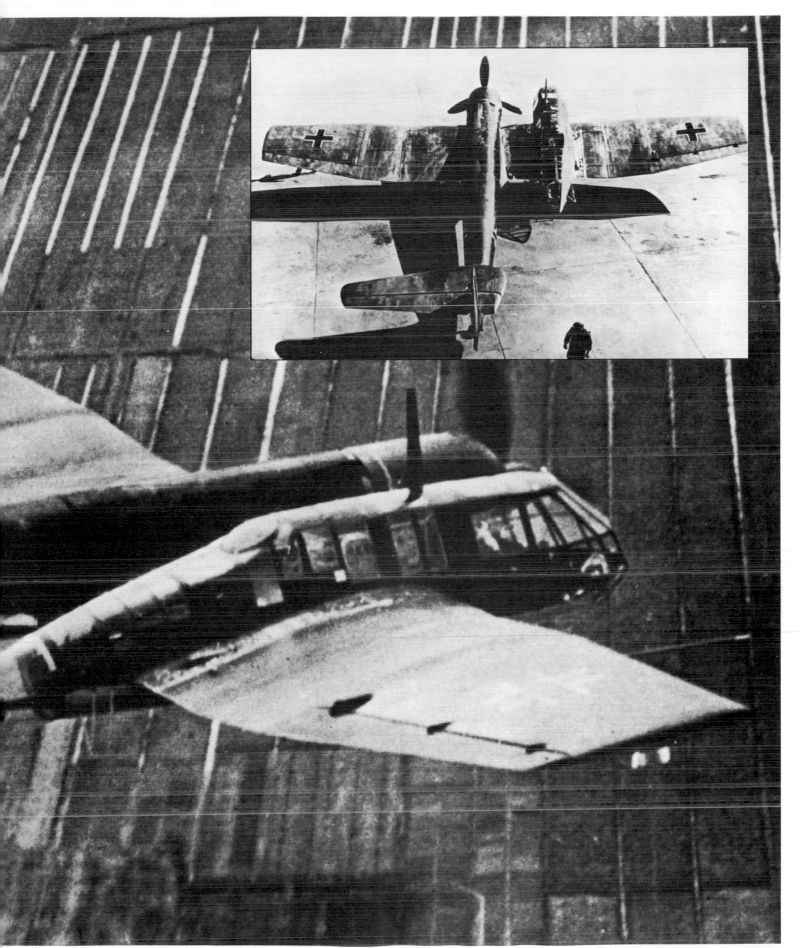

A German BV141 makes a test flight over farmland. For improved visibility, the reconnaissance plane had its cockpit on the wing and only one rear stabilizer.

EXPERIMENTS THAT WENT AWRY

Not every secret weapon dreamed up by wartime scientists bore the mark of genius. In fact, many sure-fire "war winners" were positively foolish or dangerous, and some even violated elementary laws of physics.

A few novel weapons that were essentially good went bad through minor but insuperable faults. The Italian motorboat at left was designed to be loaded with explosives and then aimed at an Allied ship; but the pilot had to jump overboard before the boat reached its target, and the Germans scrapped the weapon because in choppy waters it could not hold a steady course without him. The asymmetric BV141 reconnaissance plane *(pages 170-171)* proved aerodynamically sound in test flights. But the Luftwaffe rejected it because its wacky shape unnerved pilots, who insisted it should not be able to fly.

Other weapons were more fundamentally flawed. A huge German glider designed to airlift troops and whole tanks silently during an invasion proved so ungainly that it defied almost every scheme for getting it aloft. The British developed a vertical flamethrower to roast Axis bombers that attacked British merchant ships. However, tests revealed that high-speed bombers passed straight through the column of fire unharmed—exactly as any child who had ever run his fingers through a candle flame might have predicted.

The line separating inspiration from disaster was rarely clear, except in hindsight. Even radar—arguably the most significant scientific breakthrough of the War—might not have been developed but for a certain madness. The scientists who conceived it initially entertained hopes of perfecting a death-ray weapon—one that would kill by focusing radio waves on a target—only to discover that the rays bounced off without doing damage. A British scheme to electrocute German invaders by laying high-tension cables along the seabed would have required enough energy to set the sea aboil before a single wading soldier had been killed. But other anti-invasion schemes, such as one for setting fire to the English Channel *(right)*, might well have worked had not the shifting tide of the War rendered them superfluous.

A German pilot test-drives an Italian explosives-laden motorboat. The pilot was supposed to leap from the craft 500 feet from its target.

A British flamethrower (top) demonstrates its destructive power on land, while others—emplaced to defend Britain's Channel ports against an expected German invasion—raise billows of flame and smoke at sea.

A GERMAN GLIDER TOO HEAVY TO TOW

The German transport glider Gigant was —well, gigantic. It measured more than 180 feet across, had as much floor space as a railway flatcar and could load cannon, trucks and tanks through its nose.

But the bulky glider proved devilishly hard to get off the ground. The bomber first used to tow it overheated; then three fighters tried lifting it together, only to crash in a tangle of cables.

At last two bombers fused like Siamese twins solved the problem, at least in the-

ory. But with other projects getting priority, only 12 twins were built—not enough to keep the 200 gliders flying. Finally, six engines were added to the Gigants themselves. That made them workable but no longer gliders, and they finished the War ingloriously carrying supplies to the Russian and North African fronts.

A prototype Gigant dwarfs the crewmen wheeling it out on a two-ton undercarriage, which was jettisoned once the craft was airborne. With a length of 93 feet, the Gigant was the largest glider produced in the War.

A four-engined Junkers-90 bomber tows the Gigant during an early test flight. The glider carried rockets under its wings to provide extra thrust during takeoff; even so, the bomber pilots often reported that they could barely maintain flying speed while lugging the giant.

Twin-engined fighters in a V formation combine to pull a Gigant harnessed to them by 300-foot-long steel cables. Many wrecks occurred because straining fighters stalled and the cables failed to disconnect.

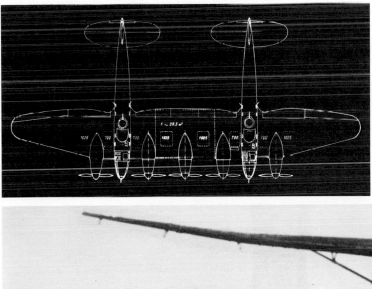

A Gigant trails behind two Heinkel-111 bombers united in a single plane especially for towing the glider. The twins had a fifth engine where the wings joined (inset); the pilot sat in the left cockpit, the copilot in the right.

Like some prehistoric creature, the converted Gigant struggles into the air under its own power. As a six-engined transport it could carry an 88mm antiaircraft gun with crew and ammunition or 120 fully equipped infantrymen and weighed nearly 50 tons when loaded.

THE WILD RIDES
OF A RIDERLESS WHEEL

Perhaps no weapon tested in World War II proved to be as intractably bad-tempered as the Great Panjandrum, a giant, rocket-powered spool designed to blast through Germany's coastal defenses in Normandy with two tons of high explosives in its axle.

In fact, the Panjandrum showed such ill will toward its Allied inventors that the German Army was spared its wrath.

Panjandrum test runs were spectacular and unpredictable occasions, for even a minor crater could throw the wheel off course at its cruising speed of 60 miles per hour. Worse still, the rockets around its rims tended to break loose and shriek across the sand. Time after time the Pan-jandrum roared down the ramp of a landing craft, plowed through the sea and careered wildly out of control.

The monster misbehaved to the end. No expedient seemed able to guarantee speed, control, and protection from the rockets all at once. The Panjandrum ran amok for the last time during its eighth test, chasing some of its terrified masters over a small ridge and into barbed wire.

British scientists and officers stand by the Great Panjandrum before its first test, in southwest England, on September 7, 1943. Eighteen rockets were too weak to push it up the beach, and the number had to be doubled not once but twice in later tests.

Smoking away, the Panjandrum launches itself (top) down a ramp into the sea and plows toward shore (middle) during the final test. After a rocket clamp broke loose, the weapon tilted (bottom) and chased the spectators, the photographer included. It headed back for the sea but crashed en route.

AN AIRCRAFT CARRIER MADE OF ICE CUBES

One of the wackiest secret weapons was the vessel *Habbakuk,* the brainchild of Englishman Geoffrey Pyke. The name was inspired by a Biblical prophet who promised "a work which you will not believe, though it be told you."

Pyke named his vessel well. His idea was to use a mixture of ice and wood pulp, called Pykrete (Pyke's concrete), to build Britain cheap, easily assembled and bad-

ly needed aircraft carriers. Pykrete itself strained credibility. It could be hewed and hammered like wood, was as strong as concrete and, though roughly 90 per cent ice, was amazingly slow to melt. It made a believer of Winston Churchill when he tested a chunk of it in his bathtub and it refused to melt.

Plans called for the *Habbakuk* to be 2,000 feet long and displace a staggering 1.8 million tons of water—26 times the displacement of the liner *Queen Elizabeth.* The 50-foot-thick walls of the cavernous hull would enclose quarters, hangars, an

immense refrigeration plant and some 20 electric motors for power.

But further research made the task look more and more difficult—and expensive. To make and assemble the nearly 280,000 Pykrete blocks in one "bergship" would have taken 8,000 men eight months of work in arctic temperatures and would have cost an estimated $70 million. Before matters reached that pass, the need for carriers lessened, and the *Habbakuk* finally melted not at sea but on the back burner of British Combined Operations Headquarters without ever reaching completion.

COMBINED OPERATIONS HEADQUARTERS

"H A B B A K

The cutaway drawing at bottom shows a cross section of the vessel Habbakuk from the ship's hull (left) to its deck (right). The 190-foot-high Habbakuk appears in profile at left alongside the Illustrious, the largest of Britain's contemporary aircraft carriers, which barely reaches the bergship's waterline.

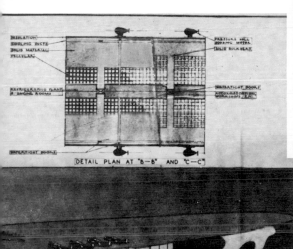

Canadian workmen build a model of the Habbakuk on Patricia Lake in Ontario. The model, put together from ice blocks in just two months by 15 men, was 60 feet long, 30 feet wide and weighed 1,100 tons.

The roofed-in model of the Habbakuk floats on the calm waters of Patricia Lake after completion in early 1943. The model was disguised to look like a boathouse in order to keep the bergship project secret.

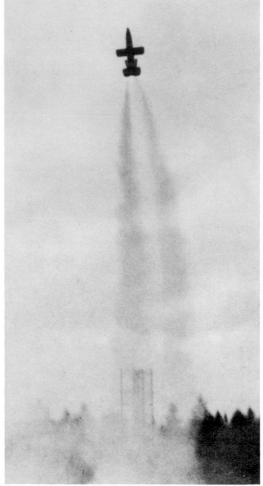

German technicians (left) prepare a Natter interceptor for a test launch from an airfield near Saint Leonhard, Austria. In flight (above), the spunky little fighter plane reached a top speed of 670 miles per hour at 16,400 feet and had a maximum range of 36 miles.

BOLD IDEAS TOO LATE TO HELP

The same rapid change in the tide of the War that swamped the *Habbakuk* brought other novel weapons to the surface—especially defensive weapons for Germany. The rocket-propelled Natter (*above and left*) combined simple construction and cheap materials with a rather bizarre recovery scheme. The pilot was to fire the 24 rockets in the nose at enemy planes and detach the forward section, ejecting himself; pilot and engine—the two most valuable parts of the weapon—would then float to earth by separate parachutes.

The futuristic flying wing shown at right was at first rejected as too radical; when it began to look better, there was no time to develop it.

The Horten V experimental flying wing, a jet-powered version of a glider, cuts the air during tests over Germany (left). The midsection below—seen from the rear, with the unfinished cockpit located between two eyelike jet engines—belonged to a Horten IX, a flying-wing fighter under construction when the War ended. It had a maximum speed of more than 600 mph at nearly 40,000 feet.

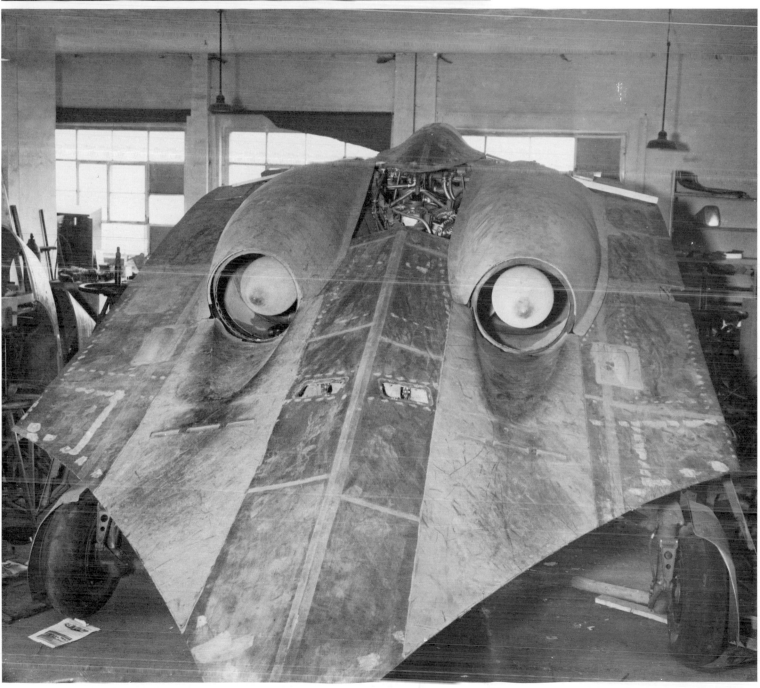

An American officer stands in front of a captured German sound cannon, a dream weapon intended to translate explosions of oxygen and methane into killing noise.

An antiaircraft wind gun crooks into the sky at the Hillersleben Proving Grounds near Stuttgart, Germany. The wind gun—which was emplaced on the Elbe River, though it was never used—took its limited power from an explosive mixture of oxygen and hydrogen.

LAST-DITCH EFFORTS THAT FAILED

Some last-ditch German weapons were not just offbeat or futuristic but plain silly as well. Such was the mine-clearing tank, a 130-ton monstrosity so heavy it could clear mines by rolling over them and ab-sorbing the blasts—but too heavy to cross most bridges or use ordinary roads.

German scientists hoped other weapons would enlist the forces of nature on the side of the Reich. The sound cannon consisted of a pair of parabolic reflectors that the Germans claimed could focus enough sound pressure to kill enemy soldiers 180 feet away—providing the soldiers were so heedless as to stay in the same place for 30 or 40 seconds.

The wind gun was supposed to blast enemy bombers out of the sky with a high-pressure plug of wind. German scientists proudly claimed it could break a one-inch board at 600 feet; targeted on aluminum bombers at 10 times that range, however, it had no effect.

American officers examine a German rifle with a detachable 90-degree barrel for shooting around corners. The Wehrmacht hoped that the curved barrel and its special sight—shown on the table at far left—would enable soldiers to defend buildings and even tanks.

A GI reaches for the top of a captured German mine-clearer. The huge armored vehicle was more than 50 feet long and 13 feet tall; it detonated mines by the sheer weight of its 130 tons, impervious to the consequences.

5

For sheer audacity, few undertakings of the secret war could match the hoaxes that were staged in the name of patriotism. Nations on both sides of the conflict expended untold energy and inventiveness not just on ferreting out the enemy's plans, but on deliberately deceiving him, in small ways and large. At one end of the spectrum was the spy who was independently such a master of deception that it was sometimes difficult for even his employers to detect where his sympathies lay. At the other extreme were government agencies that synchronized the actions of thousands to perpetrate a hoax on a grand scale.

In the opinion of Lieut. Commander Ewen Montagu of British Naval Intelligence, one of the War's grandest deceptions lies buried beneath a simple white marble tombstone in the old fishing town of Huelva, Spain, on the Gulf of Cádiz. The tombstone marks the grave of one William Martin, son of John and Antonia Martin of Cardiff, Wales. He is the same William Martin who appears in the casualty list of the London *Times* of June 4, 1943, as "Captain (Acting Major) William Martin, Royal Marines." And he is also the William Martin whose departure from London for Allied Forces Headquarters, North Africa, is noted in a top-secret German intelligence report of May 15, 1943.

To German intelligence, the major was an expert in the deployment of naval landing craft, a trusted aide to Lord Louis Mountbatten on the Combined Operations staff, an overdrawn depositor at Lloyd's Bank of London, and a lover of the good life and of a Wiltshire girl. Montagu and a small group of British intelligence officers in London knew better. To them, the major's most interesting feature was that he did not exist.

The role that the man called Major William Martin played was written and directed by Montagu himself. Montagu, who had been trained in the law, approached intelligence work with the precision of an attorney and the artistry of a painter before canvas. Indeed, he liked to use the word "artistic" to describe a particularly brilliant stroke of deception. And he was a virtuoso of dissimulation.

In the winter of 1942-1943, Montagu was attached to an interservice committee charged with liaison between a number of agencies that were mounting the forthcoming Allied invasion of Sicily. The question in everyone's mind was how to make the Germans believe the blow would fall

GRAND DELUSIONS

somewhere else—a formidable task, as Churchill observed, when "anybody but a damn fool would *know* that it was Sicily." One immediate answer was to employ the old espionage tactic of tricking the enemy by delivering falsified papers into his hands. The problem was how to deliver those papers.

Montagu remembered a bizarre suggestion that had recently been proposed for some other mission only to be discarded as farfetched. Now, as Montagu imagined the scenario, that idea suddenly seemed a possibility. "Why," he asked, "shouldn't we get a body, disguise it as a staff officer, and give him really high-level papers which will show clearly that we are going to attack somewhere else?" The corpse could be planted in the waters off some likely coast so that it would float ashore and look as if the man had been the victim of an air crash at sea.

As soon as Montagu got provisional committee approval for his plot, he called on the British pathologist Sir Bernard Spilsbury to inquire into some of the facts of life and death. Spilsbury told him over a glass of sherry at a London club that only a pathologist of enormous skill could detect that a corpse washed up on a beach had been dead before it touched the water. Much encouraged, Montagu dubbed his project Operation *Mincemeat*, and with his associates set about hunting for a suitable corpse.

Ironically, even in wartime London this proved a difficult assignment, because Montagu could hardly tell a family in the throes of bereavement—much less could he publicize—the purpose he had in mind. "There we were surrounded all too often by dead bodies," wrote Montagu in his postwar account of the project, "but none that we could take." Eventually he obtained from a London coroner the corpse of a man in his early thirties who had died of pneumonia, and hence had lungs conveniently full of a fluid that could be mistaken for sea water.

With the corpse in cold storage, Montagu worked out its last adventure. Because the Germans were known to have a highly active intelligence agent working near the port of Huelva, Montagu's group decided that the corpse should be transported there in a submarine and set afloat in the town's offshore fishing grounds. The prevailing southwesterly winds of April would almost certainly carry the corpse to the beach. Montagu was confident that the presence of a dead British officer on Spanish soil would quickly become known to German intelligence.

In determining what information should be supplied to the Germans, Montagu and his associates kept in mind two classic intelligence dicta: First, the enemy should be forced to work out for himself the false story being fed him, and second, that story should confirm suspicions already present in the enemy's mind. Reasoning that false hints would be convincing only if they came from an unimpeachable source, Montagu persuaded General Sir Archibald Nye, Vice Chief of the Imperial General Staff, to write a phony "old-boy" letter to his friend, General Harold Alexander, who was commanding the British forces fighting in northwest Africa.

"My dear Alex," the letter began, "I am taking advantage of sending you a personal letter by hand of one of Mountbatten's officers, to give you the inside history of our recent exchange of cables about Mediterranean operations and their attendant cover plans." The letter went on to hint that Sicily was going to be leaked as a cover target for something bigger. Implied but never stated was the suggestion that General Nye was referring to projected operations against Sardinia, Corsica and Greece.

Next, Montagu had to give the corpse a name and rank, and a mission to explain its presence off the coast of Spain. He decided on Captain (Acting Major) William Martin, Royal Marines, as a name sufficiently commonplace and a rank sufficiently middling not to attract undue attention. He assigned the major to the Combined Operations staff so that he could be a landing-craft expert en route to North Africa to join the staff of Admiral Sir Andrew B. Cunningham, Commander in Chief of the Mediterranean fleet.

Martin carried a letter of introduction to Cunningham from Combined Operations Chief Lord Louis Mountbatten, in which Mountbatten mentioned that the major had with him a "very urgent" letter from General Nye to General Alexander that was "too hot to go by signal." Mountbatten stressed that he would appreciate having Martin back "as soon as the assault is over," adding: "He might bring some sardines with him." Montagu was particularly proud of this last touch because he correctly guessed that the Germans would construe the mention of sardines as a labored reference to Sardinia.

Montagu and his associates then gave their man a personality, and documents to go with it. He would be newly engaged to a girl named Pam, they decided, and would have with him a bill for a diamond ring from S. J. Phillips of Bond Street, two love letters from Pam ("Darling, why did we go and meet in the middle of a war?" ran a line from one) and a snapshot of a girl in a bathing suit, posed for by a cooperative employee of the War Office. The major was fond of a good time (as evidenced by two tickets to a London show and an invitation to join the Cabaret Club) and was somewhat careless with his money (a letter from Lloyd's Bank informed him that he was overdrawn by 79 pounds, 19 shillings and twopence). Letters from the major's father and the family lawyer confirmed the major's engagement (his Edwardian father disapproved) and discussed the advisability of making a will.

It was essential that the Spanish authorities not overlook the major's documents. To be sure they did not, British intelligence provided him with a stout, locked briefcase that would be chained to the belt of his trench coat in the manner of bank messengers. The coat itself was part of a standard Royal Marines outfit, with badges of rank on the shoulders, and under it went a worn Royal Marines battle dress and used underwear—with the laundry marks removed lest German intelligence scour the major's background too thoroughly. Over the coat went a life jacket to make it appear that when the man went into the water he had expected to be picked up.

Dressing the corpse was one of the more ghoulish aspects of the undertaking. Montagu and his helpers discovered that to put the shoes on the corpse they first had to thaw its feet with an electric heater and then refreeze them. Furnishing the major with a photograph for his identity card proved to be an even more difficult task. "I defy anyone," wrote Montagu, "to take a photograph of someone who is dead and to make it look as if he could conceivably be alive." Then, by a stroke of luck, at a meeting he attended, Montagu spotted a man "who might have been the twin brother of the corpse," and persuaded the look-alike to sit for a photograph.

With that last testament to his identity, Major Martin was packed in dry ice in a canister labeled "Optical Instruments," trucked north to Greenock, Scotland, and loaded aboard the submarine *Seraph*. Twelve days later, at 4:30 on the morning of April 30, 1943, the *Seraph* surfaced a mile off the mouth of the Huelva river. The major was taken out of his canister and, after a brief, impromptu prayer service, he was consigned to the sea and the mercies of German intelligence.

Before the day was over British intelligence received the welcome news that Major William Martin had reached his destination. The information came in the form of an excited message from the British Naval Attaché in Madrid, who had learned it from the British Vice Consul at Huelva: The corpse of a British officer had been found by a Spanish fisherman. (Neither the consul nor the attaché was aware of the plot.)

Prompted by intelligence officers, the Naval Attaché in Madrid now explained to the Spaniards that the major had been carrying a black official briefcase that must quickly be returned intact. Pleading bureaucratic formalities, the Spanish authorities kept the briefcase for two weeks. When it finally was returned and forwarded to London, British intelligence officers saw to their satisfaction that its contents had been tampered with; although the envelopes containing vital letters were sealed, microscopic examination showed

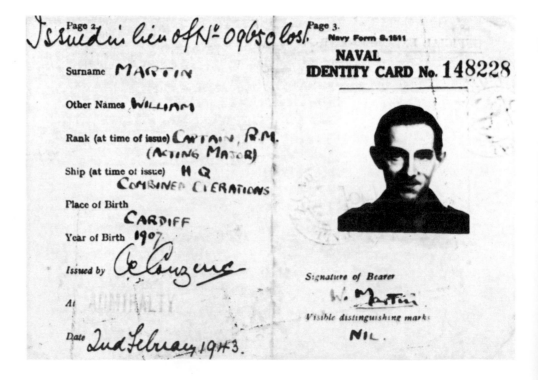

This faked identity card helped ensure the success of Operation Mincemeat, in which a dead body was used to distract the Germans from the forthcoming invasion of Sicily. "I doubt whether any 'crime' has ever been more meticulously prepared," crowed the British intelligence officer who masterminded the plot.

that the creases in the letter did not match the original folds. Montagu was certain that the letters had been photographed by the local German agent and that the copies had been sent on to Berlin (and records uncovered many years later proved him right).

"The genuineness of the captured documents is above suspicion," declared a report of May 14, 1943, to Admiral Karl Dönitz, Commander in Chief of the German Navy. Dönitz observed in his diary that Hitler himself was convinced of the authenticity of the documents, and largely as a result the Führer ruled out Sicily as the Allies' major invasion target.

Montagu did not have to wait for uncovered documents to see the effects of his hoax. In the early days of June, Axis reinforcements—some of them drawn from Sicily—were rushed to Corsica, Sardinia and Greece. The 1st Panzer Division raced across Europe from France to set up headquarters in the Greek town of Tripolis, from which it could oppose landings on the peninsula.

In the meantime, Major Martin was buried in Huelva with full military honors, and with a graveside wreath from his family and Pam. The British Vice Consul in Huelva, who was still in the dark himself, earnestly sent the family a photograph of a Spanish Naval party firing a formal salute over the grave.

Throughout the saga of Major Martin, noted Ewen Montagu, the guiding principle was to determine not how an Englishman would react to a situation, but how a German intelligence officer would see it. The aim was to assimilate so thoroughly the assumptions on which the enemy operated that "you were able to put yourself into his mind." The fictions piled upon fictions, the brilliantly elaborated details of character and circumstance were all developed with this hypothetical German in mind.

As the War progressed, hoaxes became more varied and more sophisticated, and so did the skill of the men who perpetrated them. On both sides, the demands made upon intelligence agencies grew as the War accelerated—the Allied appetite whetted by increasing success, and the German appetite by a desperate need to discover what was going wrong.

In the annals of the secret war, most hoaxers remained as anonymous as the man whose corpse became Major Martin, and as the agents who labored with Lieut. Commander Montagu to carry out that deception. Here and there, however, some spies gained notoriety—under their code names if not their real names. Among them were Cicero, Max and Josephine, who spied—or purported to spy—for the Germans, and the Grand Chef, Lucy and Ramsay, who served the Russians. Their motives varied from the mercenary to the idealistic. In some instances it appears they duped the very governments that employed them; in others they were tricked themselves. But without exception they were persuasive dissemblers.

One of the most celebrated agents on either side was the man known as Cicero, actually an Albanian by the name of Elyesa Bazna.

Bazna was a born confidence man. In the course of his 40 years he had been a petty criminal, a locksmith, a fireman, a taxi driver, and finally valet for a succession of foreign diplomats in Turkey. His career as a spy began in late 1943, when he joined the household of the British Ambassador to Turkey, Sir Hughe Knatchbull-Hugessen, an urbane and circumspect diplomat who for relaxation played the piano and composed satirical couplets about the Foreign Office. Apparently acting independently, and certainly indulging a taste for riches and adventure, Bazna used his position with his new employer to gain access to top-secret documents.

Sir Hughe kept his most secret documents in a black dispatch box in his bedroom. One morning, while the Ambassador was in the bathtub, Bazna helped himself to the keys to the dispatch box from a bedside table and made wax impressions of them. With keys made from the impressions, he later removed some of the documents, carried them to his quarters beneath the stairs and photographed them with a Leica camera by the light of a 100-watt bulb. He then offered the photographs to the German Embassy. Bazna's asking price was a princely £20,000 for the first two rolls of 26 exposures each, and £15,000 for every roll of film thereafter.

Tempted but wary, the Germans decided to test Bazna. They accepted one roll of the 35mm film from him at a nighttime meeting held in the garden tool shed of the German Embassy. Examination of the film convinced them that Bazna had access to the incoming and outgoing message file of the British Embassy. The photographs, as Bazna's German Embassy contact Ludwig Moyzisch noted, revealed documents that "a secret-service agent might dream about for a lifetime." The Germans promptly took Bazna on as an agent.

Over the next six months, Bazna delivered a steady flow of telegrams and documents photographed from the traffic passing back and forth between Ankara and the British Foreign Office in London. In recognition of this prodigious flow of messages, he was given the code name Cicero—for the eloquent Roman orator of that name.

As eagerly as they took his information, the Germans never fully trusted Cicero. They wondered how an amateur working alone could photograph documents so perfectly by the light of a single 100-watt bulb, and they questioned how someone with his limited fluency in English and scant knowledge of war strategy could select important documents so quickly and so unerringly. They concluded that either he must be working with others, or he was himself a trained agent. Yet the Germans continued to pay Cicero, because the material he supplied was so persuasive. Among his offerings were documents showing British efforts to press Turkey into the War on the Allied side, accounts of top-secret Allied staff talks at Teheran, and an advance warning of an air raid that the Royal Air Force was to make on Sofia the following January.

For these and other nuggets of intelligence, the Germans provided Bazna with a generous supply of British bank notes. For a time, he kept his accumulating currency under the carpet in his room at the British Ambassador's residence because he enjoyed the sensation of treading on money.

Eventually, as his hoard mounted to more than £300,000, he adopted the more conventional practice of stowing it in a safe-deposit box.

It is unclear whether the Germans' suspicions were correct or not. The information Bazna handed over to the Germans was of great interest but was not so momentous that it would alter the course of the War. To Ludwig Moyzisch, an attaché of the German Security Department in Ankara, the most noteworthy aspect of the documents was the impression they gave of "the determination as well as the ability of the Allies to destroy the Third Reich." Perhaps that was the message the British wanted to convey—if, in fact, Bazna was operating as a double agent. The British government declines to say.

In his own postwar account, Bazna gives no hint that he was working for anyone but himself. He had to abandon his spying activities and disappear for fear of being apprehended, he says, after Moyzisch's secretary defected to the Americans in April 1944. With his newly acquired wealth, he began to live in the style to which he thought he was entitled. He left his wife and four children, took a fashionable mistress and moved into a lavish hotel suite in the Turkish resort town of Bursa. After the War he won contracts to build a new school and a post office in Istanbul and, as he gained prominence, received invitations to dine with government officials. He was planning to construct "the most exclusive spa hotel in Turkey" when his bank called with cruel news: The fortune the Germans had given him was largely in counterfeit bills.

Wiped out and hounded by creditors, Bazna indignantly sued the government of West Germany, but to no avail. He lived in a cramped alley in Istanbul until 1971, selling

used automobiles and giving singing lessons. Elyesa Bazna died penniless—a victim of the confidence game that he had tried to play.

Quite a different sort of hoax attended a legendary spy known only as Max—a man so elusive that he has never been even tentatively identified. Max fed the Germans intelligence directly from within the walls of the nearly impenetrable Kremlin—or did he?

Max makes his appearance in the annals of espionage shortly after the German invasion of the Soviet Union in June 1941. For White Russians—the heirs and spiritual kin of the czarist regime that the Communist revolution had overthrown more than two decades before—the invasion seemed to promise hope, and some sought to exploit it. By a roundabout route now untraceable, one White Russian alerted the Germans to the existence of an informant inside the Kremlin. The Abwehr welcomed the tip, and recruited an agent named Fritz Kauders to deal with the mysterious contact, who was designated Max.

Kauders himself was an elusive Viennese. Before the War he had lived on the fringes of society, operating as a sports journalist in Zurich, Paris, Berlin and Budapest, but filling his pockets through currency transactions on the black market. By all accounts he was a plausible liar with a talent for making friends in high places. His most fruitful contact had been with the American consul in Zagreb, Yugoslavia—who had relied on him for help in buying antiques, and from whom Kauders had stolen documents that he sold to the Germans.

The Abwehr installed Kauders in a villa in Sofia, Bulgaria—the neutral capital that was closest to the Soviet Union, and the site of a large Soviet embassy. Almost from the beginning of his new assignment, Kauders elicited from Max a steady stream of messages that astounded German intelligence by their knowledge of decisions at the highest levels of Soviet power. Max radioed accounts of Allied military councils in Moscow at which both overall strategy and tactics were discussed. He described planned attacks and diversionary tactics, and he detailed troop movements: "On June 2 one rifle division, one artillery regiment, one medium tank regiment coming out of Astrakhan arrived in Tikhoretsk, supposedly going on toward Rostov."

The message that made Max famous was one he radioed on November 4, 1942, revealing decisions taken by Stalin and his military council that very day. The Soviets had decided, he reported, that four major winter offensives must be launched along the German Eastern Front by the 15th of November. These would be directed at German strong points in the Caucasus, at Voronezh in the Don River area, at Rzhev northwest of Moscow and south of Lake Ilmen, and at Leningrad. Troops for the offensives would be called up from reserves.

German Army Intelligence had already discerned that the Soviets were preparing a counteroffensive, and Max's information did nothing to tip the balance in the Germans' favor; before the end of the year the Russians had gained the upper hand over the Germans along the Eastern Front. But the promptness and the accuracy of Max's intelligence made the Abwehr think that in Max they had a man with a sure line to the highest circles in the Soviet Union. He became an overnight celebrity at German headquarters; soon his admirers in the High Command were checking to see what Max had said each day. Even Abwehr chief Wilhelm Canaris was paying attention.

As Max's presence was increasingly felt, questions about his identity inevitably arose—and, when they remained unanswered, the questions begat rumors. Some rumors depicted Max as a doctor attending Stalin, others as a Rumanian who had managed to tap the Kremlin telephones, still others as the confidant of a Japanese newspaperman who had contacts in Turkey.

Despite the multiplying rumors, the only Abwehr officer who evidenced suspicion was Colonel Otto Wagner, who was himself stationed in Sofia. Wagner determined that Kauders was not radioing to Moscow at all, and confronted Kauders with his findings. Kauders was unperturbed; he replied that he communicated with Max indirectly, through the radio section of the Bulgarian police. When Wagner pressed him further, Kauders said he sent and received messages via agents aboard cutters off the coast of Turkey. Again Wagner investigated, and again he found no proof of Kauders' claims. He concluded that Kauders must be either a fraud or a double agent or both—and conveyed as much to Canaris.

Canaris refused to be disenchanted. He doubted that Max

The dandy clutching a pair of gloves (near left) was known to German intelligence in Ankara as Cicero, an agent who sold them photographs of secret British documents; to British Ambassador Sir Hughe Knatchbull-Hugessen (far left), he was an Albanian valet named Elyesa Bazna. In April 1944 Bazna mysteriously bowed out of both roles. "Whether his greed for money was satisfied, or whether the work had become too dangerous even for him," said Cicero's German contact, "I do not know."

could have been totally fabricated by Kauders; the Max files were too knowing and too detailed for that. To quiet Wagner, Canaris agreed to have Kauders put under surveillance, but ordered that his work should not be interfered with. It was not—even by the Russians, who were curiously indifferent when they learned of Max's existence from British agents monitoring Kauders' transmissions to Berlin. The mysterious messages from Max continued to be funneled to Germany through Sofia almost daily until virtually the end of the War.

Was Max a source within the Soviet Embassy in Sofia leaking information to Kauders? Or was Kauders a Russian double agent, feeding the Germans enough information to pique their interest without giving away anything that would hurt the Russians? Although his reports appeared superficially to be crammed with detail, in fact they offered little significant data of use to field commanders. They failed, for example, to mention strategic maneuvers, such as the Soviet pincers attack on Stalingrad, which had proved to be a crucial factor in one of the four November offensives. Kauders himself seems to have vanished by War's end, and the answers to those questions vanished with him.

For sheer number of reports, Max is eclipsed by another code name among German spies: Josephine. No other German spy is so frequently mentioned in the more than 5,000 pages of the German High Command's war diary. Not only were the Josephine reports voluminous, but from June to August of 1943 German intelligence circles considered them indispensable to the planning of the Luftwaffe's bombing campaigns against England.

Josephine's reports came to the Abwehr via a tall, good-looking young German lawyer named Karl-Heinz Krämer. Krämer was a natural entrepreneur with a taste for power and intrigue, and a gift for charming women; he kept a number of mistresses, apparently more for what information they could provide than for romance. He had joined the Nazi Party while a student at the University of Hamburg in 1937. When war broke out, he was drafted into the armed forces and soon assigned to intelligence work at the Abwehr post in Hamburg. After stints in Istanbul, the Low Countries and Budapest, he was transferred in 1942 to Stockholm, a choice listening post because as the capital of a resolutely neutral nation it had travelers of all nationalities passing through it regularly.

Krämer had not been there long before he was furnishing the Abwehr with fascinating reports on Allied invasion intentions, the organization of the Royal Air Force and Allied aircraft production. The data came from sources that Krämer code-named Hector, Siegfried A, Siegfried B and Josephine. Josephine was the most prolific and the most accurate of the lot.

Krämer's sources enabled him to send an enormous amount of material to Berlin; in 1943 alone he sent almost 1,000 reports on numerous aspects of the Allied war effort. He told about Allied bombing policy, about the arrival in British waters of American convoys, about the disposition of munitions depots in England, and about the Allied decision in 1943 not to risk an invasion of the Continent until the consequences of the strategic-bombing campaign over Germany were known. So accurate and detailed were the reports that it sometimes seemed that Krämer—or Jose-

At a lake in Austria in 1959, a diver loads a boat with bogus money—a fraction of the £140 million printed by the Reich between 1942 and 1945, and thrown out at the War's end. The hoax had a double purpose—to undermine the British economy (a goal that failed) and to pay Abwehr agents in neutral countries (a dirty trick that succeeded in deceiving a spy or two).

phine—had penetrated the British Ministries of Air, Supply, and Aircraft Production, perhaps even the headquarters of Churchill himself.

But who was Josephine? When his curious superiors at Abwehr headquarters queried him, Krämer resolutely refused to say. He intimated that all of his sources were people in high places. Undoubtedly some of them were. But Krämer also relied on Swedish airport employees, and on sailors plying the route between Sweden and Britain. When the Abwehr pressed him to disclose his sources, Krämer threatened to resign.

One hint of Josephine's identity comes from British intelligence. In 1943 the British had discovered that secret information was being leaked through Sweden, and had traced some of the leaks to two men—Major S. E. Cornelius and Count J. G. Oxenstjerna, Sweden's Air and Naval Attachés in London. As trusted officers of a neutral nation, both had access to much British military information, which they passed on to the Swedish Defense Ministry in Stockholm. One of Krämer's mistresses was a secretary at that ministry. Could she have been the conduit for the information that Cornelius and Oxenstjerna relayed from London? No one could prove it.

Late in 1943, British intelligence agents of the Double Cross Committee began feeding the two Swedish attachés credible but inaccurate information; one item had to do with a fictitious diplomatic mission to Moscow to plan an Anglo-Russian invasion of Norway. Soon thereafter the Abwehr noticed that the Josephine reports were becoming less accurate. As doubts about Josephine and Krämer set in, German intelligence decided to test Krämer by inventing a British aircraft plant north of Worcester and asking him to provide information about it. Krämer obliged with a report from Josephine that the plant employed 2,000 workers and manufactured Napier-Sabre motors for Typhoons, British fighter-bombers.

That false step was followed by others. In June 1944 Krämer told the Abwehr that eight airborne divisions had been formed in the United States; the Germans learned there were only five. In October he asserted that the U.S. Fourteenth Army would be arriving in France; no such army existed. Together these mistakes largely discredited Krämer in the eyes of the Abwehr, yet try as it would the Abwehr

could not prove his reports a hoax. For a time his suspicious superiors had him shadowed in an effort to discover his sources, but Krämer covered his tracks too well. "He would not do anything during the day," recalled German Intelligence Chief Walter Schellenberg after the War. "But maybe a couple of times a week he would go out to some party, and he always knew how to disappear for three or four hours and then the next morning he would be back and start dictating."

The lapses notwithstanding, Krämer remained in Stockholm until April 1945. He returned to Germany when the Reich was in its death throes and there was captured by the British, who took him to England and placed him in a maximum-security prison. But the British, despite repeated interrogations, were no better able to pin Krämer down on his sources than the Germans had been.

Once a spy came under suspicion, he had to rely on his own fast thinking and fast talking to survive. For many a spy that meant switching allegiance—a course that was neither uncommon nor surprising, for in the world of institutionalized deception few loyalties are binding or likely to endure. But one spy in particular shifted allegiance with a finesse that astonished men and women who had known him for years and left history baffled. He was Leopold Trepper, a Soviet agent whom the Nazis captured in German-occupied Paris in 1942.

Trepper had every reason to hate the Nazis. He was a Polish Jew who had left school as a teenager in 1920 to work in the iron mines of Silesia, in southwest Poland. The working conditions there were oppressive, and Trepper was drawn to the Communist Party because it appeared to promise a better future for working-class people like himself, and for Jews.

As a member of the Communist Party, Trepper quickly became involved in espionage, and as a naturally gifted conspirator he rose in the ranks. By July of 1940 he was in France and was known as the *Grand Chef,* or Great Chief; he was senior field officer of the French section of what the Germans called the Red Orchestra. This was a mammoth Soviet spy apparatus that had networks flung out over virtually every country of Europe; one of them had even infiltrated the German High Command. Seven networks existed in

France alone, all of them under Trepper's direction. His spies penetrated high places and low; one of them worked in the Wehrmacht's Central Billeting Office in Paris and provided information about the deployment of German forces in France.

But the very extensiveness of Trepper's apparatus jeopardized it, and somebody spied on the master spy himself. Trepper was seized by German agents as he sat in a dentist's chair in Paris on November 24, 1942. Trepper took his arrest with the aplomb befitting a *Grand Chef*. "Bravo!" he told his captors. "You've done your work well." And, as he was being led away, Trepper offered to collaborate. Asked to demonstrate his good faith, he picked up the phone, called Hillel Katz, his assistant, and told him to meet the *Grand Chef* at the Madeleine station of the Metro, Paris' subway. When Katz arrived, he too was arrested: "We must work with these gentlemen," Trepper told him impassively. "The game is up."

Having become a turncoat, Trepper worked as energetically for the Germans against the Russians as he had formerly worked for the Russians against the Germans. He told the Abwehr in detail the principles on which the Red Orchestra operated. Command was decentralized so that few agents (except of course Trepper himself) could identify the others. Agents were required to live in the suburbs, where surveillance by the enemy could be more easily detected than in the cities. Messages were transmitted by marking public-telephone directories and by sending postcards—not letters—because postcards are so open that they arouse no suspicions.

That was not all; Trepper helped the Germans seize dozens of Red Orchestra agents—or "violinists," as they were called—all over France. The important captured agents were given the choice of continuing with the Red Orchestra—but now under German direction, to feed back false intelligence to the Russians, after the fashion of Operation *Double Cross* in Britain—or of being executed. The rest were tried and sentenced. In exposing these agents, Trepper was uninhibited by past confidences; when a particular friend and aide, Leon Grossvogel, proved elusive, the *Grand Chef* turned over the name of Grossvogel's mistress, who eventually led the Gestapo to him. Grossvogel was tried, and sentenced to death.

To all appearances, Trepper lived out the rest of the War double-crossing the nation he had initially served. But after the War he gave that betrayal a surprising twist. He had not been a double agent, he avowed when he wrote his memoirs, but a triple agent. With Moscow's concurrence, Trepper claimed, he had divulged only such names and details of his own organization as were necessary to secure the trust of the Germans; he had tried to protect those persons within the French Orchestra whose work Moscow did not want obstructed.

Was Trepper telling the truth, or was he compounding the hoax? The conundrum must remain unsolved. Gestapo officer Heinz Pannwitz, who remembered watching Trepper at work, wrote: "When he thought he was not being observed, he looked very tough and distrustful, cold and aloof. The moment someone paid attention to him, his appearance changed and he became an actor playing a role. If someone pressed him with questions, he would put his hand on his heart in order to remind his listener that he had a heart condition." A good spy was nothing if not a consummate actor, and Trepper kept his true allegiance permanently locked in his ailing heart.

Though the Germans caught Trepper, and through him netted so many French "violinists," their seine did not reach as far as Switzerland. There one section of the Red Orchestra played on for another two years, with some deft performances by Rudolf Rössler, a German-born émigré who went by the code name Lucy.

Rössler was a small, middle-aged, mild-mannered man who looked, as his confederate Alexander Foote noted, "like almost anyone to be found on any suburban train almost anywhere in the world." He was born into a middle-class family in Bavaria, then served in the German Army during the First World War, and after that became editor of an Augsburg newspaper and an agitator for social reform. Rössler took a dim view of Hitler's rise to power, and in 1933, when he found the freedom of the press curtailed by the Nazi regime, he left Germany. Now a political refugee, Rössler settled in Lucerne—his code name may have been derived from his place of residence—where he established a small publishing company that produced anti-Nazi pamphlets.

When the War started in 1939, Rössler decided to put his anti-Nazi sentiments to work at espionage, and before long he found his way to the Red Orchestra. By the spring of 1943 he had become a full-fledged Soviet agent and by any reckoning a successful one. One British intelligence officer asserted that Rössler "must be ranked among the great spies of all time."

Rössler won that accolade for the great quantity of intelligence he produced. In regular transmissions that eventually added up to 12,000 typed pages, he reported on the Germans' development of jet planes and on the V-1 and V-2 missiles *(pages 156-169)*. Even more valuable to the Russians were the Lucy reports that were sent after the invasion of the Soviet Union. By means still not fully known, Rössler managed to give the Russians accurate reports on German High Command decisions in regard to the Eastern Front within 24 hours of the time those decisions were made. One German commander who led a successful assault on the Russian-held town of Lomza in northwest Poland was astonished to find a copy of his own attack orders when he occupied the enemy position. But even when that startling fact was reported to the German High Command, the Germans could not trace the leak.

Where then did Rössler's information come from? Not even his Russian contacts could guess. They knew only that he had four principal sources in Germany, and that they were code-named Werther, Teddy, Olga and Anna.

Rössler never betrayed his informants. But at least one of them must have been very highly placed in Germany. Without the collusion of powerful figures in the Abwehr or the German Army or both, hardly anyone could have transmitted such sensitive information as Rössler did for two years and gone unapprehended. A French account of the episode suggested that Rössler had been the "spiritual conscience" of a number of disaffected German generals, who found in Lucy a convenient instrument for thwarting Hitler's conquest.

Whoever Rössler's sources were, they did their work well as long as the Germans held the offensive in the Russia campaign. In December 1944 the war in the east turned against the German forces, and they retreated so rapidly that intelligence could neither predict nor keep pace with their move-

Eight staff members of the German Air Ministry gather around a table in Berlin in 1941. Seven of them were unaware of a leading Soviet agent in their midst—Harro Schulze-Boysen (second from left). The Red Orchestra, the spy network to which he belonged, infiltrated most other German government ministries and even the High Command.

ments. When that happened, Lucy ceased to exist, and Rössler dropped out of espionage for the remainder of the War. He died in Lucerne in 1958.

Of all the War's great deceivers, Russia's chief of espionage in Japan, Richard Sorge, operated the longest. He quietly and patiently assembled a small but effective spy ring that for eight years supplied the Soviet Union with a steady stream of information about the intentions and capabilities of the Japanese.

Sorge was a man of startling contrasts. The impression he gave, recalled a Soviet agent who had worked with him, was of "a very calm, cold-blooded man." Yet he retained to the end of his life a passionate, almost messianic faith in Communism and imminent world revolution. He could be emotional and reckless in his personal life; he often got very drunk, passing through stages that one friend described as "high spirits, tearful misery, aggressiveness, persecution mania, megalomania, delirium, semiconsciousness." Despite his excesses, Sorge was capable of remarkable self-control: When he smashed his motorcycle into a Tokyo wall one evening after swilling more than a bottle of whisky, he remained lucid and professional long enough to summon a confederate—to whom he could turn over coded documents he was carrying—before he lost consciousness.

This mass of contradictions was born in Russia of a Russian mother and a German father. Sorge grew up outside Berlin and served with distinction in the army of Kaiser Wilhelm II during World War I. Two severe wounds he received while fighting on the Eastern Front started Sorge questioning not only the logic of the War but the goals of the Kaiser's Germany. While recovering he read Karl Marx, and by the time he was demobilized he had become a dedicated Communist. His wounds left him with a permanent limp but did nothing to slow him down.

As a young student and Communist agitator in postwar Germany, Sorge proved so energetic that he came to the notice of the Comintern Intelligence Division, a branch of Soviet Military Intelligence that was then enlisting a carefully screened group of agents in the campaign to extend Comintern influence over Communist parties abroad. The Comintern invited Sorge to Moscow, and gave him special training in political and military espionage and in the use of codes and ciphers. He spent the next six years as a freelance writer in Scandinavia and China—simultaneously but inconspicuously serving the Soviet Union as a spy. In 1933 he went to Tokyo, and in 1936 he became a foreign correspondent for the German newspaper *Frankfurter Zeitung.* By then Sorge was one of the most valued agents in the service of Soviet Military Intelligence.

In Tokyo, Sorge applied himself diligently to learning all he could about his new venue. He collected a priceless library of more than 1,000 volumes of Japanese literature and history, and an equally priceless circle of friends. Among the latter were a Japanese newspaperman who had the ear of Prime Minister Prince Konoye, and Eugen Ott, German Ambassador to Japan. Sorge made such friends easily. He was a wit and a good companion, a man who could poke fun at the Nazis without offending party members.

A small number of Sorge's friends—only five—were agents he had hand-picked to assist him in spying for the Soviet Union. But Ambassador Ott was not privy to Sorge's secret life, and Sorge exploited his friendship with Ott to gain free access to the German Embassy. Unbeknownst to his host, he used that privilege to purloin and photograph telegrams and state documents.

Over the years Sorge sent Moscow a wealth of intelligence on subjects ranging from the activities of ultranationalist groups in Japan to the hierarchy of the Japanese Army and official Japanese estimates of Soviet forces stationed along the Siberian frontier. In the spring and summer of 1941 he transmitted two choice pieces of information. The first, in March, was a microfilm containing telegrams from German Foreign Minister Joachim von Ribbentrop in Berlin informing Ott of the proposed attack on the Soviet Union scheduled for the middle of June. The second, sent in mid-May, was a radio message giving Moscow the exact date of the attack, the 22nd of June.

Seldom did spies pick up such authoritative information as that, and Sorge naïvely expected plaudits from the Kremlin for his coup. Days passed, and he asked a friend in dismay, "Why has Stalin not reacted?" When on June 22 the Germans rolled into Russia as expected and his message still had not been acknowledged, Sorge wept.

He had a worse disappointment in store. The following autumn Sorge informed Moscow that the Japanese general staff had abandoned a plan to invade Siberia and would strike to the south instead. Sorge's accurate prediction of Japanese intentions helped the Soviet high command decide to send most of its two-million-man Siberian Army west to the defense of Moscow. Again he had every reason to congratulate himself. Ironically, just at this moment his spy ring was exposed through the arrest of a minor Communist functionary. Sorge was seized in a morning raid and taken still in his pajamas to the Tokyo jail. There he was visited by Ott: "Mr. Ambassador," said Sorge, "this is our last meeting." Ott was clearly distressed; he saluted his friend and departed.

During the long interrogation and trial that followed, Sorge insisted that he was not a spy, but an idealist hopeful of preserving peace between Japan and the Soviet Union. He confidently expected the Russians would secure his release or exchange. In fact, the Comintern seemed chiefly anxious to forget him. Richard Sorge met the fate for which every spy must be prepared. He was hanged at Sugamo Prison on November 7, 1944—betrayed by the cause to which he had devoted more than 20 years.

With betrayal and trickery so much a part of the secret war, the wonder is that any person or agency trusted another sufficiently for anything to be accomplished. But in fact the most crucial undertaking of the War depended on a superb-

ly synchronized combination of hoaxes that made the work of solo spies seem insignificant by comparison. The undertaking was the Allied invasion of Europe.

By the winter of 1943, both sides knew that an Allied invasion somewhere in Northern Europe was imminent, and both knew that much of its success or failure would depend on Germany's ability to predict when and where the blow would fall. To John Masterman and other chiefs of Allied intelligence, this was the moment for "the grand deception"—the "one great coup that would repay us many times over for all the efforts of the previous years."

Nobody underestimated the difficulties involved. Considering the huge forces enlisted in the invasion plan, some of the best minds in British and American intelligence doubted that either concealment or deception were possible. Yet as Churchill pointed out, there was little choice: The alternative to what he called "legerdemain" was likely to be "sheer slaughter."

In fact, planning for the monumental legerdemain codenamed Operation *Bodyguard* had already begun early in 1943, when 14 men met in a small conference room at Storey's Gate, Churchill's subterranean headquarters in Westminster. They constituted the command staff of the innocuously named London Controlling Section (LCS), which Churchill had established as a central bureau responsible for coordinating the deceptive operations revolving around *Bodyguard*.

Commanding the LCS were two English aristocrats, Colonel John Bevan and Lieut. Colonel Sir Ronald Wingate. Bevan had been decorated in the First World War, worked as a stockbroker afterward, and was serving as an intelligence officer in the Second. He was by both birth and marriage a member of the small, hereditary clique that virtually ruled England through family connections and alliances in the worlds of politics, diplomacy and finance. He and Churchill often sat together over brandy, recalled an LCS officer, and "pulled out what were all the old tricks of Eton and Harrow and polished them up for the task at hand."

Wingate came from a notable family; his father, General Sir F. Reginald Wingate, had been Pasha of Egypt and the Sudan, and an uncle was Governor of Malta. Wingate had learned the techniques of intrigue during years of service as a British political officer in the Arab nations. Under the two

Russian master spy Richard Sorge playfully flouts the command on a "Hands Off" sign in the garden of his Tokyo residence, from which he radioed secret information to the Soviet Union. Sorge's output was prodigious; in 1940 alone, he sent 30,000 coded messages to Moscow.

men, the LCS worked closely with all of the intelligence agencies in Britain and America, but most particularly with MI-6 and with MI-5 and the Double Cross Committee.

When Bevan, Wingate and their associates began work beneath the pavements of Westminster, the Allies had already decided to invade Europe by way of the Normandy beaches sometime in the spring of 1944. The object of Operation *Bodyguard* as conceived by the LCS was to make Hitler believe that the invasion could not possibly come before July, and that when it came it would be directed at Scandinavia, the Balkans, the Pas-de-Calais coast of France—anywhere but Normandy.

To this end, Operation *Bodyguard* engaged in some stunning deceptions. It used the men of the Double Cross Committee, which had honed its skills since its inception in 1941. It also deployed fake aircraft, landing craft, trucks, tanks and artillery, created nonexistent fleets and armies, simulated military wireless traffic and mounted diversionary hit-and-run raids. As with the calculated clues that were planted on the corpse of Major Martin in the Gulf of Cádiz, nothing was conveyed to the enemy directly; everything was leaked in thousands of bits and pieces that the Germans would presumably assemble into a catastrophically misbegotten jigsaw of Allied intent.

The two obvious targets for a cross-Channel invasion were the Pas-de-Calais coast and the Caen sector of the Normandy coast. At which target did the Germans expect the Allies to strike? Here Ultra interceptions—decodings of secret German wireless communications—proved essential. They revealed that virtually everyone of account in the German High Command, including Field Marshal Gerd von Rundstedt, commanding the armies in the west, believed that the crossing would occur at the narrowest section of the English Channel—and that the assault would open at the Pas-de-Calais, from which Allied landing craft could make the round trip to Dover most rapidly and over which fighter planes based in England could provide uninterrupted air cover. The Pas-de-Calais also provided the shortest access to the German industrial heartland of the Ruhr. Recognizing the vulnerability of the area, the Germans had made the Pas-de-Calais the most heavily fortified sector of their Atlantic Wall, the staggered line of steel-and-concrete strong points they had erected from the shores of Norway to the frontier of Spain.

Yet Allied intelligence also knew from Ultra interceptions that a number of German strategists were not convinced the Pas-de-Calais was the place to watch. Field Marshal Erwin Rommel, for one, suspected that only Normandy had the broad beaches a large-scale invasion would require. He recognized that the Allies would need to capture a major port quickly. The Pas-de-Calais had none that would qualify, but Normandy had an excellent port in Cherbourg and an adequate one in nearby Le Havre. Somehow, Allied intelligence realized, the doubters had to be persuaded that Normandy was not the target. And the deception must be so effective that even after the landings took place in Nor-

AN ACTOR IN A THEATER OF WAR

THE REAL GENERAL BERNARD L. MONTGOMERY

LIEUTENANT M. E. CLIFTON JAMES, IMPERSONATOR

The two steadfast lines of officers and the cheering crowd of Spanish civilians who greeted General Sir Bernard L. Montgomery at Gibraltar on May 26, 1944, would have been surprised to learn that they were honoring a fake. Montgomery was almost 1,000 miles away, in England. The man on the airstrip was Clifton James, an actor on the London stage. Just before D-Day he was engaged by Operation *Bodyguard* to impersonate Monty and was flown with much ado to the Mediterranean to add to Hitler's distractions.

How Hitler reacted to the news of Montgomery's presence in the Mediterranean is unrecorded. But James had learned his model's every quirk so well—the way he pinched his cheek when deep in thought, the long stride with hands clasped behind his back, the jaunty salute—that some at Allied headquarters were fooled. "I can't get over it," an old friend of the general who was in on the plot told James. "Why, you *are* Monty!"

mandy the Germans would still believe that the main blow was yet to come.

All told, Operation *Bodyguard* comprised six major deceptive plans, 36 subordinate ones and a welter of related stratagems. The deception plan specifically involving the Normandy invasion was code-named *Fortitude*. It was conceived in two parts: a northern plan *(Fortitude North)* designed to pin down the 27 German divisions in Scandinavia by threatening an Allied invasion of Norway, and a southern plan *(Fortitude South)* that would keep the German Fifteenth Army tied to the Pas-de-Calais.

The success of *Fortitude North* depended on making the Germans believe that an expeditionary force of more than 250,000 men was massing in Scotland to launch an attack on Norway with American and Russian support. Thus the British Fourth Army was born—a phantom force that in fact consisted of 28 overage officers and 334 enlisted men, many of them radio operators headquartered in rooms beneath Edinburgh Castle.

These men set about creating the Fourth Army out of radio reports—filling the airwaves with the detailed and sometimes chaotic traffic characteristic of an army assembling for a major operation. Seeded through the traffic were veiled references to what could only have been a rugged, northern country: "Captain R. V. H. Smith, 10th Cameronians, will report to Aviemore for ski training forthwith"; "II Corps Car Company requires handbooks on engine functioning in low temperatures and high altitudes."

Before long, a German fighter plane came roaring over Edinburgh and strafed the Fourth Army's wireless station. No serious damage was done, and the inventors of the bogus army had proof that they were being listened to. Meanwhile, wedding and sports announcements involving personnel of the Fourth Army were appearing in the local press, and British spymasters were asking their agents in Norway about the disposition of German garrison troops and the snowfall in the Kjölen Mountains.

Radio traffic and newspaper reports were only the beginning of Operation *Bodyguard's* deceptions. Throughout the spring of 1944, British special units mounted a series of hit-and-run raids, typical of preinvasion tactics, against industrial and military installations in Norway. Ships were sunk, power stations knocked out, railways disrupted and an oil refinery was blown up. At the same time, Soviet submarines were being sighted by the Germans in Norwegian waters, and Allied reconnaissance planes flew in increasing numbers over Norwegian territory. In neutral Sweden, British and American military engineers turned up and began gathering information about railbeds, airfields and port facilities that might accommodate armored forces in transit from Norway to the Baltic Sea.

Allied intelligence knew that the success or failure of *Fortitude North* would finally depend on what kind of corroboration the Germans could get. Inevitably, they would turn to their most trusted agents in Britain—all of whom by the end of 1943 were enlisted in the Double Cross network. All told, the British had 20 double agents under control at the beginning of 1944. Two of the best, from the Allied point of view, were the agents code-named Mutt and Jeff—both of whom had begun collaborating in 1941. Queried about the increasing commotion in Scotland by his German contacts, Mutt named the units stationed in his immediate vicinity and added that a Soviet military mission was at Edinburgh coordinating plans for an invasion of Scandinavia. Jeff described for the Germans the insignia of the Fourth Army, which he said was a gold, truncated figure 8 resembling the Anglo-Saxon rune for the name Ethel and superimposed on a field of red and blue.

Largely because of their misplaced trust in their agents in Britain, the Germans did indeed leave their 27 divisions in Scandinavia rather than transfer them to the south (where they would later be desperately needed). German intelligence officers were so convinced of the existence of the fictitious Fourth Army that when agents reported it was slated to join the First U.S. Army Group (FUSAG) in southeast England by mid-August 1944, they did not question the news.

There was indeed a FUSAG in southeast England; it comprised the Canadian First Army and the American Third Army and was prominently assembled in coastal areas across the Channel from the Pas-de-Calais. The unit not only presented a cross-Channel invasion threat but drew attention from the actual Normandy invasion force, General Sir Bernard Montgomery's Twenty-first Army Group, which was secretly assembling in the southwest.

But FUSAG was to start moving its forces to France in the

second week of June, after the initial invasion, to support the offensive. The Fourth Army that Operation *Bodyguard* was purporting to send to southeast England by August would be joining a phantom at an evacuated post. The Germans would not know that. *Fortitude South* intended to make them so sure that the main thrust was to be at the Pas-de-Calais that two months after the Normandy landings they would still believe the real invasion was yet to come.

The FUSAG deception was extraordinarily daring, for it involved an entire army group of 13 divisions, some 200,000 men. The putative commander of the group was Lieut. General George S. Patton. Beneath him, there had to be a whole roster of legitimate staff officers whose names would not arouse suspicion when German intelligence began to scrutinize the list.

The fake FUSAG made its presence known to the Germans by radio traffic, just as the phantom Fourth Army had done, but it also staged some highly sophisticated visual tricks in order to deceive German aerial reconnaissance. During May, German pilots began to detect recently added oil docks, hospitals, field kitchens and troop encampments at the post, and they observed guns, planes and tanks massing in the fields. What they could not discern was that all this equipment was faked—made of canvas, plywood,

papier-mâché and inflated rubber. False landing craft built at a motion-picture studio near London were moored in the rivers and smoke spewed from their funnels. At night, lights outlined imaginary rail yards and port facilities. And everywhere simulated tank and truck tracks led into the woods to suggest that additional quantities of equipment were stored under the trees.

Leaks to the press further corroborated the phantom FUSAG. Angry debate raged in newspaper letters columns about the "vast number of foreign troops" that had recently come into the area. But the main responsibility for selling FUSAG to the Germans fell to selected double agents under the aegis of the Double Cross Committee. The agents had to be carefully chosen because of the enormous damage that one slip could do to the whole *Bodyguard* operation, and of course they could be given no notion at all of the full dimensions of the vast scheme to which they were contributing. Nevertheless, they dutifully fed the Germans such information as Double Cross decreed they should.

One double agent in particular played a key role in overcoming the Germans' initial suspicions of FUSAG. He was the Yugoslav Dusko Popov, who went by the code name Tricycle. In February 1944 he went to Lisbon to give his German controller, a certain Karsthoff, the complete order

of battle of the FUSAG forces. Double Cross took a calculated risk in giving Popov such an assignment, for if he raised suspicions, FUSAG might be exposed as a hoax. Indeed Karsthoff did have doubts about Popov's report. He called it "warmed-over gossip." Fortunately for Operation *Bodyguard,* Karsthoff's superiors in Berlin disagreed; Popov's details matched their own operational picture and therefore seemed to them authentic. Thereafter FUSAG was a reality in the minds of Hitler and his intelligence staff.

Another star double agent was a Pole known as Brutus. He told his controller that he had been assigned to General Patton's headquarters to serve as liaison officer between the Polish high command and FUSAG. Every night shortly before midnight Brutus sent a wireless message detailing the FUSAG order of battle, noting changes of units and commands, and giving his German audience the exciting sense of seeing FUSAG from within. A number of other spies played lesser roles in the hoax. An agent code named Tate provided the Germans with the rail schedule for moving the FUSAG forces to the invasion embarkation ports in August.

In the spring of 1944, a young Argentinian woman code-named Bronx used a cipher system given her by the Germans to send artfully misleading intelligence embedded in innocuous telegrams addressed to the Bank of the Holy Ghost in Lisbon, where she had an account. On May 15, 1944, she wired for £50 to be used for dental expenses, thus signifying—according to a code in which sums of money stood for invasion sites—that the invasion would be in the Bordeaux area, where the German 11th Panzer Division was quartered. The German High Command decided to keep the division where it was.

British intelligence even found a way to send a message to the Germans by means of a captured German officer— General Hans Kramer, last commander of the Afrika Korps. Kramer's health was deteriorating, which prompted the British to send him home in May through a Swedish Red Cross repatriation program. En route from a detention camp in Wales to the interrogation center in London he was taken by a roundabout route to southwest England past the military build-up that was going on for the Normandy landings— and deluded into thinking he was in the southeast, where the Germans assumed FUSAG was assembling.

While the stratagems revolving around FUSAG were en-

gulfing the Germans in confusion on the eve of the invasion, other schemes were adding to their distraction. Within the main design of Operation *Bodyguard,* deceptive plans for the Mediterranean area went under the code name *Zeppelin.* The most important of these plans involved the Balkans. By calculated leaks, word was passed that at Stalin's request the Allies had agreed to defer the invasion of Europe until the late summer of 1944 in order to attack the Balkans first and force Hitler's allies out of the War.

In the complex scenario worked out by the *Zeppelin* planners, most of the phony assaults were assigned to the British Twelfth Army—a force that, like FUSAG, was enlarged by fictitious divisions. The fake strategy called for a series of landings that would enable the Allies to threaten the Balkans from several directions. In the first stage the British would land in Crete and the Greek Peloponnesus; the fictitious Polish III Corps would land in Albania, and the U.S. Seventh Army, which was real and was stationed in Sicily, would land on the Istrian Peninsula in northern Yugoslavia. Shortly thereafter would come amphibious operations against the Rumanian coast along the Black Sea, followed by a British move into Turkey.

To make the plan credible, air attacks were increased in the Balkan countries and on Axis shipping in the Aegean

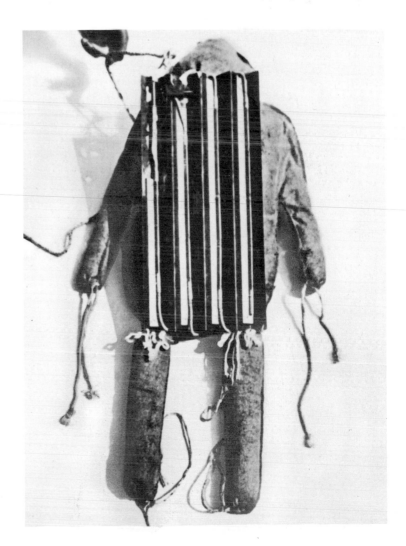

Four British soldiers shoulder a Sherman tank—a feat made possible because the tank was a rubber decoy. To German planes spying over England's southeast coast from 30,000 feet, such decoys seemed to pose a threat to the Pas-de-Calais, directly across the Channel.

This dummy paratrooper played a role in the D-Day hoax. To befuddle the Germans and draw their defenses away from Normandy, the Allies scattered several hundred such counterfeit soldiers along the coast of France from Cherbourg to Dieppe for 24 hours after the Normandy landings started. The dummies were a mere three feet tall, but as they drifted through a perspectiveless sky they looked life-sized enough.

Sea; the naval radio station at Tobruk, Libya, simulated the sort of traffic that precedes an amphibious assault, and dummy landing craft began to appear around the southern rim of the Mediterranean and in the Strait of Gibraltar. The *Zeppelin* planners even thought to hire Middle Eastern printers known for their loose tongues to print leaflets describing the invasion areas for the attacking troops. To keep the deception alive, the planners named dates for the fictitious invasions and then postponed them three times on various pretexts—one of them being that the Russians wanted a delay of a month so that they would be in a position to invade Bulgaria simultaneously.

Strange to say, it never seems to have occurred to the Germans that all three major plans—*Fortitude North* in Scandinavia, *Fortitude South* at the Pas-de-Calais and *Zeppelin* in the Balkans—could not possibly take place at once. Presumably they were too harried to see through the ruses. For the Allies, the full effect of the stratagems would not be known until after the War, but Ultra interceptions and communications with Double Cross agents quickly made it apparent that the Germans were badly disoriented and confused—and would remain so longer than the planners of Operation *Bodyguard* had dared to hope. At the end of May, when the Allies had only 38 divisions in the Mediterranean theater, the Germans believed the number was 71 divisions—an error representing 250,000 men.

Bodyguard tried another set of ruses in the western Mediterranean, but without much success. Two deceptions failed to convince the Germans that an invasion of the South of France was imminent. One problem was that because a genuine invasion of southern France was planned for August 1944, Allied intelligence wanted its deception to be only partly persuasive—enough to keep German troops from being sent north to Normandy, but not so convincing that German reinforcements would be sent south.

Nevertheless, the overall effect of *Zeppelin* was impressive. The Germans took the threat to the Balkans so seriously that after February 1944, when the *Zeppelin* deception was launched, not a single German division was moved north to Normandy. On the contrary, four crack divisions—including three of Hitler's best panzer divisions—were shifted from France to Eastern Europe.

All of the Allies' plots were fragile in the extreme; the whole structure of lies could have been brought down in an instant—as became chillingly apparent on the very eve of the invasion. In May 1944, the Germans kidnapped Johann Jebsen, an Abwehr agent who had come under Double Cross control in 1943 while he was living in Lisbon. Under the code name Artist, Jebsen had provided the British with much valuable information, particularly on the German intelligence system and the rocket program. For reasons still not clear, German intelligence became suspicious of Jebsen and seized him at his villa outside Lisbon, drugged him, stuffed him into a trunk and transported him to Germany as diplomatic luggage.

Allied intelligence learned through Ultra that Jebsen was being interrogated, and waited under excruciating tension, wondering whether he would betray the Double Cross system and the plans for Normandy. But Jebsen held fast, thus performing one of the crucial feats of the secret war. His silence despite undoubtedly severe interrogation was one of the happier surprises in the uncertain war of nerves, where double agents could seldom be counted on for loyalty. The Allies never had a chance to show their appreciation; Jebsen was killed in a German concentration camp while trying to escape.

"Battles are won by slaughter and maneuver," wrote Winston Churchill. "The greater the general, the more he contributes in maneuver, the less he demands in slaughter." The wonder of the secret maneuvering for D-Day was not only that it deluded the Germans, but that it did so while the biggest military build-up in history was taking place under the noses of their reconnaissance planes. While German intelligence was pursuing nonexistent armies, the Allies were assembling in England a real invasion force of two million men, supplied with three million tons of stores and matériel. When D-Day dawned on June 6, 1944, the troops bound for Normandy crossed the Channel in 5,000 transports supported by 600 warships and 10,000 aircraft.

Major Friedrich August Baron von der Heydte, commander of the German 6th Parachute Regiment located 30 miles south of Cherbourg, never forgot his first glimpse of the invasion fleet. He climbed the steeple of the village church at Saint Côme-du-Mont at dawn on June 6 and saw the fleet before him, filling the sea from shore to horizon. The sight was, he recalled, "overwhelming."

But the complex hoax that made it all possible went on and on. When the Germans took prisoners from the real FUSAG formations included in the Normandy forces, they found that the troops belonged to units already reported to them by their agents—a seemingly irrefutable confirmation of the existence of the phantom FUSAG.

The Double Cross agents continued on the job. Garbo, the Spaniard who had put himself at the disposal of MI-5 (page 28), performed some of his most valuable work after D-Day. He told the Germans that he was now functioning as a translator in the Iberian section of the British Ministry of Information, where a vast amount of highly confidential material was available to him because he had access to the secrets of Brendan Bracken, a confidant of Prime Minister Churchill.

Perhaps Garbo's most brilliant stroke was a report on D-Day-plus-1. Only hours after the invasion, Allied leaders had gone on the air with brief statements that referred to the landings as the "first in a series"; the purpose was to reinforce the German expectation of further strikes. But General Charles de Gaulle, leader of the movement to liberate France from German occupation, alarmed the perpetrators of Bodyguard by referring to Normandy as "the supreme battle."

Was it not possible, German intelligence demanded of Garbo, that other threats were mere feints and that all available force should be rushed to the Normandy battlefront? Not at all, replied the resourceful Garbo. He then quoted from a fabricated directive he claimed the Ministry of Political Warfare had issued two days before. It discouraged speculation about other landings precisely because they were so imminent. Although many Allied leaders had been careless in their language, Garbo went on, de Gaulle had

followed the directive to the letter. Garbo argued the case so persuasively that his appreciative German superiors recommended him for the Iron Cross.

The intelligence battle was only partly won when the invasion forces hit the beaches. There still remained the ultimate question of what Hitler would do. Would he fall for the Fortitude South ruse and keep the Fifteenth Army tied to the Pas-de-Calais? Or would he invoke a contingency plan and hurl his panzer divisions from the Pas-de-Calais and other parts of France against the Normandy beaches? If he chose the latter course, there was every likelihood that the beachheads would be destroyed and the invasion army driven back into the sea.

For five days after D-Day, the British intelligence chiefs hovered anxiously about the Operations Room at Storey's Gate, closely following via Ultra interceptions the twists and turns of Hitler's wavering intentions. Lieut. Colonel Wingate, recalling those stress-filled days and nights, wrote that he and his colleagues lived in an atmosphere "heavy with tension and pipe and cigarette smoke." On June 10, the chiefs were joined by Churchill and General George C. Marshall, U.S. Army Chief of Staff. They were studying the war maps when a secretary came in with an Ultra message that made all the weary months and years of intrigue and planning worthwhile. It revealed that Hitler was not moving his forces out of the Pas-de-Calais. "We knew then that we'd won," recalled Wingate. "There might be very heavy battles, but we'd won."

Many strategists on both sides have attributed the success of D-Day largely to the magnificent hoax of Operation Bodyguard. Because of the ruse, the enemy was "paralyzed into indecision," noted General Omar N. Bradley, and it lured him into the irreversible tactical error of "committing his forces piecemeal." Ninety German divisions—nearly one million men—were deployed all over Europe far from the Normandy beachhead, waiting for invasion forces that never came. So artful was the planning that up until the end of the War the German general staff continued to think of the Normandy landings as a diversionary tactic that by sheer luck had grown into something bigger.

BIBLIOGRAPHY

Accoce, Pierre, and Pierre Quet, *A Man Called Lucy.* Transl. by A. M. Sheridan Smith. Coward-McCann, 1967.

Angelucci, Enzo, and Paolo Matricardi, *World War II Airplanes,* Vols. 1 and 2. Rand McNally, 1977.

Arct, Bohdan, *Poles against the "V" Weapons.* Warsaw: Interpress Publishers, 1972.

Babington-Smith, Constance, *Air Spy: The Story of Photo Intelligence in World War II.* Harper & Brothers, 1957.

Barrett, David D., *Dixie Mission: The United States Army Observer Group in Yenan, 1944.* Center for Chinese Studies, University of California, Berkeley, 1970.

Batchelor, John, and Ian Hogg, *Artillery.* Charles Scribner's Sons, 1972.

Bazna, Elyesa, and Hans Nogly, *I Was Cicero.* Transl. by Eric Mosebacher. Harper & Row, 1962.

Beesly, Patrick, *Very Special Intelligence: The Story of the Admiralty's Operational Intelligence Centre, 1939-1945.* Doubleday, 1978.

Best, S. Payne, *The Venlo Incident.* Hutchinson, 1950.

Blackstock, Paul W., and Frank L. Schaf Jr., *Intelligence, Espionage, Counterespionage, and Covert Operations: A Guide to Information Sources* (International Relations Information Guide Series, Vol. 2). Gale Research Company, 1978.

Brown, Anthony Cave, *Bodyguard of Lies.* Harper & Row, 1975.

Brown, Anthony Cave, ed., *The Secret War Report of the OSS.* Berkley Publishing, 1976.

Calvocoressi, Peter, *Top-Secret Ultra.* Pantheon Books, 1980.

Carter, Carolle J., *The Shamrock and the Swastika.* Pacific Books, 1977.

Churchill, Winston S., *Their Finest Hour.* Bantam Books, 1962.

Clark, Ronald, *The Man Who Broke Purple: The Life of Colonel William F. Friedman, Who Deciphered the Japanese Code in World War II.* Little, Brown, 1977.

Colby, William, and Peter Forbath, *Honorable Men: My Life in the CIA.* Simon and Schuster, 1978.

Collier, Basil, *The Battle of the V-Weapons, 1944-45.* William Morrow, 1965.

Colvin, Ian, *Master Spy.* McGraw-Hill, 1951.

Connell, Brian, *Return of the Tiger.* Doubleday, 1960.

Cruickshank, Charles:
  Deception in World War II. Oxford University Press, 1979.
  The Fourth Arm: Psychological Warfare, 1938-1945. London: Davis-Poynter, 1977.

Dasch, George J., *Eight Spies against America.* Robert M. McBride Company, 1959.

Deacon, Richard:
  A History of the British Secret Service. London: Frederick Muller, 1969.
  A History of the Russian Secret Service. London: Frederick Muller, 1972.

Deacon, Richard, and Nigel West, *Spy!* London: British Broadcasting Corporation, 1980.

Deakin, F. W., and G. R. Storry, *The Case of Richard Sorge.* Harper & Row, 1966.

Delmer, Sefton, *Black Boomerang.* Viking Press, 1962.

Dornberger, Walter, *V-2.* Transl. by James Cleugh and Geoffrey Halliday. Viking Press, 1958.

Dulles, Allen:
  The Craft of Intelligence. Harper & Row, 1963.
  The Secret Surrender. Harper & Row, 1966.

Dunlop, Richard, *Behind Japanese Lines: With the OSS in Burma.* Rand McNally, 1979.

Eggleston, Wilfrid, *Scientists at War.* Oxford University Press, 1950.

Ellis, L. F., *Victory in the West,* Vol. 1, *The Battle of Normandy.* London: Her Majesty's Stationery Office, 1962.

Fairbairn, W. E., *Get Tough! How to Win in Hand-to-Hand Fighting as Taught to the British Commandos and the U.S. Armed Forces.* Paladin Press, 1942.

Farago, Ladislas, *The Game of the Foxes.* London: Hodder and Stoughton, 1971.

FitzGibbon, Constantine, *Secret Intelligence in the Twentieth Century.* Stein and Day, 1976.

Flower, Desmond, and James Reeves, eds., *The Taste of Courage: The War, 1939-1945.* Harper & Brothers, 1960.

Foot, M. R. D., *SOE in France: An Account of the Works of the British Special Operations Executive in France, 1940-1944.* London: Her Majesty's Stationery Office, 1966.

Foot, M. R. D., and J. M. Langley, *MI-9.* London: The Bodley Head, 1979.

Ford, Brian:
  Allied Secret Weapons: The War of Science. Ballantine Books, 1971.
  German Secret Weapons: Blueprint for Mars. Ballantine Books, 1969.

Ford, Corey, *Donovan of OSS.* Little, Brown, 1970.

Ford, Corey, and Alastair MacBain, *Cloak and Dagger: The Secret Story of the OSS.* Random House, 1945.

Gallo, Max, *The Poster in History.* Transl. by Alfred and Bruni Mayor. American Heritage, 1974.

Gander, Terry, and Peter Chamberlain, *Weapons of the Third Reich.* Doubleday, 1979.

Ganier-Raymond, Philippe, *The Tangled Web.* Transl. by Len Ortzen. Pantheon Books, 1968.

Garliński, Józef:
  Hitler's Last Weapons: The Underground War against the V1 and V2. London: Julian Friedman, 1978.
  Intercept: The Enigma War. London: J. M. Dent & Sons, 1979.
  Poland, SOE and the Allies. Transl. by Paul Stevenson. London: George Allen and Unwin, 1969.

George, Willis, *Surreptitious Entry.* D. Appleton-Century, 1946.

Haldane, R. A., *The Hidden War.* St. Martin's Press, 1978.

Hartcup, Guy, *Camouflage: A History of Concealment and Deception in War.* Charles Scribner's Sons, 1980.

Haswell, Jock, *The Intelligence and Deception of the D-Day Landings.* London: B. T. Batsford, 1979.

Hearings before the Committee on Foreign Relations, U.S. Senate, 92nd Congress, on "Causes, Origins and Lessons of the Vietnam War." May 9, 10, 11, 1972. U.S. Government Printing Office, 1973.

Hinsley, F. H., *British Intelligence in the Second World War: Its Influence and Operations,* Vol. 1. London: Her Majesty's Stationery Office, 1979.

Hogg, I. V., *German Secret Weapons of World War II.* London: Arms and Armour, 1970.

Hogg, Ian V., and J. B. King, *German and Allied Secret Weapons of World War II.* London: Phoebus Publishing, 1976.

Höhne, Heinz:
  Canaris. Transl. by J. Maxwell Brownjohn. Doubleday, 1979.
  Codeword: Direktor: The Story of the Red Orchestra. Transl. by Richard Barry. Coward, McCann & Geoghegan, 1971.

Höhne, Heinz, and Hermann Zolling, *The General Was a Spy: The Truth about General Gehlen and His Spy Ring.* Transl. by Richard Barry. London: Pan Books, 1972.

Holmes, W. J., *Double-Edged Secrets: U.S. Naval Intelligence Operations in the Pacific during World War II.* Naval Institute Press, 1979.

Hughes, Terry, and John Costello, *The Battle of the Atlantic.* The Dial Press, 1977.

Hutton, Clayton, *Official Secret: The Remarkable Story of Escape Aids—Their Invention, Production—and the Sequel.* Crown, 1961.

Huzel, Dieter K., *Peenemünde to Canaveral.* Prentice-Hall, 1962.

Hyde, H. Montgomery, *Room 3603: The Story of the British Intelligence Center in New York during World War II.* Farrar, Straus, 1962.

Hymoff, Edward, *The OSS in World War II.* Ballantine Books, 1972.

Infield, Glenn B., *Disaster at Bari.* New English Library, 1971.

Innes, Brian, *The Book of Spies: 4,000 Years of Cloak and Dagger.* London: Bancroft, 1966.

James, M. E. Clifton, *I Was Monty's Double.* London: Rider and Company, 1954.

Johnson, Brian, *The Secret War.* London: British Broadcasting Corporation, 1978.

Johnson, Chalmers, *An Instance of Treason: Azaki Hotsumi and the Sorge Spy Ring.* Stanford University Press, 1964.

Jones, R. V., *The Wizard War: British Scientific Intelligence, 1939-1945.* Coward, McCann & Geoghegan, 1978.

Kahn, David:
  The Codebreakers: The Story of Secret Writing. Macmillan, 1967.
  Hitler's Spies: German Military Intelligence in World War II. Macmillan, 1978.

Kennan, George F., *Russia, the Atom and the West.* Harper & Brothers, 1958.

Klee, Ernst, and Otto Merk, *The Birth of the Missile: The Secrets of Peenemünde.* Transl. by T. Schoeters. E. P. Dutton, 1965.

Kozaczuk, Wladyslaw, *W Kregu Enigmy.* Warsaw: Ksiazka i Wiedza, 1979.

Laurence, William L., *Dawn over Zero: The Story of the Atomic Bomb.* London: Museum Press, 1947.

Lewin, Ronald, *Ultra Goes to War: The First Account of World War II's Greatest Secret Based on Official Documents.* McGraw-Hill, 1978.

Lord, Walter, *Day of Infamy.* Henry Holt, 1957.

Lovell, Stanley P., *Of Spies and Stratagems.* Prentice-Hall, 1963.

Lusar, Rudolf, *German Secret Weapons of the Second World War.* Transl. by R. P. Heller and M. Schindler. Philosophical Library, 1959.

McGovern, James, *Crossbow and Overcast.* William Morrow, 1964.

McLean, Donald B., *The Plumber's Kitchen: The Secret Story of American Spy Weapons.* Normount Technical Publications, 1975.

Manvell, Roger, and Heinrich Fraenkel, *The Canaris Conspiracy: The Secret Resistance to Hitler in the German Army.* David McKay, 1969.

Manvell, Roger, advised by Heinrich Fraenkel, *SS and Gestapo: Rule by Terror.* Ballantine Books, 1969.

Masterman, J. C., *The Double-Cross System.* Avon Books, 1972.

Merrick, K. A., *Halifax: An Illustrated History of a Classic World War II Bomber.* London: Ian Allan, 1980.

Millis, Walter, *This is Pearl! The United States and Japan—1941.* William Morrow, 1947.

Montagu, Ewen:
  Beyond Top-Secret Ultra. Coward, McCann & Geoghegan, 1978.
  The Man Who Never Was. Bantam Books, 1953.

Moon, Thomas N., and Carl F. Eifler, *The Deadliest Colonel.* Vantage Press, 1975.

Moore, Dan Tyler, and Martha Waller, *Cloak and Cipher.* Bobbs-Merrill, 1962.

Morgenstern, George, *Pearl Harbor: The Story of the Secret War.* Devin-Adair, 1947.

Morison, Samuel Eliot, *History of United States Naval Operations in World War II:*
  Vol. 1, *The Battle of the Atlantic: September 1939-May 1943.* Little, Brown, 1970.
  Vol. 3, *The Rising Sun in the Pacific: 1931-April 1942.* Little, Brown, 1948.
  Vol. 4, *Coral Sea, Midway and Submarine Actions: May 1942-August 1942.* Little, Brown, 1949.
  The Two-Ocean War. Little, Brown, 1963.

Mosley, Leonard, *The Druid.* Atheneum, 1981.

Moyzisch, L. C., *Operation Cicero.* Transl. by Constantine FitzGibbon and Heinrich Fraenkel. Coward-McCann, 1950.

Muggeridge, Malcolm, *Chronicles of Wasted Time, Chronicle 2: The Infernal Grove.* William Morrow, 1974.

Murphy, Robert, *Diplomat among Warriors.* Doubleday, 1964.

Niehaus, Werner, *Die Radarschlacht: 1939-1945.* Stuttgart: Motorbuch Verlag, 1977.

Ordway, Frederick I., III, and Mitchell R. Sharpe, *The Rocket Team.* Thomas Y. Crowell, 1979.

OSS Special Weapons, Devices and Equipment. Office of Strategic Services, Research and Development Branch, Washington, D.C., 1975.

Parris, Thomas, and S. L. A. Marshall, eds., *The Simon and Schuster Encyclopedia of World War II.* Simon and Schuster, 1978.

Paul, Doris A., *The Navajo Codetalkers.* Dorrance, 1973.

Pawle, Gerald, *The Secret War: 1939-45.* William Sloane Associates, 1957.

Peers, William R., and Dean Brelis, *Behind the Burma Road: The Story of America's Most Successful Guerrilla Force.* Little, Brown, 1963.

Peis, Günter, *Mirror of Deception.* Pocket Books, 1976.

Perrault, Gilles, *The Red Orchestra.* Transl. by Peter Wiles. Simon and Schuster, 1969.

Persico, Joseph E., *Piercing the Reich.* Viking Press, 1979.

Piekalkiewicz, Janusz, *Secret Agents, Spies and Saboteurs.* Transl. by Francisca Garvie and Nadia Fowler. William Morris, 1973.

Popov, Dusko, *Spy/Counterspy: The Autobiography of Dusko Popov.* Grosset & Dunlap, 1974.

Price, Alfred, *Instruments of Darkness: The History of Electronic Warfare.* London: Macdonald and Jane's, 1977.

Purcell, John, *The Best-Kept Secret: The Story of the Atomic Bomb.* Vanguard Press, 1963.

Ramsay, Winston G., ed.:
"The V-Weapons." *After the Battle* magazine, No. 6. London: Battle of Britain Prints, 1974.
"German Spies in Britain." *After the Battle* magazine, No. 11. London: Battle of Britain Prints, 1976.

Reit, Seymour, *Masquerade: The Amazing Camouflage Deceptions of World War II.* Hawthorn Books, 1978.

Rhodes, Anthony, *Propaganda, The Art of Persuasion: World War II.* Chelsea House, 1976.

Rohwer, Jürgen, and Eberhard Jäckel, *Die Funkaufklärung und Ihre Rolle im Zweiten Weltkrieg.* Stuttgart: Motorbuch Verlag, 1979.

Roskill, S. W., *The War at Sea, 1939-1945:*
Vol. 2, *The Period of Balance.* London: Her Majesty's Stationery Office, 1956.
Vol. 3, Pt. 1, *The Offensive, 1st June 1943-31st May 1944.* London: Her Majesty's Stationery Office, 1960.
The Rote Kapelle. The CIA's History of Soviet Intelligence and Espionage Networks in Western Europe, 1936-1945. University Publications of America, 1979.

Russell, Francis, "Waiting for the End." *Horizon* magazine, Spring 1975, Vol. 17, No. 2, American Heritage.

Ryan, Cornelius, *A Bridge Too Far.* Popular Library, 1974.

Sanger, E., and J. Bredt, "A Rocket Drive for Long-Range Bombers." Transl. by M. Hamermesh, Radio Research Laboratory. Reproduced by Technical Information Branch, Bauer, Navy Department, 1974.

Sayers, Michael, and Albert E. Kahn, *The Great Conspiracy: The Secret War against Soviet Russia.* Little, Brown, 1946.

Schellenberg, Walter, *The Labyrinth: Memoirs of Walter Schellenberg.* Harper & Brothers, 1956.
Secrets and Spies: Behind-the-Scenes Stories of World War II. The Reader's Digest Association, 1964.

Seth, Ronald:
Secret Servants: A History of Japanese Espionage. Farrar, Straus, 1957.
Unmasked! The Story of Soviet Espionage. Hawthorn Books, 1965.

Sevareid, Eric, *Not So Wild a Dream.* Alfred A. Knopf, 1946.

Shirer, William L., *The Rise and Fall of the Third Reich: A History of Nazi Germany.* Simon and Schuster, 1960.

Simon, Leslie E., *Secret Weapons of the Third Reich.* WE, INC., 1971.

Smith, R. Harris, *OSS: The Secret History of America's First Central Intelligence Agency.* Dell, 1972.

Stephan, Enno, *Spies in Ireland.* Transl. by Arthur Davidson. Stackpole Books, 1963.

Stephens, Frederick J., *Fighting Knives: An Illustrated Guide to Fighting Knives and Military Survival Weapons of the World.* Arco Publishing, 1980.

Tompkins, Peter, *A Spy in Rome.* Simon and Schuster, 1962.

Trefousse, Hans L., "Failure of German Intelligence in the United States, 1935-1945." *The Mississippi Valley Historical Review,* Vol. 62, No. 1, June 1955. The Mississippi Valley Historical Association.

Trepper, Leopold, *The Great Game: Memoirs of the Spy Hitler Couldn't Silence.* McGraw-Hill, 1977.

Van Der Rhoer, Edward, *Deadly Magic: A Personal Account of Communications Intelligence in World War II in the Pacific.* Charles Scribner's Sons, 1978.

Von Braun, Wernher, and Frederick I. Ordway III, *History of Rocketry and Space Travel.* Thomas Y. Crowell, 1966.

War Department.
War Report of the OSS (Office of Strategic Services). Walker Publishing, 1976.
The Overseas Targets: War Report of the OSS (Office of Strategic Services), Vol. 2. Walker Publishing, 1976.

West, Nigel, "When A Spy Was Trapped." London: *Telegraph* Sunday magazine, No. 173, January 13, 1980.

Whiting, Charles, *Gehlen: Germany's Master Spy.* Ballantine Books, 1972.

Wighton, Charles, and Günter Peis, *Hitler's Spies and Saboteurs.* Aware Books, 1973.

Willoughby, Charles A., *Shanghai Conspiracy: The Sorge Spy Ring.* E. P. Dutton, 1952.

Winterbotham, F. W., *The Ultra Secret.* Dell, 1974.

Wohlstetter, Roberta, *Pearl Harbor: Warning and Decision.* Stanford University Press, 1962.

Woytak, Richard A., *On the Border of War and Peace: Polish Intelligence and Diplomacy in 1937-1939 and the Origins of the Ultra Secret.* East European Quarterly, Columbia University Press, 1979.

Wykes, Alan, *Heydrich.* Ballantine Books, 1973.

Zacharias, Ellis M., *Secret Missions: The Story of an Intelligence Officer.* G. P. Putnam's Sons, 1946.

ACKNOWLEDGMENTS

For help given in the preparation of this book, the editors wish to express their gratitude to Philip Arnold, Saint Louis, Missouri; Aaron Bank, San Clemente, California; Dürriye Bazna, Munich; Patrick Beesly, Lymington, England; Véronique Blum, Chief Curator, B.D.I.C., Musée des Deux Guerres Mondiales, Paris; Commander Marc' Antonio Bragadin, Italian Navy (Ret.), Rome; Anthony Cave Brown, New York; Squadron Leader S. F. Burley, RAF, Gosfield, England; William L. Cassidy, Intelligence Studies Foundation, Oakland, California; Dennis V. Cavanaugh, Laguna Beach, California; Jeannette Chalufour, Archives Tallandier, Paris; Keith C. Clark, Washington, D.C.; G. Clout, Imperial War Museum, London; William E. Colby, Washington, D.C.; Cécile Coutin, Curator, Musée des Deux Guerres Mondiales, Paris; Paul Cyr, Fairfax Station, Virginia; Gerald W. Davis, Fort Myers, Florida; Lieut. Colonel John Duggan, Dublin; Richard Dunlop, Arlington, Virginia; Captain Thomas H. Dyer, USN (Ret.), Sykesville, Maryland; Captain Hamish Eaton, Intelligence Corps, Brampton, England; Phil Edwards, National Air and Space Museum, the Smithsonian Institution, Washington, D.C.; Dr. Carl Eifler, Salinas, California; Alger C. Ellis, Arlington, Virginia; Dr. Eugene J. Fisher, Washington, D.C.; David Floyd, London; John Friedman, Plainfield, New Jersey; Major General J. D. Frost, C.B., D.S.O., M.C., Liphook, England; Józef Garlinski, London; Randy Hackenberg, Assistant Curator, United States Army Military History Institute, Carlisle Barracks, Pennsylvania; Major D. J. D. Haswell, Lyminge, England; Rudolf Heinrich, Deutsches Museum, Munich; E. C. Hine, Imperial War Museum, London; James J. Hitchcock, Bethesda, Maryland; Ian Hogg, Upton-upon-Severn, England; Heinz Höhne, Grosshansdorf, West Germany; Alfredo Hummel, Publifoto, Milan; Lieut. Colonel K. Iranek-Osmecki, London; John Jacob, George C. Marshall Research Foundation, Lexington, Virginia; Brian Johnson, BBC, London; Geoffrey M. T. Jones, President, Veterans of the OSS, New York; W. J. Peter Kin, Sumner, Washington; Heidi Klein, Bildarchiv Preussischer Kulturbesitz, Berlin (West); Dr. Roland Klemig, Bildarchiv Preussischer Kulturbesitz, Berlin (West); Don Kloster, the Smithsonian Institution, Washington, D.C.; Louis Kruh, Middleburg, Michigan; Joseph E. Lazarsky, Middleburg, Virginia; Gerard Le Marec, Meudon-la-Forêt, France; Ronald Lewin, East Horsley, England; H. W. Little, Bellair Beach, Florida; Pierre Lorain, Paris; Roster Lyle, George C. Marshall Research Foundation, Lexington, Virginia; Lieut. Colonel J. K. MacFarlan, O.B.E., Yeovil, England; Barry Maschado, Washington and Lee University, Lexington, Virginia; Keith Melton, Intelligence Studies Foundation, Oakland, California; Françoise Mercier, Institut d'Histoire du Temps Présent, Paris; Paul Mero, Wilmette, Illinois; Uta Merzbach, the Smithsonian Institution, Washington, D.C.; Brün Meyer, Bundesarchiv/Militärarchiv, Freiburg, West Germany; The Honorable E. S. Montagu, C.B.E., Q.C., D.L., F.R.S., London; Tim Mulligan, National Archives and Records Service, Washington, D.C.; Daphne M Mundinger, Paris; Meinrad Nilges, Bundesarchiv, Koblenz, West Germany; J. W. Pavey, Imperial War Museum, London; Gerald Pawle, Penzance, England; Lieut. General William R. Peers, USA (Ret.), Kentfield, California; Joseph Persico, Washington, D.C.; Janusz Piekalkiewicz, Rösrath-Hoffnungsthal, West Germany; Neil Pilford, Imperial War Museum, London; Polish Underground Movement (1939-1945) Study Trust, London; Professor Lucio Puttin, Director, Museo Civico, Treviso, Italy; Hannes Quaschinsky, ADN-Zentralbild, Berlin, DDR; Winston Ramsay, *After the Battle* magazine, London; Michel Rauzier, Institut d'Histoire du Temps Présent, Paris; Professor Dr. Jürgen Rohwer, Bibliothek für Zeitgeschichte, Stuttgart; Manfred Sauter, Luftschiffbau Zeppelin, Friedrichshafen, West Germany; Hanfried Schliephake, Königsbrunn, Augsburg, West Germany; Axel Schulz, Ullstein Bilderdienst, Berlin (West); J. Simmonds, Imperial War Museum, London; Maurice Southgate, La Celle-Saint-Cloud, France; Robert Staver, Los Altos, California; Enno Stephan, Deutschlandfunk, Cologne; Regina Strother, Defense Audiovisual Agency, Marine Corps Historical Center, Washington, D.C.; Robert L. Stroud, Falls Church, Virginia; John Taylor, National Archives and Records Service, Washington, D.C.; Fernand Thirion, Secrétariat d'État aux Anciens Combattants, Paris; A. W. Tickner, Senior Archival Officer, National Research Council of Canada, Ottawa; Gordon Torrey, Bethesda, Maryland; Fritz Trenkle, Fürstenfeldbruck, West Germany; William E. Trible, Office of Congressional and Public Affairs, Federal Bureau of Investigation, Washington, D.C.; James H. Trimble, Archivist, National Archives, Still Photo Branch, Washington, D.C.; Ufficio Storico, Stato Maggiore Marina, Rome; Benoit Verny, Paris; Waldemar Werther, Ahrweiler, West Germany; Nigel West, London; William C. Wilkinson, Largo, Florida, M. J. Willis, Imperial War Museum, London; Brian Winkel, Albion, Michigan; Group Captain F. W. Winterbotham, C.B.E., Kingsbridge, England; Hans Wolf, Koblenz, West Germany; Jennifer Wood, Imperial War Museum, London; Werley A. Wright, Silver Spring, Maryland.

The index for this book was prepared by Nicholas J. Anthony.

PICTURE CREDITS

Credits from left to right are separated by semicolons, from top to bottom by dashes.

COVER and page 1: U.S. Army.

THE URGENT NEED FOR SECRECY—6, 7: Dmitri Kessel, courtesy Musée des Deux Guerres Mondiales, B.D.I.C. (Universités de Paris), Paris. 8: Bildarchiv Preussischer Kulturbesitz, Berlin (West). 9: Dmitri Kessel, courtesy Musée des Deux Guerres Mondiales, B.D.I.C. (Universités de Paris), Paris. 10: Foto Piccinni, courtesy Museo Civico "L. Bailo," Treviso, Italy; Bildarchiv Preussischer Kulturbesitz, Berlin (West). 11: Eileen Tweedy, poster by Fougasse, courtesy Imperial War Museum, London. 12, 13: Dmitri Kessel, courtesy Musée des Deux Guerres Mondiales, B.D.I.C. (Universités de Paris), Paris. 14: Foto Piccinni, courtesy Museo Civico "L. Bailo," Treviso, Italy. 15: Bildarchiv Preussischer Kulturbesitz, Berlin (West).

A BODYGUARD FOR TRUTH—18: Wide World. 19: Süddeutscher Verlag, Bilderdienst, Munich. 20: Bildarchiv Preussischer Kulturbesitz, Berlin (West). 22: Historical Research Unit, Kings Sutton nr. Banbury, Oxfordshire, England. 23: Ullstein Bilderdienst, Berlin (West). 25, 26: Courtesy Mrs. Harold Deardon, Herefordshire, England.

GERMANY'S MASTER SPY—30, 31, 33: Courtesy Colonel Otto Wagner (Ret.), Bad Säckingen, Federal Republic of Germany. 34, 35: Ullstein Bilderdienst, Berlin (West), except bottom left, National Archives. 36: Historical Research Unit, Kings Sutton nr. Banbury, Oxfordshire, England. 37: Bundesarchiv, Koblenz—Süddeutscher Verlag, Bilderdienst, Munich. 38, 39: Bundesarchiv, Koblenz; Süddeutscher Verlag, Bilderdienst, Munich—from German Military Intelligence by Paul Leverkuehn, published by Frederick A. Praeger, Inc., 1954.

AGENTS IN THE FIELD—40, 41: Federal Bureau of Investigation. 42: From They Spied On England: Based on the German Secret Service War Diary of General von Lahousen by Charles Wighton and Günter Peis, © 1958, Hamlyn Publishing Group Ltd., London. 43: William Vandivert for Life. 44: National Archives (No. 862.20235/4-2545)—courtesy Enno Stephan, Cologne. 45: Bottom left, courtesy Enno Stephan, Cologne. 46, 47: Heinz Kutscha Collection, Kiel, Federal Republic of Germany. 48, 49: Federal Bureau of Investigation. 52: Federal Bureau of Investigation; UPI; Federal Bureau of Investigation; UPI. 53: Federal Bureau of Investigation. 54, 55: Federal Bureau of Investigation (2); Myron Davis for Life.

EAVESDROPPING ON THE ENEMY—58: UPI. 59: National Archives. 61: Courtesy Franklin D. Roosevelt Library. 64: U.S. Navy. 65: Mainichi Shimbun, Tokyo—National Archives (No. 80-G-413507). 67: National Archives (No. 80-G-60948). 68: Bundesarchiv, Koblenz. 71: Tonftunislap Pgrabinska, Warsaw. 72: Dr. T. Lisicki, London. 73: Private collection, England. 74: Brian Johnson, London. 75: British Crown Copyright, courtesy Brian Johnson, London. 76: Joan Bright Astley, London.

A PIONEER IN CRYPTOLOGY—78-81: The Friedman Collection, George C. Marshall Research Foundation. 82: Courtesy Verna Lehman Silvermann—The Friedman Collection, George C. Marshall Research Foundation (2). 83: The Friedman Collection, George C. Marshall Research Foundation—UPI. 84, 85: National Archives (No. 64-M-276); The Friedman Collection, George C. Marshall Research Foundation; National Archives.

COMMUNICATING IN THE FIELD—86, 87: Bundesarchiv, Koblenz. 88: Cartoon by Fougasse, David Kahn Collection. 89: U.S. Marine Corps. 90: National Security Agency, courtesy the Smithsonian Institution, © 1981. 91: U.S. Army—National Security Agency, courtesy the Smithsonian Institution, © 1981 (2). 92: National Security Agency, courtesy the Smithsonian Institution, © 1981. 93: National Archives (No. 242-GAP-33H-2); National Security Agency, courtesy the Smithsonian Institution, © 1981. 94: Ullstein Bilderdienst, Berlin (West)—Jack Savage, courtesy The Philip Mills Arnold Semeiology Collection, Washington University Libraries, Saint Louis. 95: Dmitri Kessel, courtesy Maurice Southgate, La Celle-Saint-Cloud, France—U.S. Army.

LOW TRICKS FOR HIGH STAKES—99: © National Geographic Society. 101: Courtesy H. Montgomery Hyde, Kent, England. 103: Published with permission of Princeton University Library. 104: Courtesy Gordon H. Torrey. 106: Courtesy Carl

Strahle. 108, 110: Courtesy Richard Dunlop from Behind Japanese Lines: With the OSS in Burma by Richard Dunlop, © 1979 by Rand McNally & Company. 111: Courtesy Richard Dunlop from Behind Japanese Lines: With the OSS in Burma by Richard Dunlop, © 1979 by Rand McNally & Company; Charles Phillips, courtesy Joseph Lazarsky. 112: Lieut. General William R. Peers, U.S. Army (Ret.).

AN AMERICAN COVERT FORCE—114, 115: Tom Moon Collection. 116: Wide World. 117: Courtesy Richard Dunlop from Behind Japanese Lines: With the OSS in Burma by Richard Dunlop, © 1979 by Rand McNally & Company. 118: Philip K. Allen, West Coast Training Center (OSS)—Leon Dishman, courtesy Library of Congress (3). 119: Courtesy Mrs. Robert G. Mundinger, Paris. 120, 121: William J. Rader; courtesy Richard Dunlop from Behind Japanese Lines: With the OSS in Burma by Richard Dunlop, © 1979 by Rand McNally & Company; Wilbur J. Peterkin—U.S. Army. 122, 123: National Archives (No. SQ/R3N28); Colonel Gerald W. Davis, U.S. Army (Ret.)—courtesy Angelo Lygizos. 125: Top right, Lieut. General William R. Peers, U.S. Army (Ret.).

AN ARSENAL FOR AGENTS—126, 127: Fil Hunter, courtesy Joseph F. Canole. 128: Courtesy Intelligence Studies Foundation. 129: Ben Benschneider, courtesy Intelligence Studies Foundation—courtesy Intelligence Studies Foundation. 130, 131: Ben Benschneider, courtesy Intelligence Studies Foundation. 132, 133: Ben Benschneider, courtesy Intelligence Studies Foundation, except X-ray, courtesy Intelligence Studies Foundation. 134, 135: Ben Benschneider, courtesy Intelligence Studies Foundation, except bottom left, Erich Lessing, courtesy The Niels Bohr Institute, Copenhagen.

THE WIZARDS' WAR—138, 141: R. V. Jones, Aberdeen, Scotland. 142: Courtesy U.S. Army Military History Institute. 144, 145: British Crown Copyright Photograph. 147: Bundesarchiv/Militärarchiv, Freiburg, Federal Republic of Germany. 148, 149: Popperfoto, London. 151: Imperial War Museum, London. 152: Courtesy Peter Masters. 154: Fritz Goro for Life.

VENGEANCE FROM HITLER—156, 157: U.S. Army photo, courtesy U.S. Air Force. 158: Imperial War Museum, courtesy Brian Johnson, London. 159-161: Deutsches Museum, Munich. 162: Top, courtesy Janusz Piekalkiewicz, Rösrath-Hoffnungsthal, Federal Republic of Germany. 163: U.S. Air Force. 164, 165: From Hitler's Last Weapons: The Underground War Against the V1 and V2 by Józef Garlinski, © 1978, published by Julian Friedman Publishers Ltd., London; courtesy Lieut. Colonel Robert Staver, A.U.S. (Ret.); Deutsches Museum, Munich—courtesy Janusz Piekalkiewicz, Rösrath-Hoffnungsthal, Federal Republic of Germany. 166: Courtesy R. V. Jones, Aberdeen, Scotland—The Museum of Denmark's Fight for Freedom 1940-1945, Copenhagen. 167: Brian Johnson, London—Józef Garlinski, courtesy Polish Institute and Sikorski Museum, London. 168: Imperial War Museum, London. 169: R. V. Jones, Aberdeen, Scotland.

A GALLERY OF WONDER WEAPONS—170, 171: C. G. B. Collection, National Air and Space Museum, the Smithsonian Institution; inset, the Smithsonian Institution (Neg. No. 78-7598). 172: Bundesarchiv, Koblenz. 173: Imperial War Museum, London. 174: Imperial War Museum, courtesy Brian Johnson, London. 175: RLM Manual, courtesy National Air and Space Museum, the Smithsonian Institution; Imperial War Museum, courtesy Brian Johnson, London—MBB Archiv, Munich—Bundesarchiv, Koblenz. 176, 177: Imperial War Museum, London (2)—Imperial War Museum, courtesy Brian Johnson, London (2). 179: Two right pictures, National Research Council of Canada, Ottawa. 180: U.S. Army. 181: U.S. Air Force—U.S. Army. 182: U.S. Army—from Secret Weapons of the Third Reich: German Research in World War II by Leslie E. Simon, © 1971, published by Paladin Press, a division of Paladin Enterprises, Inc. 183: David Scherman for Life (2)—U.S. Army.

GRAND DELUSIONS—186: From The Man Who Never Was by Ewen Montagu, published by Evans Brothers Ltd., London, 1953. 188: Hart Preston for Life; courtesy Dürriye Bazna, Munich. 190: Stern, Hamburg. 193: ADN-Zentralbild, Berlin, DDR. 195: Black Star, London. 196: UPI; Syndication International Ltd., London. 198: Dunlop Archive Project, London. 199: British Crown Copyright, Public Records Office, London (AIR 24/281).

205

206